General editors: Andrew S. Thompson and Alan Lester

Founding editor: John M. MacKenzie

When the 'Studies in Imperialism' series was founded by Professor John M. MacKenzie more than thirty years ago, emphasis was laid upon the conviction that 'imperialism as a cultural phenomenon had as significant an effect on the dominant as on the subordinate societies'. With well over a hundred titles now published, this remains the prime concern of the series. Cross-disciplinary work has indeed appeared covering the full spectrum of cultural phenomena, as well as examining aspects of gender and sex, frontiers and law, science and the environment, language and literature, migration and patriotic societies, and much else. Moreover, the series has always wished to present comparative work on European and American imperialism, and particularly welcomes the submission of books in these areas. The fascination with imperialism, in all its aspects, shows no sign of abating, and this series will continue to lead the way in encouraging the widest possible range of studies in the field. 'Studies in Imperialism' is fully organic in its development, always seeking to be at the cutting edge, responding to the latest interests of scholars and the needs of this ever-expanding area of scholarship.

Creating the Opium War

Manchester University Press

SELECTED TITLES AVAILABLE IN THE SERIES

WRITING IMPERIAL HISTORIES
ed. Andrew S. Thompson

GENDERED TRANSACTIONS
Indrani Sen

EXHIBITING THE EMPIRE
ed. John McAleer and John M. MacKenzie

BANISHED POTENTATES
Robert Aldrich

MISTRESS OF EVERYTHING
ed. Sarah Carter and Maria Nugent

BRITAIN AND THE FORMATION OF THE GULF STATES
Shohei Sato

CULTURES OF DECOLONISATION
ed. Ruth Craggs and Claire Wintle

HONG KONG AND BRITISH CULTURE, 1945–97
Mark Hampton

Copyright © Hao Gao 2020

The right of Hao Gao to be identified as the author of this work has been asserted by him in accordance with the Copyright, Designs and Patents Act 1988.

Published by Manchester University Press
Oxford Road, Manchester M13 9PL
www.manchesteruniversitypress.co.uk

British Library Cataloguing-in-Publication Data is available

ISBN 978 1 5261 3342 7 hardback
ISBN 978 1 5261 6365 3 paperback

First published by Manchester University Press in hardback 2020

This edition published 2022

The publisher has no responsibility for the persistence or accuracy of URLs for any external or third-party internet websites referred to in this book, and does not guarantee that any content on such websites is, or will remain, accurate or appropriate.

Typeset by Toppan Best-set Premedia Limited

Creating the Opium War

BRITISH IMPERIAL ATTITUDES
TOWARDS CHINA, 1792–1840

Hao Gao

MANCHESTER UNIVERSITY PRESS

For my family

CONTENTS

Acknowledgements—viii

Introduction ... 1

Part I – The embassies

1 The Macartney embassy ... 21
2 The Amherst embassy ... 51

Part II – Prelude to the Opium War

3 The EIC versus free traders ... 95
4 'Show of force' ... 122
5 Justifying the Opium War ... 145

Conclusion ... 180

Bibliography—185
Index—204

ACKNOWLEDGEMENTS

There are many people whom I would like to thank. My first order of gratitude is to Professor Harry Dickinson, who has guided and inspired me over many years. Without his invaluable advice and generous help, this book could not have been possible. I am grateful to Professor Henry French for taking on the laborious work of reading the full revised manuscript, and Professor James Mark for providing comments and suggestions on various versions of some chapters. Their scholarship and kindness have greatly helped to improve the manuscript. I also thank the following colleagues or former colleagues who contributed in various ways to the completion of this book: Andrew Thompson, Andrew Thorpe, Richard Toye, Kate Fisher, Martin Thomas and David Thackeray of the University of Exeter, and Richard Follett, Vinita Damodaran, Maurizio Marinelli and Claire Langhamer of the University of Sussex. My special thanks go to Miles Taylor, Alexandra Walsham, Alvin Jackson, Frances Dow, Matthew Cragoe, Kent Deng and Naomi Tadmor for their support and encouragement over a long time. I pay tribute to my previous supervisor in Peking University Professor Qian Chengdan, who guided me in the study of world history.

Over the course of this research, I benefited from the expertise of several people who provided advice and helpful conversation, especially Henrietta Harrison, Peter Kitson, John Carroll, Julia Lovell, Hans van de Ven, David Clayton, Anthony Howe, Antonia Finnane, Felix Boeking, Stephen McDowall, Wu Yixiong, Xu Kai and Guo Weidong. The two anonymous reviewers for Manchester University Press provided extremely valuable comments which considerably improved this book. Also of great help were the questions and feedback from participants in conferences, workshops or seminars at Edinburgh, Cambridge, Institute of Historical Research (London), Exeter, Sussex, Newcastle, Glasgow and Tsinghua (Beijing). I acknowledge my appreciation to the University of Exeter and the Institute for Advanced Studies in the Humanities at the University of Edinburgh for granting me generous research leave and fellowship to see this book through to completion. Some of the material and arguments that appear in this book have previously appeared in the following journals: *Historical Research, History, Diplomacy & Statecraft, The Journal of Imperial and Commonwealth History* and *Britain and the World*. Chapter 5 is a much expanded version of an essay that appeared in *Imagining Britain's*

ACKNOWLEDGEMENTS

Economic Future, c. 1800–1975, published by Palgrave Macmillan in 2018. More details of these works can be found in the bibliography.

Last but not least, I must thank my wife Dr Huang Shuo for her love, care, support and understanding. A big thank you to my father Professor Gao Dai for always believing in me and being proud of me. The unwavering support from the rest of my family was also crucial to the completion of this book. I dedicate this book to every member of my family.

Introduction

On 1 October 1839 – exactly a hundred and ten years before Mao Zedong proclaimed the establishment of the People's Republic of China to a huge crowd in Tiananmen Square – a secret cabinet meeting was held behind closed doors in Windsor Castle, England. On this occasion, ministers of the Whig government led by Prime Minister Lord Melbourne and Foreign Secretary Lord Palmerston made a historic decision to send a military expedition to China for the protection of British commerce, interests and honour. This decision effectively resulted in the First Anglo-Chinese War (1840–2), popularly referred to as the 'Opium War'. Although the conflict has been de-emphasised by some scholars as the dividing line between modern and premodern Chinese history,[1] it is still widely recognised as a deeply consequential event in the history of Sino-Western relations. The war not only substantially 'opened up' China to the West but also marked the beginning of a 'century of humiliation' for the Chinese.

As such a defining moment, the Opium War has been much commented upon by historians. In explaining its origins, some emphasised the irreconcilability of Britain's economic expansion and China's containment policies.[2] Scholars of this school maintained that a war was inevitable, while opium was but an instrument of British commercial expansion: 'Had there been an effective alternative to opium, say molasses or rice, the conflict might have been called the Molasses War or the Rice War'.[3] Another school of historians believed that the military conflicts between Britain and China in the mid-nineteenth century were indeed unavoidable, but they were primarily the outcome of a clash of opposing cultures.[4] Pre-Opium War China was considered as backward, stagnant, irrational and unable to understand Britain's 'modern' civilisation. In the late 1960s, John K. Fairbank famously suggested that the war was caused by the wide cultural differences between the conservative East and the progressive West.[5] Almost a decade later, Tan Chung, a Chinese historian based in India, explored the connections between the opium traffic and British imperialism in Asia. With a strong anti-imperialist tone, Tan pointed out that the vital importance of the opium trade had been underestimated as a cause of the war by Fairbank and others, whereas the Sino-British cultural differences had been exaggerated. After a careful investigation into the triangular trade between Britain, India and China, Tan concluded that the clash of socio-economic interests around the opium traffic was the primary cause of the First Anglo-Chinese War.[6] In 1998, J.Y. Wong endorsed Tan's views by conducting sophisticated statistical analysis into Britain's commerce with China. Focusing on the importance of the opium trade to the maintenance of the British Empire, his research confirmed that opium sales to China were extremely important for British rule in India and for the development of British imperialism in general. For this reason, Wong maintained that both Opium Wars – the 1840–2 war and the 1856–60 *Arrow* War (commonly known as the Second Opium War) – arose from Britain's need to protect the crucial opium trade, rather than from a general commercial or cultural conflict.[7] As an overall explanation for the origins of the Opium War, this war-due-to-opium theory has been probably the most widely accepted one in recent decades. 'The evidence overwhelmingly suggests', as Julia Lovell has recently summarised, 'the principal cause of the war was ... Britain's determination to maintain its illegal, profitable opium trade between Britain, India and China, in the face of the Qing government's resolution to ban drug smuggling'.[8]

In addition to these interpretations, which sought to pinpoint the fundamental cause of the Opium War, other scholars have mentioned some less discernible but still significant causes. Peter Fay, for example, claimed that the determination of Protestant missionaries to 'open up' China was crucial to the outbreak of the war.[9] Glenn Melancon pointed out that Britain's concern for its national honour and the domestic political crisis facing the Whig government in the late 1830s were also important factors in influencing Britain's decision to go to war with China.[10] Lydia Liu's study on the translation of the Chinese character *yi* has analysed the manner in which translingual communication influenced Sino-British encounters. Her work has shown that negative connotations were produced when the British translated *yi* as 'barbarian' and how this discourse created anger and indignation on the British side to fuel the drift to the Opium War.[11] Li Chen, in his sophisticated work *Chinese Law in Imperial Eyes*, has added a legal dimension to the study on the origins of the war.[12] Chen is concerned with British and Western conceptions of sovereignty, extraterritoriality and international law, as well as how the British strove to justify a war of highly questionable legality within their own legal framework. Chen's work illustrated how the discourses on Chinese and international law came to influence the causes, decision-making and long-term results of the Opium War. Chen revealed that 'the popular perception of Chinese judicial administration as despotic and barbaric' encouraged defiance of Chinese laws and that Charles Elliot's intervention in the opium crisis of 1839 helped convert the Chinese anti-opium campaign into 'an unjust aggression against British lives, liberty, property and national dignity'.[13] These legal notions, according to Chen, provided an opportunity for key British actors to legitimise British military action against China. With respect to the identities of these 'key British actors', Song-Chuan Chen has recently added that a group of British merchants in Canton, known as the 'warlike party', should be held primarily responsible for the outbreak of war between the two nations.[14] His book *Merchants of War and Peace* is helpful in expanding the existing knowledge on the British mercantile community in Canton in the 1830s, by providing very useful contextual information on the making of the Canton system, the debate on the translation of *yi* (barbarian/stranger), the formation of the Society for the Diffusion of Useful Knowledge in China and so on. Chen, however, refused to accept that the opium trade or the crisis in 1839 was the origin of the war. 'The war's origin', he insisted, 'lay in the Warlike party's actions to force the Whig government to respond'.[15]

These existing studies have revealed many interesting aspects of the Opium War, but they also share some common weaknesses. In particular, in explaining the causes of the war, previous research has produced either grand narratives which have overlooked some important historical details (such as Fairbank's case challenged by Tan),[16] or specific 'short-term (*courte durée*)' studies of the kind which 'centred on the drama of "great events"'[17] only. Much research concentrating on the war itself has traced its origins back no earlier than the rise of the opium trade and more attention has therefore been paid to the immediate triggers of hostilities.[18] Moreover, some researchers of the Opium War appear to be keen to identify *the* principal cause of the conflict – either the general expansion of Britain's trade, or the opium trade in particular, or a clash of Western and Eastern cultures, or the need to safeguard Britain's national honour, or the war campaigns waged by the 'warlike party'. In contrast, some underlying but equally important questions remain unclear: how was China perceived in the British eyes before the war idea was formed? How was the China question discussed in a longer duration prior to the war? On the basis of these perceptions and attitudes, how exactly was the idea of the Opium War created, developed and justified in the British minds? To answer these questions, I argue for the necessity of surveying a medium-term (*moyenne durée*) period – a nearly half-century timespan before the war – to examine British imperial attitudes formed as a result of Sino-British encounters both before and during the years in which the opium trade became a serious concern. The purpose of this study, however, is not to replace the existing theories on the causes of the war with a brand new one. Its aim is to explore some hitherto under-researched aspects of Sino-British relations through a new perspective, to analyse the important factors *without* which open hostilities between Britain and China could *not* have been possible, in order to understand the origins of the Opium War more fully.

It needs to be pointed out that independent from the above-mentioned scholarship, which largely consists of diplomatic and commercial histories, there is another relevant body of literature offering cultural investigations of early British–Chinese relations. This field of cultural studies, however, has not previously been brought into dialogue with the former in a sustained manner. Some early publications of this scholarship often do not differentiate clearly between Britain and the West or between China and Asia.[19] In 1998, a group of Chinese historians published an edited volume entitled *The Vision of China in the English Literature of the Seventeenth and Eighteenth Centuries*,[20] in which they began to comment on the positive and negative images of China presented by English writers. Since the beginning of the new millennium, there has been a significant increase in work from Western scholars on early British perceptions of China. Rachel Ramsey and Robert Batchelor, in their respective papers, have discussed how individuals in Britain used China as an imaginary space to advocate for change at home.[21] By analysing John Webb's *An Historical Essay*,[22] for example, they have revealed that the Chinese system of meritocracy, as opposed to aristocracy in Britain at the time, served as an enviable model for the British middle and upper classes to criticise Britain's government bureaucracy. Focusing on the years from 1600 to 1730, Robert Markley has challenged the assumptions of earlier scholars that China was technologically, economically and culturally inferior to Europe in the English imagination during the discussed period.[23] In Markley's study, a range of English writings, including those of John Milton, John Dryden and Daniel Defoe, have been utilised to demonstrate that a sense of admiration for China's wealth and power clearly existed in the minds of early modern English writers. These perceptions of China, according to Markley, helped shape national and individual identities in seventeenth- and early eighteenth-century English literature.

INTRODUCTION

In addition to these general studies on British/English cultural representations of China, other scholars tend to focus on more specific themes. Beth Kowaleski-Wallace and Kristin Bayer, for instance, have analysed how British consumption of Chinese tea defined notions of gender, class and opinions of China in the eighteenth and nineteenth centuries.[24] David Porter, Elizabeth Hope Chang and Eugenia Zuroski Jenkins have examined the British/English cultural awareness of China from the perspectives of aesthetic practice, consumer tastes and material culture.[25] Porter, in particular, has explored the process by which Chinese aesthetic ideas were assimilated within English culture through imports of Chinese goods such as porcelain and furniture. He agrees with Kowaleski-Wallace and Bayer that because the trade in and the consumption of Chinese products were largely associated with the English female, they gave rise to a feminisation of China in the English imagination. It, in turn, contributed to the increasingly negative views of China and Chinese culture in England in the early nineteenth century. To understand this shift from positive to negative attitudes, William Christie and Logan Collins have investigated the representations of China in British periodicals.[26] They are concerned with the roles that were played by the writers and editors of periodical journals in constructing images of China in the minds of the British reading public, the former concentrating on the representation of the Macartney embassy, while the latter surveying how China was defined in major British periodicals from 1793 to 1830.

This scholarship of cultural histories has substantially enriched our understanding of Sino-British cultural exchange in the centuries and decades before the Opium War, but one common feature of these studies is that they tend to dwell on how China as a civilisation was understood by the literate public, especially by intellectuals.[27] These impressions were not formed by those who had visited China or who possessed political influence as a direct result of early Sino-British encounters. In 1992, Mary Louise Pratt pointed out in *Imperial Eyes* the importance of studying cross-cultural perceptions from the perspective of a 'contact zone'.[28] This approach has been adopted more recently by Ulrike Hillemann, who has indicated that changing British knowledge of its empire in Asia might have made a military attack on China more imaginable.[29] Peter J. Kitson's *Forging Romantic China* is probably the best study so far in analysing the works of those individuals who had first-hand experience in China through embassies, trade and missionary work during the British Romantic period, demarcated by Kitson as c.1760 – c.1840.[30] Kitson has shown how new British perceptions of China were constructed by these so-called 'China experts', as a response to the previous images of China transmitted by Jesuit missionaries, or formed through the acquisition of Chinese commercial goods as discussed by Porter and others. Kitson's methodological focus, however, is not exclusively on the writings and translations of these Britons who were acknowledged as authorities in interpreting China. He is also concerned with the process in which these new understandings of China were mediated via a dynamic print culture to a variety of British poets, essayists, novelists and dramatists, including Jane Austen, Thomas Percy, William Jones and George Colman who had never been to China. Kitson's emphasis, therefore, is not the question of *political* reception. The possible connection between the changing British attitudes towards China and the drift to the Opium War remains unexplored.

This book makes the first attempt to connect the two largely separate bodies of literature – the diplomatic and commercial histories of the Opium War and the cultural studies of early British representations of China. It explores the complex interplay between cultural representations and policy towards China, as a way of understanding the origins of the Opium War. This study examines the crucial half-century before the war, a medium-term period which Kitson and Markley have recently compared in importance with that of American and French Revolutions and the Napoleonic Wars.[31] This period produced a range of Sino-British political moments of connection, from the Macartney embassy (1792–4), through the Amherst embassy (1816–17) to the Napier incident (1834) and the lead-up to the opium crisis (1839–40). To grasp more fully how the idea of war against China developed as a result of changing attitudes, this book focuses on the perceptions formed by those who had first-hand experience of China or possessed political influence in Britain. In comparison with the multifarious representations of China's image created by the British writers 'at home', whose impact on policies is somewhat difficult to ascertain, Britain's direct discoveries in China clearly received much attention from the policy-makers. From Amherst to Napier, as well as some Members of Parliament who participated in the debates on the opium question, many of them had declared that they placed emphasis on the 'local experience' obtained by British travellers to and residents in China.[32] These first-hand observations were also more likely to have had a greater influence on the opinions of those who later travelled to China or helped to shape the development of British–Chinese relations. Li Chen's and Song-Chuan Chen's works have demonstrated that the views of Charles Elliot, Britain's Superintendent of Trade in China 1836–41, and William Jardine, one of the leading opium traders, were key to convince Palmerston of the necessity to go to war against the Middle Kingdom.[33] For these reasons, this book examines a wealth of primary materials, some in more detail than ever before, with a special focus on how British observers perceived and

INTRODUCTION

interpreted aspects of China, such as its government, society and people, when these were met and confronted. By using these sources in such a way, this study seeks to discover how changing images of China were connected to British discussions over whether to adopt a pacific or aggressive policy towards the Qing court. Only by investigating how key opinion-formers and decision-makers developed and justified their views on this matter can we ascertain how the idea of open warfare against China gradually became acceptable and why the First Anglo-Chinese War broke out at such a point in time. On this basis, this book eventually illuminates the underlying causes as well as immediate triggers of the Opium War from a perceptional point of view.

This book starts with a brief introduction to British knowledge of China before official Sino-British encounters took place. The main body of this book consists of two parts (in five chapters). In Part I, two British royal embassies to China, the Macartney and the Amherst missions, are investigated and analysed. Since they both failed to achieve their diplomatic and commercial goals, these two early contacts with China are conventionally regarded as unsuccessful. Nevertheless, if we take into consideration their impact on the development of British attitudes towards China, these embassies can be considered of much greater long-term importance. In general, they not only encouraged initial official contacts with the Chinese government but led to more visits into the interiors of many Chinese cities and rural areas by British travellers. This experience helped the British participants in these embassies to obtain more in-depth perceptions of China's circumstances at the time. On the basis of this newly acquired knowledge, however, the two embassies reached contrasting opinions on whether Britain should abandon the conciliatory attitude towards China that had previously been adopted. A more aggressive policy towards the Qing government, as a result, was becoming more imaginable to the British on the one hand, but on the other hand it was also developing into a controversial issue.

In Part II, British perceptions of China during the 1830s, the immediate pre-Opium War period, are closely examined. From the debate between the East India Company [EIC] advocates and free traders in the early 1830s, to the controversy over the opium crisis at the end of the decade, the perception of a Chinese government manipulated by a capricious and despotic monarchy was developed and seen as the primary cause of China's backwardness. China was increasingly interpreted as an isolated 'other' that could not be communicated with through normal diplomatic negotiations. As a consequence, a firm attitude, supported by a British naval force, became seen as a necessary approach to safeguard the wellbeing of British interests in China as well as that of the Chinese common people. This part, in the end, shows how the continuity and changes in British imperial attitudes towards China through this critical period shaped Britain's final decision to attack the Chinese empire.

Early British knowledge of China

Before examining British attitudes towards China during the early British–Chinese encounters, it is necessary to sketch what a Briton such as Lord George Macartney (1737–1806) could have read about China, or what second-hand knowledge of China an informed British public could have gained, prior to the two countries' official encounters. As stated above, there has been considerable research on early European perceptions of China, but, generally speaking, such information might have reached Britain from the following sources. First of all, Catholic missionaries, especially the Jesuits who visited the Chinese empire in the seventeenth and eighteenth centuries, are well-known for transmitting rather favourable images of China to Europe. In order to convert the Chinese to Catholicism, these missionaries believed that it was essential to adapt to the culture and society of China in the first place. They not only learned the Chinese language but also spent much time studying China's orthodox histories, philosophical works and religious texts. As a result of these dedicated efforts, as well as their expertise in Western science and technology, some of these missionaries, such as Matteo Ricci (1552–1610) and Ferdinand Verbiest (1623–88), won the friendship of the Chinese literati and consequently gained favour at the imperial court. Partly because of this close relationship with elite Chinese society, and partly because of the necessity to justify their unconventional approach to converting the Chinese, the Jesuit writings were mostly laudatory of Chinese culture and government. China, according to these accounts, was a powerful and wealthy empire with advanced political and moral systems. In Louis Le Comte's (1656–1729) *Nouveaux mémoires sur l'état present de la Chine* (1696), an influential work that was translated into English in 1697, the author spoke highly of the great empire in the East. Le Comte particularly praised the antiquity of Chinese civilisation, which he believed 'furnishes us [the Europeans] with an infinite number of examples of conspicuous wisdom'.[34] Another monumental work, the four-volume *Description geographique, historique, chronologique et physique de l'empire de la Chine et de la Tartarie chinoise* (1735),[35] edited by Jean Baptiste Du Halde, was the largest and most comprehensive single product of Jesuit scholarship on China. Du Halde was immensely positive about China and he appreciated almost every aspect of Chinese society. Du Halde claimed that China was governed in such a philosophic and enlightened way that material prosperity as well as mental contentment could be achieved for a vast population. In addition to Le Comte's and Du Halde's works, the Jesuit sinophilic series, *Lettres édifiantes et curieuses des missions étrangères par quelques missionaires de la Compagnie de Jesus*, which was published between 1702 and 1776,[36] was another important reference work for information about China. This series was clearly subjected to careful selection and editing, so that a similar idealised image of China was presented to its European readers.[37]

Under the influence of the Jesuits, some key philosophers of the Enlightenment became enthusiastic about China. From the mid-seventeenth to the late eighteenth century, the Jesuit reports on China were widely read by European intellectuals. As a result, China was seen by many as an ideal model, which might be a rational alternative to the existing order of royal autocracy and religious intolerance in Europe. The German logician and mathematician Gottfried Wilhelm Leibniz (1646–1716) for example, was fascinated by Chinese culture. In particular, he admired the Kangxi emperor (1654–1722, r. 1662–1722), who was known to have tolerated Christianity and to have shown a strong interest in mathematics, philosophy and European science. Leibniz regarded the Kangxi emperor as a model of a benevolent monarch, because, although 'being a god-like mortal, ruling all by a nod of his head', he was 'educated to virtue and wisdom … thereby earning the right to rule'.[38] Voltaire (1694–1778), prince of the *philosophes*, was also famously laudatory of Chinese institutions. Since it was illegal to criticise openly the state or the church in his time, Voltaire employed China as a polemical weapon to cloak his attacks on obscurantism and misgovernment in France. In *Essai sur les moeurs et l'esprit des nations* (1756), Voltaire offered a panegyric on the rationality of Chinese culture and philosophy. He extolled the secular nature of Confucianism, because the religion of the emperors and the tribunals had never been troubled by priestly quarrels.[39] China, moreover, was appreciated by Voltaire as a great ancient civilisation that was founded upon paternal authority and governed by an enlightened literary class, recruited by competitive examination not by noble birth. Like Leibniz and Voltaire, François Quesnay (1694–1774), the leader of the Physiocratic school, was an ardent admirer of China. Quesnay and his fellow Physiocrats highly valued the fact that 'in China … agriculture has always been held in veneration, and those who profess it have always merited the special attention of the emperor'.[40] Quesnay also eulogised the Chinese constitution as founded on wise and irrevocable laws so that even 'the emperor himself is not immune from … censure when his conduct offends the laws and rules of the state'.[41] Quesnay, unlike Voltaire, did not deny that the Chinese government was in essence despotic, but he asserted that the power of the Chinese emperor did not prevent China from having the best form of government, because 'It is a generally established maxim among the people ... that as they should have a filial obedience toward their sovereign, he in turn should love them like a father'.[42] Although Quesnay's high regard for China's enlightened despotism was not shared by some other great European thinkers, such as Montesquieu (1689–1755), who condemned the oppressiveness of the Chinese government and discredited the Jesuits' accounts, European intellectuals' admiration for China, on the whole, was striking from the mid-seventeenth to the mid-eighteenth centuries.

Along with the appeal of Chinese moral and political systems, a general fascination with Chinese artistic tastes became a notable feature of European culture at this time. As trade with China increased significantly from the late seventeenth century onwards, Chinese objects were more widely circulated throughout Europe. A lively vogue for Chinese fashions, which was later known as 'Chinoiserie',[43] spread over much of Europe. In consequence, not only were Chinese porcelain, lacquer ware, silk cloth and wallpaper extensively imported and copied but a number of Chinese summer houses, pavilions, pagodas and bridges were constructed, as ornaments to royal parks and aristocratic estates throughout Europe. It is worth noting that Britain excelled in Chinese-style garden designs. Sir William Chambers (1723–96), a Scottish-Swedish architect who had twice visited Canton (Guangzhou), was the foremost authority on Chinese architecture and gardening at this time. Chambers published in 1757 his *Designs of Chinese Buildings, Furniture, Dresses, Machines and Utensils* and, several years later, he produced a more detailed *Dissertation on Oriental Gardening* (1772). Both of these books drew much attention from within and beyond Britain. In the early 1760s, according to his notions of naturalistic style of Chinese gardening, Chambers redesigned Kew Gardens in the vicinity of London. The famous Great Pagoda, which was designed by Chambers and still remains, was considered the most accurate reconstruction of a Chinese building in Europe at the time.

On the basis of the favourable accounts written by Jesuits and enlightened philosophers, as well as the enthusiasm for Chinese material culture, Britain developed a considerable admiration for China, especially in the second half of the seventeenth century. Nevertheless, unlike Voltaire and Quesnay who were activists for social progress and political reforms, British admirers of China were sceptical about the achievements of their own age and tended to believe that British society and institutions were in a worsening state. China, for this reason, was interpreted by British commentators as a venerable and ancient civilisation that 'had kept its pristine excellence to a remarkable extent in a world prone to deterioration'.[44] John Webb (1611–72), for example, praised the antiquity of Chinese civilisation. In *An Historical Essay*, Webb justified his admiration for China upon a biblical footing. Webb claimed that, prior to the Confusion of Tongues (*confusio linguarum*), Noah carried the world's primitive language into the Ark with him and settled in the East. Because of the superiority and hence the independence of Chinese civilisation, the Chinese language had kept the original tongue that was common to the world before the Flood. In this respect, Emperor Yao, a legendary Chinese ruler, was even recognised by Webb as no other than Noah himself.[45] Sir William Temple (1628–99), Britain's most famous sinophile in the seventeenth century, agreed with the antiquity of Chinese civilisation by maintaining that the seeds of Grecian learning and institutions could be easily found in ancient China. Temple pointed out that China in his own age was 'the greatest, richest, and most populous kingdom now known in the world', because, ever since ancient times, the 'admirable constitution of its government' had been 'established upon the deepest and wisest foundations'.[46] As with some Enlightenment thinkers on the Continent, Temple wrote very highly of the Chinese form of government, which was believed to have been established upon the wisdom of Confucius. Together with the fair and efficient system of its civil service examinations, the Chinese political system overall was regarded 'in practice to excel the very speculations ... and all those imaginary schemes of the European wits, the institutions of Xenophon, the republic of Plato, the Utopia's, or Oceana's of our modern writers'.[47] As a result of Temple's vigorous efforts to promote such positive images of China, Britain's enthusiasm for Chinese culture reached its peak in English literature during the seventeenth century.

Despite the fact that a similar esteem for Chinese culture and institutions can be detected in the British Isles as on the Continent, European respect for China declined first in Britain. From the beginning of the eighteenth century, the excellence of Chinese civilisation began to be doubted by British commentators. Publications censorious of China increased markedly, especially during the second half of the century. Some reasons can be offered to explain this shift in British attitudes towards China at this particular time. Most immediately, because of the Rites Controversy, the Kangxi emperor banned Christian missions in China in 1721. It deprived the Jesuits of the imperial patronage which they had long enjoyed at the Chinese court and most missionaries were expelled from China in the following years. In 1773, the Society of Jesus was formally dissolved in Europe on the orders of Pope Clement XIV. These events resulted in Jesuit writers on China being unsupported by the authorities both in China and in Europe. Moreover, to the British, who were largely Protestant, the Society of Jesus had always been a suspicious body which could not be fully trusted. Jesuit admiration for China was therefore undermined and could no longer be so relied upon to offer a positive image of the government of China.

The values of British society and its changing preoccupations also helped to cause mounting scepticism about China and things Chinese. From the very beginning, British fascination with China, especially among intellectuals, had been weaker than on the Continent. Compared with Voltaire and others in France who produced a romanticised image of China in order to veil their criticisms of the French government, the British were generally more satisfied with their own political system. Particularly after the Glorious Revolution, Britain basically lost the 'motivation to hold up China for utopian contrast with the home country which was prevalent among the French *philosophes*'.[48] Moreover, in the eighteenth century, as British society was undergoing rapid but mainly positive changes, which reinforced the pride and sense of superiority of the British nation, far fewer Britons adhered to the belief that Britain's civilisation was in decline. Instead, 'change' or 'progress' was widely accepted as the natural expectation of society. For this reason, the antiquity and changelessness of Chinese civilisation, which were appreciated by Webb and Temple, lost their attractions in Britain. Increasingly, 'China was not judged by how well it adhered to its ancient traditions but by how it performed at the present time in terms of military power, effective government, scientific knowledge, technological skill and the living standards of the mass of the population'.[49] A stagnant and backward image of China began to take shape. Adam Smith (1723–90), for instance, admitted that China used to be 'one of the richest, that is, one of the most fertile, best cultivated, most industrious and most populous countries in the world', but '[it] seems ... to have been long stationary'.[50] In order to avoid such a stagnant state, Smith pointed out the value of cultivating an extensive foreign trade. If China decided to engage in such foreign trade, it would be able to 'learn the art of ... different machines made use of in other countries, as well as the other improvements of art and industry which are practised in all the different parts of the world'.[51] Daniel Defoe (1660–1731), the author of *Robinson Crusoe*, was more straightforward in his contempt for China. As he put it in Crusoe's words, the Chinese people were 'a contemptible herd or crowd of ignorant, sordid slaves, subjected to a government qualified only to rule such a people'.[52] In a similar tone, Defoe belittled Chinese cities, architecture, commerce and so on. Even the Chinese mode of husbandry, which had been particularly eulogised by previous commentators, was now deemed as 'imperfect and impotent'[53] according to European standards. Like Defoe, Sir William Jones (1746–94), the great Orientalist, held completely negative views of Chinese civilisation.

INTRODUCTION

In a speech he delivered to the Asiatic Society, in 1790, Jones stated that:

> Their popular religion was imported from India in an age comparatively modern; and their philosophy seems yet in so rude a state, as hardly deserve the appellation; they have no ancient monuments; ... their sciences are wholly exotick; and their mechanical arts have nothing in them characteristic of a particular family ... They have indeed, both national music and national poetry, and both of them beautifully pathetick, but of painting, sculpture, of architecture, as arts of imagination, they seem (like other Asiaticks) to have no idea.[54]

It was probably owing to these unfavourable views of China, which were becoming commonly held in eighteenth-century Britain, that Samuel Johnson (1709–84), in sharp contrast to Temple, categorised the Chinese as 'East-Indian barbarians'. Although Johnson still acknowledged the Chinese people as 'great, or wise', this was 'only in comparison with the nations that surround them',[55] rather than in comparison to Britain or any other major European state.

Another reason for the worsening British impressions of China in the eighteenth century was the rapid growth of Britain's China trade. As a considerable number of Britons were now able to set foot on Chinese soil, merchants, instead of Catholic missionaries, became the principal source of the images of China that were transmitted to Britain. The main contacts of these new visitors to China were no longer the upper or middle classes of Chinese society but the Chinese merchants and seamen who belonged to the lower classes and who were much more disposed to take advantage of foreigners engaged in commerce with them. As a result, reports about deceitful Chinese tradesmen were constantly on the rise. George Anson's *Voyage Round the World* (1748), according to Mackerras, was 'the first full-scale attack on the rosy images of China which the French Jesuits were pushing'.[56] Although Anson only skirted the coast of Canton, he formed a range of negative views of the Chinese character diametrically different from those which had appeared in the accounts of earlier missionaries. Anson was particularly incensed at the dishonest Chinese practices he encountered, such as cramming ducks and chickens with stones and gravel to bloating hogs with water. On the basis of these experiences, Anson concluded that 'these instances may serve as a specimen of the manners of this celebrated nation, which is often recommended to the rest of the world as a pattern of all kinds of laudable qualities'.[57] In addition, as China's external trade at this time was confined only to the south-east coast, the local authorities there, who operated thousands of miles from the central government, also tended to be interested in soaking the foreign traders for money. With the increase in British–Chinese commerce, the East India Company's employees in China gradually discovered that, whatever might be the theory, many Chinese officials were in fact grasping extortionists rather than enlightened governors. In one of the Company's reports to the Westminster Parliament, the Chinese government was characterised as 'the most corrupt in the universe'.[58] Probably as a result of these new first-hand findings, the notion that the Chinese were in fact a crafty and avaricious nation gradually spread in Britain. Anti-Chinese writings kept emerging and their tone generally became ruder.

In sum, from the seventeenth to the middle of the eighteenth century, Jesuits and Continental philosophers had inspired considerable enthusiasm for China in Europe. With the changing values of British society and the increasing first-hand knowledge about the Chinese, however, eighteenth-century Britain experienced a gradual decline in its admiration for China. Although the balance between favourable and unfavourable views was shifting away from the former and towards the latter, it should be noted, as Marshall and Williams have pointed out, that 'at any time in the eighteenth century British readers were never wholly dependent on one set of sources rather than another'.[59] By the end of the eighteenth century, despite the mounting scepticism about China, the British public still 'enjoyed some freedom to choose what published version of China it would or would not believe'.[60] It was in this context that Macartney and his retinue embarked on their journey to the East, by which Britain, for the first time, began to take the lead in informing Europe about China.

Notes

1 Philip Kuhn, for example, has doubted whether the modern period of China's history can be demarcated by largely external events. Instead, he suggests that 'we can reasonably seek the beginning of the old order's decline ... no earlier than 1864, the year the Taiping Rebellion was destroyed'. See Philip A. Kuhn, *Rebellion and Its Enemies in Late Imperial China: Militarization and Social Structure, 1796–1864* (Cambridge, MA: Harvard University Press, 1970), pp. 5, 8.
2 See, for example, W.C. Costin, *Great Britain and China: 1833–1860* (Oxford: Clarendon Press, 1937); Michael Greenberg, *British Trade and the Opening of China 1800–42* (Cambridge: Cambridge University Press, 1951); Hsin-pao Chang, *Commissioner Lin and the Opium War* (Cambridge, MA: Harvard University Press, 1964); and Gerald S. Graham, *The China Station: War and Diplomacy 1830–1860* (Oxford: Clarendon Press, 1978).
3 Chang, *Commissioner Lin and the Opium War*, p. 15.
4 Some of these works were first published in the early twentieth century and then reprinted in the 1970s. See, for example, James Bromley Eames, *The English in China: Being an Account of the Intercourse and Relations between England and China from the Year 1600 to the Year 1843 and a Summary of Later Developments* (1909; reprinted, London: Curzon, 1974); Earl Pritchard, *Anglo-Chinese Relations during*

INTRODUCTION

the Seventeenth and Eighteenth Centuries (Urbana, IL: University of Illinois Press, 1929; reprinted, New York: Octagon Books, 1970); Earl Pritchard, The Crucial Years of Early Anglo-Chinese Relations, 1750–1800 (Washington, DC: Pullman, 1936; reprinted, New York: Octagon Books, 1970); P.C. Kuo, A Critical Study of the First Anglo-Chinese War with Documents (Shanghai: The Commercial Press, 1935; reprinted, Westport, CT: Hyperion, 1973); Evan Luard, Britain and China (London: Chatto & Windus, 1962); John K. Fairbank, Trade and Diplomacy on the China Coast: The Opening of the Treaty Ports, 1842–1854 (Stanford, CA: Stanford University Press, 1969).

5 Fairbank, Trade and Diplomacy on the China Coast, p. 74.
6 Tan Chung, China and the Brave New World: A Study of the Origins of the Opium War 1840–42 (Durham, NC: Carolina Academic Press, 1978).
7 J.Y. Wong, Deadly Dreams: Opium, Imperialism and the Arrow War (Cambridge: Cambridge University Press, 1998).
8 Julia Lovell, 'Introduction to the English Edition', in Mao Haijian, The Qing Empire and the Opium War: The Collapse of the Heavenly Dynasty, trans. Joseph Lawson, Craig Smith and Peter Lavelle (Cambridge: Cambridge University Press, 2016), p. xvi.
9 P.W. Fay, 'The Protestant Mission and the Opium War', Pacific Historical Review, 40 (1971), 145–61.
10 Glenn Melancon, 'Honour in Opium? The British Declaration of War on China, 1839–1840', International History Review, 21 (1999), 855–74; and Glenn Melancon, Britain's China Policy and the Opium Crisis: Balancing Drugs, Violence and National Honour, 1833–1840 (Aldershot: Ashgate, 2003), pp. 5–6, 133–9. Harry Gelber agreed with Melancon's view. See Harry G. Gelber, Opium, Soldiers and Evangelicals: Britain's 1840–42 War with China, and Its Aftermath (New York: Palgrave Macmillan, 2004).
11 Lydia H. Liu, The Clash of Empires: The Invention of China in Modern World Making (Cambridge, MA; London: Harvard University Press, 2004), pp. 31–69.
12 Li Chen, Chinese Laws in Imperial Eyes: Sovereignty, Justice, and Transcultural Politics (New York: Columbia University Press, 2016).
13 Ibid., p. 239.
14 Song-Chuan Chen, Merchants of War and Peace: British Knowledge of China in the Making of the Opium War (Hong Kong: Hong Kong University Press, 2017).
15 Ibid., p. 123.
16 Other long-term studies that have covered the pre-Opium War period include: Hosea Ballou Morse, The Chronicles of the East India Company Trading to China, 1635–1834 (5 vols, Oxford: Clarendon, 1926; reprinted, London: Routledge, 2000); Hosea Ballou Morse, The International Relations of the Chinese Empire (3 vols, London: Longmans, 1910–18; reprinted, Folkestone: Global Oriental, 2008); Wolfgang Franke, China and the West (Oxford: Blackwell, 1967); Joanna Waley-Cohen, The Sextants of Beijing: Global Currents in Chinese History (New York; London: Norton, 1999); John S. Gregory, The West and China since 1500 (Basingstoke: Palgrave Macmillan, 2003); and D.E. Mungello, The Great Encounter of China and the West, 1500–1800 (Oxford: Rowman & Littlefield, 2006). These works have offered wide-ranging narratives of China's engagement with the outside world over the centuries, but they have focused principally on the major trends in political and commercial factors. Stephen Platt's popular book Imperial Twilight, indeed, vividly tells many detailed stories on both the Western and the Chinese sides about the lead-up to the Opium War and the decline of the Qing from the peak of its power. The book, however, is not concentrated on identifying what caused the conflict between Britain and China. See Stephen R. Platt, Imperial Twilight: The Opium War and the End of China's Last Golden Age (New York: Alfred A. Knopf, 2018).
17 Fernand Braudel, On History, trans. Sarah Matthews (London: Weidenfeld and Nicolson, 1980), p. 28.
18 See, for example, Peter Ward Fay, The Opium War 1840–1842 (New York; London: Norton, 1975); James M. Polachek, The Inner Opium War (Cambridge, MA: Harvard

University Press, 1992); W. Travis Hanes III and Frank Sanello, *The Opium Wars: The Addiction of One Empire and the Corruption of Another* (Naperville, IL: Sourcebooks, 2002); Gelber, *Opium, Soldiers and Evangelicals*; Julia Lovell, *The Opium War: Drugs, Dreams and the Making of China* (London: Picador, 2011); and Mao, *The Qing Empire and the Opium War.*

19 See, for example, Donald Lach, *Asia in the Making of Europe* (3 vols, Chicago: University of Chicago Press, 1965–93); P.J. Marshall and Glyndwr Williams, *The Great Map of Mankind: Perceptions of New Worlds in the Age of Enlightenment* (Cambridge, MA: Harvard University Press, 1982); Henry A. Myers (ed.), *Western Views of China and the Far East* (2 vols, Hong Kong: Asian Research Service, 1982); and V.G. Kiernan, *The Lords of Human Kind: European Attitudes towards the Outside World in the Imperial Age* (London: Serif, 1995).

20 Adrian Hsia (ed.), *The Vision of China in the English Literature of the Seventeenth and Eighteenth Centuries* (Hong Kong: The Chinese University Press, 1998).

21 Rachel Ramsey, 'China and the Idea of Order in John Webb's *An Historical Essay*', *Journal of the History of Ideas*, 3 (2001), 483–503; Robert Batchelor, 'Concealing the Bounds: Imagining the British Nation through China', in *The Global Eighteenth Century*, ed. Felicity Nussbaum (Baltimore, MD: Johns Hopkins University Press, 2003), pp. 79–92.

22 John Webb, *An Historical Essay Endeavoring a Probability that the Language of the Empire of China is the Primitive Language* (London: Nath. Brook, 1669).

23 Robert Markley, *The Far East and the English Imagination, 1600–1730* (Cambridge: Cambridge University Press, 2009).

24 Beth Kowaleski-Wallace, *Consuming Subjects: Women, Shopping, and Business in the Eighteenth Century* (New York: Columbia University Press, 1997); Kristin Bayer, 'Contagious Consumption: Commodity Debates over the Eighteenth and Nineteenth Century China Trade', *International Journal of Asia Pacific Studies*, 8 (2012), 73–94.

25 David Porter, *The Chinese Taste in Eighteenth-Century England* (Cambridge: Cambridge University Press, 2010); Elizabeth Hope Chang, *Britain's Chinese Eye: Literature, Empire and Aesthetics in Nineteenth-Century Britain* (Stanford, CA: Stanford University Press, 2010); Eugenia Zuroski Jenkins, *A Taste for China: English Subjectivity and the Prehistory of Orientalism* (Oxford: Oxford University Press, 2013). See also: Catherine Pagani, 'Chinese Material Culture and British Perceptions of China in the Mid-nineteenth Century', in *Colonialism and the Object: Empire, Material Culture and the Museum*, ed. Tim Barringer and Tom Flynn (London; New York: Routledge, 1998), pp. 28–40.

26 William Christie, 'China in Early Romantic Periodicals', *European Romantic Review*, 1 (2016), 25–38; Logan P. Collins, 'British Periodical Representations of China: 1793–1830' (MA thesis, University of Houston, 2014).

27 Other studies which do not distinguish Britain from the West include: Colin Mackerras, *Western Images of China* (Oxford: Oxford University Press, 1989); Raymond Dawson, 'Western Conceptions of Chinese Civilization', in *The Legacy of China*, ed. Dawson (Boston, MA: Cheng & Tsui, 1990), pp. 1–27; Gregory Blue, 'China and Western social thought in the modern period', in *China and Historical Capitalism: Genealogies of Sinological Knowledge*, ed. Timothy Brook and Gregory Blue (Cambridge: Cambridge University Press, 1999), pp. 57–109; Jonathan D. Spence, *The Chan's Great Continent: China in Western Minds* (London: Penguin, 2000).

28 Mary Louise Pratt, *Imperial Eyes: Travel Writing and Transculturation* (London: Routledge, 1992).

29 Ulrike Hillemann, *Asian Empire and British Knowledge: China and the Networks of British Imperial Expansion* (Basingstoke: Palgrave Macmillan, 2009), pp. 104–5. She has not, however, explored this specific aspect in great detail.

30 Peter J. Kitson, *Forging Romantic China: Sino-British Cultural Exchange 1760–1840* (Cambridge: Cambridge University Press, 2013).

31 Peter J. Kitson and Robert Markley, 'Introduction: Writing China', in *Writing China: Essays on the Amherst Embassy (1816) and Sino-British Cultural Relations*, ed.

INTRODUCTION

Kitson and Markley (Woodbridge: Boydell & Brewer, 2016), p. 2. They have also attached importance to the Second Opium War (1856–60).

32 For example, British Library, London: India Office Library and Records (hereafter IOLR): India Office Amherst Correspondence, Lord Amherst's Embassy, 1815–17, G/12/197/271. Letter from Amherst to George Canning, 28 Feb. 1817; George T. Staunton, *Miscellaneous Notices Relating to China, and Our Commercial Intercourse with that Country* (London: John Murray, 1822), p. 238; Napier to Palmerston, 9 Aug. 1834, in *Correspondence Relating to China, Presented to Both Houses of Parliament, by Command of Her Majesty* (London: T.R. Harrison, 1840), p. 8; and *Hansard's Parliamentary Debates*, House of Commons, 9 Apr. 1840, Third series, vol. 53, 937.

33 Chen, *Chinese Laws in Imperial Eyes*, pp. 232–5; Chen, *Merchants of War and Peace*, pp. 118–22.

34 Le Comte, *Nouveaux mémoires sur l'état present de la Chine* (Paris, 1696), p. 125. See Qian Zhongshu, 'China in the English Literature of the Eighteenth Century', in *A Collection of Qian Zhongshu's English Essays* (Beijing: Foreign Language Teaching and Research Press, 2005), p. 151. This article was originally published in *Quarterly Bulletin of Chinese Bibliography*, new series, 2 (1941), 7–48, 113–52.

35 There are two English translations of this book: one published by John Watts in 1736 under the title *The General History of China*, the other published by Edward Cave between 1738 to 1741 in two folio volumes, which was entitled *A Description of the Empire of China and Chinese Tartary*.

36 It has a selective English translation entitled *Travels of the Jesuits into various parts of the World*. This book was edited by the English author John Lockman. The first edition appeared in two volumes in 1743 with a second one in 1762.

37 It is worth noting that, while the Jesuit accounts were influential, they were also contested by the Franciscan and Dominican missionaries.

38 Donald F. Lach, 'Leibniz and China', *Journal of the History of Ideas*, 6 (1945), 440.

39 Voltaire, *Essai sur les moeurs et l'esprit des nations et sur les principaux faits de l'histoire depuis Charlemagne jusqu'à Louis XIII* (1756; reprinted, Paris, 1963), p. 69, in Mackerras, *Western Images of China*, p. 38.

40 Lewis A. Maverick, *China: A Model for Europe* (San Antonio, TX: Paul Anderson, 1946), p. 206. This work was originally published in two volumes, the second of which is the author's translation of Quesnay's works.

41 Quesnay, in *ibid.*, p. 216.

42 Quesnay, *Le despotisme de la Chine* (1767), II, 226, in William Joseph Eaton, 'The Old Regime and the Middle Kingdom: The French Physiocrats and China as a Model for Reform in the Eighteenth Century, a Cautionary Tale', *Tamkang Journal of International Affairs*, 10 (2006), 75.

43 'Chinoiserie' as a term to describe a European fantasy vision of China was not known in the seventeenth and eighteenth centuries. It is an expression of relatively recent invention, which first appeared in dictionaries in 1883. See David Beevers, '"Mand'rin only is the man of taste": 17th and 18th Century Chinoiserie in Britain', in *Chinese Whispers: Chinoiserie in Britain 1650–1930*, ed. Beevers (Brighton: The Royal Pavilion and Museums, 2008), p. 13.

44 Marshall and Williams, *The Great Map of Mankind*, p. 132.

45 Webb, *An Historical Essay*, pp. 15–26, 44, 60, see Qian Zhongshu, 'China in the English Literature of the Seventeenth Century', in *The Vision of China*, ed. Hsia, p. 46. Qian's article was originally published in *Quarterly Bulletin of Chinese Bibliography*, new series, 1 (1940), 351–84.

46 William Temple, *The Works of Sir William Temple* (4 vols, London: J. Brotherton, 1770; reprinted, New York: Greenwood, 1968), III, 41, 328.

47 *Ibid.*, III, 332.

48 Myers (ed.), *Western Views of China and the Far East*, I, 38.

49 Marshall and Williams, *The Great Map of Mankind*, p. 175.

50 Adam Smith, *An Inquiry into the Nature and Causes of the Wealth of Nations*, ed. R.H. Campbell and A.S. Skinner (2 vols, Oxford: Oxford University Press, 1976), I, 89.

51 *Ibid.*, II, 681.
52 Daniel Defoe, *The Life and Adventures of Robinson Crusoe* (1719; reprinted, Edinburgh: James Ballantyne, 1812), p. 395.
53 *Ibid.*
54 William Jones, *The Works of Sir William Jones* (6 vols, London: G.G. and J. Robinson, 1799), I, 102.
55 James Boswell, *Boswell's Life of Johnson: Together with Boswell's Journal of a Tour to the Hebrides and Johnson's Diary of a Journey into North Wales*, ed. L.F. Powell (6 vols, Oxford: Clarendon, 1934–50), III, 339; IV, 188.
56 Mackerras, *Western Images of China*, p. 43.
57 George Anson, *A Voyage Round the World in the Years 1740–1744* (London: John and Paul Knapton, 1748), p. 525.
58 East India Company, *Three Reports of the Select Committee, Appointed by the Court of Directors to Take into Consideration the Export Trade from Great Britain to the East Indies, China, Japan, and Persia* (London: J.S. Jordan, 1793), p. 82.
59 Marshall and Williams, *The Great Map of Mankind*, p. 174.
60 *Ibid.*

PART I

The embassies

CHAPTER ONE

The Macartney embassy

The Macartney embassy of 1792–4, also known as the Macartney mission, was the first official encounter between Britain and China, the greatest Western and Eastern powers in the late eighteenth century. After the War of American Independence concluded in 1783, significant changes occurred in the structure of the British Empire. Growing importance was attached to Asia, and the trade with China became increasingly important for the expansion of British commerce overseas. Nevertheless, from the mid-seventeenth century, the imperial government of China began to apply a highly restrictive policy to its foreign trade. In 1757, the Qing court further confined the country's external trade to a small area outside the city of Canton and restricted it to being conducted through a handful of authorised merchants. This so-called 'Canton system' resulted in a trade balance unfavourable to the British. On the one hand, the fact that Britain had no access to the wider Chinese market made it almost impossible for the British to import into China the same manufactured products that were sold in India. On the other hand, since China accepted only silver and gold as payment for its products, and had little demand for British goods, an ever-increasing desire for Chinese tea in Britain resulted in a drain of precious metals from the country. Meanwhile, in Britain, the theories of Adam Smith and Jeremy Bentham promoted the benefits of free trade. The free competition and reciprocity of trade were deemed beneficial not only to the British but to the whole of humankind. Government control over commerce, such as the Canton system of China, became more and more unacceptable to British manufacturers and merchants, who were keen to open up new markets for their products. In these circumstances, a British embassy was first formed in 1788 to travel to the imperial court of China, with the object of gaining greater trade rights and even establishing Western-style diplomatic relations with the Qing.[1] It was called off, however, because of the sudden death of the ambassador, Charles Cathcart, before he reached Chinese waters. Shortly after that, another embassy was appointed by the British government – this time led by Lord George Macartney. Macartney had experience dealing with an autocratic ruler, Catherine II, when he was Britain's envoy to Russia in 1764. He also served as the governor of Madras (now Chennai) from 1781 to 1785 and was believed to be somewhat familiar with 'oriental' diplomacy. Considered as the most suitable diplomat to lead the mission, Macartney set sail with his embassy on 26 September 1792 from Spithead, England.

The standard narrative of the Macartney embassy's experience in China is as follows. In June 1793, the embassy arrived in China with various presents from the British monarch, George III, including a range of state-of-the-art scientific apparatus. Under the pretext of wishing to pay respects to the Qianlong emperor (1711–99, r. 1735–96) on his eighty-second birthday, the embassy was granted an imperial audience at the emperor's summer resort of Jehol (Rehe, now Chengde) in September. The Qing court at this time had little idea of Western diplomacy or the principle of free trade. In this context, Macartney failed to launch any official negotiation on the commercial and diplomatic objectives of the embassy. Instead, his refusal, or at least reluctance, to perform kowtow, a ceremony that involves kneeling and knocking the forehead against the floor, before the emperor created much controversy. According to the British accounts, the Qianlong emperor made a compromise in allowing Macartney to kneel upon only one knee, but no such record can be found from the archives of the Qing. The later Jiaqing emperor (1760–1820, r. 1796–1820) claimed that Macartney did kowtow and he had witnessed the occasion. No matter whose words are true, shortly after the imperial audience, Macartney received strong hints that the embassy should leave Beijing immediately, as its official business had been concluded. In early October, Macartney felt obliged to request permission to depart from the Chinese capital. Although the Qing government treated the British very well during the embassy's return journey across China (partly to prevent them from causing trouble), none of its primary goals had been achieved.

As a monumental event in the history of Sino-Western encounters, the Macartney embassy has attracted extensive scholarship, especially since the early 1990s when its bicentennial anniversary was commemorated by researchers from China and the West. To appreciate its significance, some historians have maintained that it marked a missed opportunity for China to move towards some kind of accommodation with the West,[2] while others have argued that its failure was due to a clash of world views which were almost irreconcilable.³ In particular, the issue of the kowtow ceremony was in the forefront of scholarly attention. The well-known debate between James Hevia and Joseph Esherick has prompted widespread discussion in both Western and Chinese academia to research and interpret the court ritual of the Qing.⁴ As a result of this literature, culture and ritual were placed by historians at the heart of the scholarship on the Macartney embassy for an extended period of time. Meanwhile, scholars slowly but gradually realised the need to go beyond the study of the kowtow controversy. Joanna Waley-Cohen and Maxine Berg have paid attention to the presents offered to the Qing court by the Macartney embassy. The former concentrates on how the Qing perceived British science and technology in the late eighteenth century,⁵ while the latter discusses the attitudes of British manufacturers and government officials towards their own products and technologies.⁶ In recent years, William Christie and Logan Collins have explored how the Macartney embassy and the images of China were presented in British periodicals.⁷ Both of them are interested in the process in which British writers, editors and reviewers at home helped mediate the embassy's findings about China. Henrietta Harrison, in her outstanding paper published in *American Historical Review*, has added that archivists were also important 'co-creators' of history in the choices they made about what to keep and what to exclude from the archive.⁸ That the Macartney embassy has been remembered and researched in the present ways, according to Harrison, is partly because the issue of diplomatic protocol was a key concern in the culture of eighteenth-century Britain,⁹ partly because the political context of early twentieth-century China, the editors' preoccupations and the structure of the archive itself heavily influenced the Chinese archivists' decision in the 1920s on what documents were to be released about the embassy.

Despite this rich literature, there is still room to study further the Macartney embassy and what it meant to the development of Sino-British relations. Notably, in terms of British imagination of China, contemporary scholars have recognised that it became increasingly critical from the seventeenth to the nineteenth century, but they have not reached consensus on when exactly the balance between favourable and unfavourable views began to shift from the former to the latter. Song-Chuan Chen has maintained that a 'paradigm shift' occurred dramatically in the 1830s, largely due to the warlike party's campaigns for war.¹⁰ Peter Kitson disagrees with this view, believing that the shift happened decades earlier. He has shown that a definitive move away from the earlier Jesuit-inspired writing on China resulted from the Macartney embassy, which generated a mass of textual commentary that signalled the emergence of a new British or 'Romantic Sinology'.[11] In this respect, Kitson's view seems more reasonable, because, despite the failure of its official business, the Macartney embassy did provide a unique opportunity for the British to contact with various people in China, as well as to travel through the interior of the empire during its return journey from Beijing to Canton. Such experience definitely allowed members of the Macartney embassy to bring back to Britain a variety of first-hand observations of China, which became the source of new knowledge about the country for the British at home. Based on available primary sources, this chapter focuses on some hitherto overlooked perceptions formed as a result of this first official encounter between Britain and China.

Moreover, as shown above, historians have recently investigated the power of archivists, editors and reviewers in 'creating' knowledge about China at second hand, but less effort has been made to question the reliability of first-hand materials. For those who did challenge the trustworthiness of primary sources, the work has been conducted mainly on Chinese sources. In 1993, Joanna Waley-Cohen famously contested the traditional interpretation of the Qianlong emperor's letter to King George III as a sign of China's arrogance, isolationism and resistance to progress. She suggested that the emperor's expression of disdain for Western goods was actually for the purpose of domestic politics.[12] This approach of treating the Chinese official documents with caution has now been adopted more widely by historians when digesting Chinese materials; however, as Li Chen has pointed out, the same kind of caution was rarely exercised towards the English-language primary sources.[13] In this chapter, I argue that it would be equally erroneous to take British accounts at face value. By comparing different accounts of the Macartney embassy, this chapter shows that the leaders of the embassy also attempted to gloss over or withhold certain information about their mission, in order to cast their experience in China in a light favourable to themselves. These representations, in turn, helped shape Britain's attitudes and policy towards China in the decades to come.

Pride and prejudice

Six members of the Macartney mission published accounts of their visits to China. When the embassy returned to Britain in 1794, Lord Macartney did not release his own journal. Instead, he gave his diary and correspondence to his deputy, Sir George Leonard Staunton, and urged him to produce an 'official' account of the embassy experience. This book, entitled *An Authentic Account of an Embassy from the*

King of Great Britain to the Emperor of China, remained the most authoritative account of the Macartney mission until 1962, when the Canadian historian J.L. Cranmer-Byng edited and published Macartney's own journal.[14] Two middle-ranking persons, John Barrow and James Dinwiddie, also printed records of their experiences with the embassy. The former, the comptroller of the mission, published his *Travels in China* in 1804.[15] The journal of the latter, the embassy's technician and a well-known scientist, was published by his grandson, William Jardine Proudfoot, in 1868. In addition, Lord Macartney's valet, Aeneas Anderson, and a sergeant-major in Macartney's guard named Samuel Holmes also had their diaries printed for the public. These two accounts appeared only a few years after the conclusion of the embassy, but they have been criticised either as having been 'vamped up by a London bookseller as a speculation'[16] or as 'nothing of value'.[17] Among these works, it is the first three that have received most scholarly attention, especially on the sections in relation to the kowtow controversy. A broader reading of these sources, however, can tell us much more about the embassy.

To begin with, as shown in the introduction, scholars of British cultural representations of China have agreed that there was a gradual decline in British admiration for China in the eighteenth century. This view often leads to an assumption that, by the time of the Macartney embassy, British society had by and large reached a consensus on a negative image of the Chinese empire. This impression can probably be sustained if we examine only Macartney's and Staunton's accounts, especially in light of their expectations for the mission. In the late years of the eighteenth century, as industrial advances were rapidly transforming the British landscape and society, enlightened ideas prevailed among the British elite. Just like other celebrated figures such as Samuel Johnson, Macartney and Staunton, the former a member of the eminent Literary Club, the latter a Fellow of the Royal Society and an honorary doctoral degree holder of Oxford University, were convinced of Britain's superiority over China. In Macartney's diary, we can find that he did entertain an apparent distaste for China's political and cultural practices before he set foot on Chinese soil. Throughout the embassy, Macartney was keen to impress the Chinese with Britain's superior learning and power. For example, he claimed that:

> One great advantage indeed of the embassy is the opportunity it afforded of showing the Chinese to what a high degree of perfection the English nation had carried all the arts and accomplishments of civilized life; that their manners were calculated for the improvement of social intercourse and liberal commerce; that though great and powerful they were generous

and humane, not fierce and impetuous like the Russians, but entitled to the respect and preference of the Chinese above the other European nations, whom they have any knowledge of.[18]

This statement shows that Macartney, as the leader of the embassy, did have unfavourable preconceptions of China. Although one objective of the mission was to discover the secrets of silk, tea and porcelain production in China, to demonstrate the strength and ingenuity of Britain was one of Macartney's main concerns.

It is important to note, however, that this sentiment was not shared by all members of the Macartney mission. As William Christie has recently analysed, 'it would be wrong to assume that by the end of the eighteenth century, the ideological debate about China was settled'.[19] In contrast to the negative views of China held by Macartney and supposed to have been typical in the late eighteenth century, rather positive expectations about China did exist, particularly in the minds of some middle- and lower-ranking persons of the embassy. Barrow, for instance, recorded that, prior to the voyage, he was informed that 'The Chinese ... are superior to all the Asiatic nations, in antiquity, in genius, in the progress of the sciences, in wisdom, in government, and in true philosophy; may, moreover, ... enter the lists, on all these points, with the most enlightened nations of Europe'.[20] Although Barrow acknowledged that there were doubts about these views, 'upon the whole, the British embassy left England under a favourable impression of the people it was about to visit'.[21] Dinwiddie, a committed scientist whose main job was to impress the Chinese with European technology, was one of those who were excited about the prospect of exploring China. He wrote, 'To visit such a country – to have an opportunity of examining into the state and arts and manufactures there – was a theme of overpowering interest in the mind of an ardent philosopher, and it is easy to guess the feelings with which those favoured individuals, whom Government had honored on this occasion, set sail'.[22]

Henry Eades, the embassy's metallurgist, entertained the belief that China possessed some forms of cutting-edge technology which were unknown to the rest of the world. Eades believed that some artisans in Beijing knew a method of making a kind of tinsel that did not tarnish, or could be kept without tarnishing much longer than anything of its kind in Europe. Although he died on the road to the Chinese capital, Eades had long cherished the hope that, once he had obtained such techniques, he would be able to generate considerable wealth for his family. As Staunton recalled, 'he [Eades] thought it not too much to shorten his own life, in a perilous voyage, for the sake of being able to communicate to his offspring, what would be the means of their prosperity'.[23] Although in the late eighteenth century elite Britons such as Macartney might hold a belief that China was inferior to Britain, their sense of pride as 'superior' Britons was not necessarily shared by others. Other members of the embassy held diverse expectations of what might be discovered in China and their views were more inclined to be favourable. The assumption that the Macartney embassy at large came to China with negative preconceptions cannot be sustained.

In fact, the strong sense of pride that can be found in Macartney and Staunton before their arrival in China can be detected throughout their accounts of the mission. It certainly influenced the ways in which they represented their experience. Just as the early twentieth-century Chinese archivists had done to the Qing documents about the embassy (as recently discovered by Harrison), the two leaders carefully selected what was to be recorded and what to be left out to suit their own purposes. A notable example is their narratives of the embassy's departure from Beijing. In early October 1793, the Qing court sent clear signals to Macartney that the official business of the embassy was over and the British should leave Beijing immediately. This message was delivered in such a hasty and determined manner that Macartney's request for a delay of even two days was rejected. To most of the embassy members, who had been expecting to spend the winter in the Chinese capital, this rapid dismissal was surprising and disappointing. Some of them recorded that the unexpected order to the embassy to leave without delay caused 'a state of indescribable confusion'[24] within the British delegation. Anderson noted that 'the manner in which the Ambassador was *dismissed* from Pekin [Beijing] was ungracious and mortifying in the extreme'.[25] He wrote:

> Our surprise at such unexpected intelligence may be readily conceived, but the mortification which appeared throughout the palace on the occasion, was at least equal to the astonishment: ... while our fatiguing pilgrimage was to be renewed, not only with all the humiliation that accompanies a forced submission to peremptory power, but with the painful despondency which arises from the sudden annihilation of sanguine and well-grounded hope. ... But, though we might, in the first moments of surprise, be disposed to feel something for ourselves, superior considerations soon succeeded, and we forgot the trifle of personal inconvenience, in the failure of a political measure which had been pursued with so much labour, hazard, and perseverance; had been supported with such enormous expense, and to which our country looked with eager expectation, for the aggrandizement of its commercial interests.[26]

This general sentiment within the embassy, however, was concealed in the narratives produced by Macartney and Staunton. No words can be found in Macartney's account to show that he also shared such feelings. Macartney's diary entries for these few days, however, were unusually short. He simply explained that the reason given by the Chinese government was the coldness of Beijing's winter. In just a few lines, he justified his decision to request to leave: 'It is now beyond a doubt, although nothing was said upon the subject, that the Court wishes us to be gone, and if we don't take the hints already given, they may possibly be imparted to us in a broader and coarser manner, which would be equally unpleasant to the dignity of the Embassy and the success of its objects'.[27] Staunton, in comparison, gave a fuller explanation for the need to leave Beijing, but his attempt to gloss over the displeasure within the embassy is equally obvious. Among other reasons, Staunton pointed out that, due to the probable outbreak of war between Britain and France, a warship was needed to convey the British merchant ships back home. Since the embassy's flagship, the sixty-four-gun *Lion*, was the best available for the time being, the embassy could not afford to lose time in joining the *Lion*'s Captain, Sir Erasmus Gower, at Zhoushan. With regard to the disappointment within the embassy, Staunton wrote:

> So sudden a removal was a disappointment to several persons of the Embassy, who had made their arrangements for passing the winter at Pekin. Judging of its temperature by the latitude of the place, a few minutes under forty degrees north, they were not aware of the violent effect of the great range of high Tartarian mountains, covered perpetually with snow, upon that capital, where the average degree of the thermometer, is under twenty in the night during the winter months, and even in the day time considerably below the freezing point.[28]

In this manner, Staunton not only described the degree of frustration among only 'several persons' but implied agreement with the Qing court's justification. If we take Staunton's and Macartney's words at face value, the embassy's departure from Beijing would appear to be rather a sensible 'decision' based on rational advice than a forced and ungracious dismissal. It is, however, hard to imagine that, without even starting discussion about the embassy's real objectives, the two proud leaders of the mission should not have felt much regret for not remaining in the Chinese capital any longer. Although, at this point, the departure from Beijing would have meant that the embassy had failed, neither Macartney nor Staunton chose to make extensive comments on its implication. The bustle and depression across much of the embassy was significantly understated in their published accounts. The request to leave Beijing, by contrast, was described as neither unreasonable nor inconsistent with the interests of Britain.

The leaders' attempts to interpret their encounters in China in a favourable light were even more apparent when it came to their overall assessment of the embassy. In particular, unlike Anderson and others who claimed that the unwilling departure from Beijing had indicated the failure of the mission, Macartney and Staunton neither mentioned that they were aware of such a view nor seemed to agree with it. Throughout the return journey, however, the two leaders of the embassy appeared keen to prove such a claim wrong without even referring to it. They presented a variety of viewpoints and constructed a series of images to defend the view that the mission had not been a failure.

First, both of them maintained that, during the return journey, despite the great distance from the imperial court, Macartney actually obtained a much more effective channel of communication with the emperor than he would have done by staying at Beijing. This was because the two Chinese officers conducting them in these few months, Song Yun and Chang Lin,[29] appeared to be very kind to the embassy. According to Staunton, since these officers held a regular, almost daily, correspondence with the emperor, contact with the Chinese sovereign 'was in fact maintained ... more intimately ... than while he [Macartney] remained in the middle of his court'.[30] Because of this 'favourable' channel, Macartney noted that he eventually had a chance to mention some of the real purposes of his mission, including the extension of Sino-British trade and the establishment of a permanent ambassadorship in Beijing. Although these requests were all turned down, Macartney suggested that it was due to the invariable laws and usages of China, rather than any ill feelings occasioned by his embassy. In his diary, Macartney repeatedly stressed that Song Yun and Chang Lin were keen to impress upon him the opinion that the emperor was well disposed towards the embassy. He also spared no effort in collecting every sign that might sustain such an interpretation. For example, the civility with which the embassy was treated on the return journey was taken as evidence that not only was the emperor not affronted by Macartney's refusal to kowtow, but he actually had a favourable opinion of the embassy as well as of the British nation. To prove this view, Macartney noted down minutely many statements made by Song Yun or Chang Lin about the emperor's wish to treat British merchants with more favour and kindness in the future. Harrison's recent research, however, has shown that this was simply the Qianlong emperor's tactic to pacify the embassy – by giving vague promises of future trade negotiations in order to avert immediate trouble that the British might cause while they were travelling through China.[31] From the existing accounts of the embassy, we cannot know to what extent Macartney was aware of this strategy or whether he had doubted the sincerity of the Chinese. He should have had a clue, because Macartney was eager to have written confirmation of Song Yun's and Chang Lin's words, but he never succeeded in obtaining one. The reason given to him was that promises made in private conversations should not be shown in an official document.

Moreover, to further interpret the embassy's 'achievements', Macartney and Staunton maintained that they had managed to improve Britain's image in the minds of the Chinese. They claimed that, as a result of their visit, Chinese prejudice against the British was considerably softened. Macartney stated that it was understandable that the Chinese, as 'one of the vainest nations in the world',[32] should have held poor impressions of the British in the past. Nevertheless, 'by my Embassy the Chinese have had, what they never had before, an opportunity of knowing us, this must lead them to a proper way of thinking of us and of acting towards us in future'.[33] Staunton added that, through recent contacts, some Chinese senior officials had become convinced that Britain had no other purpose in view than developing a mutually beneficial trade relationship with China. In addition, while the embassy was in China, many Chinese people had been given an opportunity to learn 'some of the advantages which the English now had over them'.[34] As a result, the 'superior knowledge and acquirements' of the British earned for the embassy 'admiration, esteem, and consequent good treatment'.[35] To highlight this, Macartney emphasised in the conclusion of his journal:

> It is no small advantage rising from the Embassy that so many Englishmen have been seen at Pekin, from whose brilliant appearance and prudent demeanour a most favourable idea has been formed of the country which had sent them. Nor is it any strain of vanity to say that the principal persons of rank who, from their intercourse with us, had opportunities of observing our manners, tempers and discipline very soon dismissed the prejudices they had conceived against us, and by a generous transition grew to admire and respect us as a nation and to love us as individuals.[36]

Despite these efforts to demonstrate that the embassy was not a failure, it remains the case that it did not succeed in achieving its primary objectives. Why this mission was not successful in achieving these goals hence became another important question which Macartney and Staunton had to answer. To explain it, the two leaders blamed the prejudices and hostility of a few senior ministers at the Qianlong court rather than the emperor himself. On the basis of his recently obtained 'first-hand knowledge', Macartney asserted in his diary that, contrary to the assumption that the emperor had absolute control over all state affairs, 'the power and administration of the State resided in the great councils or tribunals ... The government as it now stands is properly the tyranny of a handful of Tartars over more than three hundred millions of Chinese'.³⁷ On the basis of this belief, which was formed without reliable inside knowledge of the Qing's political system, Macartney drew a conclusion that 'I should rather imagine that the personal character of the Ministers, alarmed by the most trifling accident, the aversion they may naturally have to sudden innovation, especially at the Emperor's late period of life ... have been among the chief obstacles to my business'.³⁸

Compared to Macartney's general comment, Staunton's criticism of these principal ministers was more specific. He placed most blame on Fu Kang-an, one of the six grand councillors, and He Shen, the chief councillor. Fu Kang-an, as Staunton was informed, was a senior Manchu general who had governed a number of provinces including Guangdong. Not long before 1793, Fu Kang-an had led a military campaign against the Gurkhas on the Tibet–Nepal border, where he claimed to have met interference from the British. Perhaps for these reasons, no matter how hard Macartney attempted to please Fu Kang-an, the general remained hostile to the embassy. Fu Kang-an's animosity towards the British was so strong and obvious that Staunton could not avoid protesting that 'nothing was, perhaps, more desirable for its [Britain's] interest in China, than that he should neither be continued in the councils of the Emperor, or be sent back to the vice-royalty of Canton'.³⁹ He Shen, the minister who enjoyed the almost exclusive confidence of the Qianlong emperor, was portrayed by Staunton as '[t]he Vizier of China, who ... possess[es], in fact, under the Emperor, the whole power of the empire'.⁴⁰ Although they admitted that He Shen displayed all the good breeding and politeness of an experienced courtier, Staunton and Macartney agreed that He Shen's real attitude towards the British was the same as Fu Kang-an's. According to Macartney's diary, it was He Shen, rather than anybody else, who prevented him from communicating the real purposes of his embassy to the Qianlong emperor. As historians, we do not know what made Macartney think in this way and why he appeared so convinced. 'It is much regretted', Macartney wrote, 'that the first Minister was determined not to give me such opportunities'.⁴¹

Despite blaming these senior ministers for the failure of their embassy, Macartney and Staunton presented rather positive images of almost everybody else they met in China, particularly the Qianlong emperor himself. In their accounts, the emperor was described as a liberal, amicable and father-like figure. They repeatedly insisted that the Qianlong emperor was 'a leader of a calm judgement',⁴² who had 'a high esteem for the Ambassador and his nation ... and ... [was] determined to protect their trade'.⁴³ Even on the controversy over kowtow, Staunton claimed that 'the good sense and liberality of the emperor himself, cloyed too much perhaps with adoration, rendered him much more inclined than any of his advisers, to dispense with that ceremony in the present instance'.[44] It was a few ministers 'more than the Emperor himself, [who] adhered to this antiquated claim of superiority over other nations'.[45] In commenting upon the disposition of lower-ranking officials as well as the attitudes of the common Chinese people, Macartney noted that:

> most of the principal people, whom I have had opportunities of knowing, I have found sociable, conversable, good-humoured, and not at all indisposed to foreigners. As to the lower orders, they are all of a trafficking turn, and it seemed at the seaports where we stopped that nothing would be more agreeable to them than to see our ships often in their harbours.[46]

As a result of these constructed images, the failure of Macartney's mission (although neither Macartney nor Staunton was never willing to accept the term 'failure') seemed to be the result of the prejudices of a handful of Manchu ministers, while the vast majority of the Chinese, including their Manchu emperor, were better disposed towards both the British and Britain's trade with China. Again, it is difficult for us to make clear whether this was Macartney's and Staunton's genuine belief, but it certainly proved a convenient way for them to say 'this is not our fault'.

These interpretations (or perhaps deliberate misinterpretations) of Chinese affairs, furthermore, allowed Macartney and Staunton to formulate their answers to another self-raised question: what line of action should Britain adopt in its future relations with China? The two leaders maintained that, in terms of the primary goals of the embassy, no concession could possibly be gained all of a sudden, but, provided with time and patience, good results should follow in due course. Therefore, Britain should not rush to seek any substantial change in Sino-British relations in the near future. This attitude was largely borrowed from Father Amiot, a French missionary who had served in the Qing court since 1750. Shortly before Macartney requested to leave Beijing, Amiot wrote an unsolicited letter to Macartney with his advice on the British mission. In a friendly tone, Amiot was clearly trying to persuade Macartney to depart from the Chinese capital without delay. Amiot commented that, according to his long experience of living in China, the Chinese had no idea of free trade and Western diplomacy. They, however, 'might be rendered sensible of them if applied to and solicited without precipitation, and managed with caution and adroitness, for nothing was to be expected as attainable on the sudden'.[47] It is interesting to note that, after reading this message, neither Macartney nor Staunton questioned the intention of Amiot or attempted to check the reliability of his views. Instead, since Amiot had presented such a useful argument to allow them to argue that they had not done anything inappropriate, Macartney and Staunton accepted his advice without reservation. On this basis, they developed it into a key argument to further justify Macartney's request to leave Beijing. Staunton asserted that, since 'the present mission had made such an impression throughout the empire'[48] and the emperor entertained kind intentions towards the British, beneficial consequences could eventually be obtained 'by time and management'.[49] He continued to write that:

> such was the nature and practice of the Chinese government, that however adverse in the beginning to any new propositions, lest it should be surprised into an undue concession or improper regulation, the same matters might be brought again, when the offensive novelty of the idea was over, into a more serious and dispassionate consideration.[50]

From claims such as this, we can conclude that Macartney and Staunton were endeavouring to deliver the following message: the present embassy not only had done nothing wrong to render it less fruitful than had been hoped, but had laid favourable foundations for future British–Chinese contacts. It was the unique character of the Qing government that unfortunately prevented more positive results from the embassy being seen immediately. There was therefore nothing more this embassy could have achieved, and hence it should not be regarded as unsuccessful.

Although the leaders had tried to glorify the experience and outcome of their embassy as much as they could, their views do not seem very tenable if we examine other accounts of the mission. Dinwiddie, in particular, challenged many of Macartney's and Staunton's conclusions. In his diary, which was published seven decades after the mission, Dinwiddie maintained that, although the heads of the embassy had endeavoured to 'look upon their treatment in the most favourable light',[51] it was indisputable that the mission was treated so shamefully that 'no apology' had been able to satisfy the public when they returned home.[52] Even though general assurances were allegedly made by Song Yun and Chang Lin to the effect that Britain's trading conditions in China would be bettered, 'nothing that looks like an improvement has yet taken place'[53] and 'the Chinese are not likely to make any alteration in our trade'.[54] In this respect, in contrast to the contention that no immediate achievements could be obtained because of the unique character of the Chinese government, Dinwiddie claimed that 'the behaviour of the gentlemen of the Embassy themselves was the principal cause' of the embassy's failure.[55] Since Dinwiddie was in charge of the presents which were expected to impress the Chinese, he claimed that mistakes had been made in the selection as well as in the presentation of these gifts. Dinwiddie maintained that, because the Chinese had limited ability to appreciate British technology, in order to produce the best effect, more military contrivances rather than scientific apparatus should have been taken to China, and 'the guns ought to have been of a larger calibre'.[56] Moreover, the long process of erecting some highly sophisticated instruments, such as the planetarium, should have been concealed from the Chinese before they were presented as a whole. Otherwise, as had transpired, the sensation that they had been supposed to create was so far diminished that very few of the Chinese were impressed. Some of them even doubted the value of such instruments when the British seemed to have problems setting them up.

Dinwiddie, furthermore, pointed out in his diary that the leadership of the embassy was extremely unprofessional. Although Macartney had tried a variety of ways to please He Shen, who was famously known as the most corrupt official in China, Macartney had never attempted to give He Shen 'something considerable in a private way'.[57] Failing to bribe such a crucial figure, in Dinwiddie's opinion, was the key reason for the failure of the embassy. In addition, Dinwiddie complained that 'in all our operations, no plan or system has been adopted; no regular orders given, [or] at least adhered to'.[58] For instance, regarding whether to employ a suspicious Portuguese missionary as Dinwiddie's interpreter, a number of inconsistent and even contradictory instructions were issued by the leaders of the embassy. This resulted in much embarrassment for Dinwiddie and he was deeply annoyed for what had subsequently happened. Perhaps for this reason, Dinwiddie became further convinced that it was primarily the unprofessional leadership that had led to such disgrace.

Compared to Dinwiddie, the lower-ranked members, such as Anderson and Holmes, did not comment so much on the management or the results of the Macartney mission. Some of their observations, however, still show that certain key images introduced by Macartney and Staunton were of questionable veracity. Most importantly, Holmes was critical of the notion that most Chinese mandarins and people were on good terms with the British visitors, and that this relationship had underpinned the positive reception of the embassy amongst the majority in China. Holmes maintained that it was actually not the case at all. He pointed out that under the cover of ostensible hospitality was the Chinese people's fear of upsetting the guests whom they had to be ordered not to offend, while the Chinese, in fact, had no truly kind feelings towards the British. Holmes observed that 'though, in many instances, they treated us with singular marks of respect, yet all their attention to us seemed tempered with fear and dread; it was apparent enough that they wished us away from amongst them'.[59] To further demonstrate that the attention with which the Macartney embassy was received primarily derived from the dread of displeasing their superiors, Holmes added that, apart from the principal ministers such as He Shen and Fu Kang'an who had no fear of any authority, most mandarins indeed 'treated us with singular marks of attention and politeness, and were ever anxious to do us some acceptable piece of service'.[60] This was, however, not because they were genuinely friendly to the British, but because 'the slightest deviation from any given order is punished with such severity, without regard to the rank of the offender, that all are very cautious; and more particularly, when that order respects any Europeans or strangers, of whom they are so unaccountably suspicious and fearful'.[61] Holmes's observation now proves to be consistent with Harrison's recent discovery – the Qianlong emperor did send many orders to his officers along the embassy's returning route, instructing them to treat the embassy with great care and caution, to prevent the British from stirring up trouble.[62] It, again, does not make much sense that such a lower-ranking person as Holmes was able to question the 'friendship' demonstrated by the Chinese but a similar kind of suspicion escaped Macartney's and Staunton's accounts – unless they deliberately disguised it.

Moreover, Anderson suggested that the leaders' accounts of the mission focused too much on the civility and respect that the embassy received during the return journey, but deliberately overlooked the disrespectful manner in which they were treated at the Qing court. In particular, Anderson recorded that, before the arrival in Jehol where the imperial audience was going to take place, Macartney was anxious to create a favourable impression of his mission on those Chinese high officials who he supposed would welcome them at the city gate. To achieve this end, Macartney decided to enter the city in a glorious procession, for which repeated practices and rehearsals were made by all members of the embassy during the journey. To everyone's surprise, however, when the mission finally reached the city gate of Jehol, not only did Macartney's highly anticipated meeting with He Shen not take place but 'not a mandarin appeared to congratulate the Ambassador on his arrival, or to usher him, with that form which his dignity demanded, to the apartments provided for him'.[63] This dishonourable reception, which certainly disappointed Macartney a great deal, did not leave a trace in Macartney's or Staunton's account. Nor was any importance attached by the two leaders to the frustration it generated across the embassy. To the lesser-ranked members of the mission who had not previously been informed of the problematic nature of official relations, however, the ungracious manner with which they were received at Jehol sent them the very first signal that the success of the mission was by no means assured. Anderson wrote in his diary that 'Nothing, however, has yet transpired that could lead us to form a judgment as to the final issue of the business: as far as any opinion could be formed as to the general aspect of things, it did not bear the promise of that success which had been originally expected from it'.[64]

It can be seen that Macartney and Staunton, as leaders of the embassy, created a set of images which were essentially self-serving and 'face-saving'. These new interpretations of the Chinese affairs, however, could be misleading. The two leaders maintained that the embassy had successfully laid good foundations for future Sino-British relations, because they had won the respect of the majority of the Chinese they met, as well as the favour of the Qianlong emperor. They claimed that it was the unique character of the Qing government, which was currently dominated by a handful of hostile ministers, that prevented the embassy from achieving more positive results in 1793. A deeper and wider look into other accounts of the embassy, however, shows that most of these arguments were asserted rather than based upon solid evidence. In particular, nothing could prove that the emperor himself had a high esteem for the British and any intention of improving British trade in China. Macartney and Staunton, moreover, selectively documented and deliberately withheld a series of significant occurrences of the embassy, in order to glorify the experience and to suit their own interpretations. Although it is understandable that all commentators have their own standpoints, or a tendency to interpret things to suit their own needs, it is worth bearing in mind that these 'authoritative' accounts of the Macartney embassy greatly influenced the ways by which the British at home viewed China and Chinese affairs at the turn of the century. It was on the basis of some of these preconceptions, which were questionable in themselves, that later generations of Britons came to develop the nation's relations with China.

Discoveries in China

Although the overall picture of the Macartney embassy projected by its leaders had clearly been 'photoshopped' (to use a modern phrase), this mission did enable the British travellers to make contact with the Chinese government and people in a way that had never been achieved before. In particular, it allowed Britons to traverse the interior of China for the very first time and this opportunity to examine China so closely made new discoveries about the country possible. After they left Beijing, the embassy proceeded by barge along the Grand Canal to its southern end in Hangzhou. Macartney and the main party then travelled on inland waterways to Canton, while others followed the river from Hangzhou to the coast where the British ships waited. The observations made by the embassy during this return journey are another aspect which lacks sufficient research in recent scholarship of the Macartney embassy.[65] An examination of these first-hand British discoveries in China, however, is worth making and should prove valuable.

One of the principal discoveries made by Macartney's embassy was that China at that time was actually a country of two distinct ethnicities (or according to their word, 'nations') – the Han Chinese and the Tartars/Manchus. Unlike previous British travellers to China, such as George Anson, who had essentially conflated these two peoples under the general name of 'Chinese', members of the Macartney mission found that 'although their appearance and manners are externally the same, a closer acquaintance soon discovers that in disposition they are widely different'.[66] According to their observations, the Han Chinese were 'more regularly educated, more learned and more patient than the Tartars', while the latter 'in general ... prefer active military duty to tranquil or sedentary occupations'.[67] During the return journey, the British visitors learned that, although the Qing rulers had adopted a lot of Han Chinese manners and had retained a great part of the Ming dynasty's government administration after their conquest in 1644, they had also paid much attention to preserving their own identity and to promoting Tartar/Manchu culture within the empire. These measures, however, did not entirely merge the two ethnic groups. Instead, there had always been mutual antipathy between them. The Tartars/Manchus regarded the Han Chinese as a conquered nation, while the Han Chinese generally considered the Tartars/Manchus as barbarians. Although the Qing emperor professed impartiality and proclaimed that he made no distinction between the two, Macartney found that 'neither Tartars nor Chinese are imposed upon by the pretence'.[68] He wrote:

> whatever might be concluded from any outward appearances, the real distinction is never forgotten by the sovereign who, though he pretends to be perfectly impartial, conducts himself at bottom by a systematic nationality, and never for a moment loses sight of the cradle of his power. ... The Viceroys of the provinces, the commanders of the armies, the great officers of state are almost all Tartars. The detail of business indeed, and the laborious departments are chiefly carried on by the Chinese. ... In all the tribunals of justice and finance, in all the courts of civil or military administration, an equal number of Tartar assessors is indispensably necessary to be present, in order to watch over and control the others. A Chinese may preside at the Board, and pronounce the opinion, but the prompter and manager is a Tartar who directs and governs the performers. These regulations and precautions sufficiently disclose the sovereign's real opinion of his tenure of the empire, and how little he depends upon the affections and loyalty of his Chinese subjects.[69]

Macartney drew this information mostly from his two escort officers, Wang Wenxiong and Qiao Renjie, who were both Han Chinese. Through them, Macartney was informed that the predominance of the Tartars/Manchus and the emperor's partiality for men from his own ethnicity were common subjects of conversation among the Han Chinese whenever they met in private. In public, however, Macartney noticed that Wang and Qiao had to pay humble deference to Tartar/Manchu mandarins, insomuch that they did not even venture to sit down in the presence of a Tartar/Manchu officer of the same rank as themselves. These observations helped the British visitors form an impression that the internal conflicts between China's two 'nations' were so serious that to the Han Chinese, the majority of the population, it was like living under 'a foreign tyranny'.[70] On this basis, Barrow pointed out that the stability of the Chinese empire was becoming a serious problem for its Qing rulers and that a collapse from within was not impossible. He wrote that:

> Whether this most ancient empire among men will long continue in its stability and integrity can only be matter of conjecture: but certain it is, the Chinese are greatly dissatisfied, and not without reason, at the imperious tone now openly assumed by the Tartars; and though they are obliged to cringe and submit, in order to rise to any distinction in the state, yet they unanimously load them with 'curses, not loud, but deep, mouth-honour breath' ... Whenever the dismemberment or dislocation of this great machine shall take place, either by a rebellion or revolution, it must be at the expense of many millions of lives.[71]

This early impression that the Qing rulers were not favoured by their Han Chinese subjects and that it could potentially cause political unrest was one of the key contributions to British knowledge of China made by the Macartney embassy.

The embassy also quickly learned that the Qing government was extremely suspicious of foreigners. As soon as the delegation arrived in China, the British clearly perceived the caution and vigilance of the Qing. Macartney noted that 'we have indeed been very narrowly watched, and all our customs, habits and proceedings, even of the most trivial nature, observed with an inquisitiveness and jealousy which surpassed all that we had read of in the history of China'.[72] The Qing court took particular care to prevent the British from making contact with common people. During their journey, when members of the Macartney embassy wished to make excursions from their boats into the towns or the countryside, their wishes were seldom granted. In Beijing, Holmes recorded that, except for Lord Macartney, 'none of his train, gentle or simple, were ever allowed to leave the place appointed for them, not even to peep out of it, till permission was obtained'.[73]

THE MACARTNEY EMBASSY

As the embassy proceeded, the British visitors gradually discovered that the extreme caution and suspicion of the Qing government was applied not only to foreigners but also to its own subjects. Macartney noted that, in the Chinese capital, 'The police is singularly strict. It is indeed stretched to an extent unknown I believe in any other city, and strongly marks the jealousy of the Government, and their unceasing apprehension of danger.'[74] Staunton added that 'the provident attention of the Chinese government preserves carefully the exclusive advantage of giving information to, or withholding it, as it may deem expedient, from the body of the people'.[75] For example, although an express mail system was available, its exclusive purpose was to convey messages to and from the emperor and his court. Throughout the empire, there was no establishment of a post for the general convenience of the people. Nor were canals built in China to benefit the public. It was through this strict control of information, Macartney found, that the Qing government not only retained the idea of their own importance among the people, but also endeavoured to 'undervalue in their eyes as much as possible the superior invention of foreign nations'.[76] Macartney commented in this regard that, even though the Chinese had been acquainted with Europeans for centuries, they had generally remained 'averse to all novelties, and wish to discountenance a taste for any foreign article that is not absolutely necessary'.[77] Although historians have shown that Macartney and his contemporaries had probably misread the Qing court's real attitude towards Western technology,[78] the embassy found as a result of their journey across China that the Chinese were indeed 'centuries behind the nations of Europe'[79] in many aspects.

First of all, the 'extraordinary ignorance'[80] of the Chinese people was surprising to the Macartney embassy. According to Holmes, the ignorance of the Chinese people generally 'has no bounds'.[81] Dinwiddie even claimed that 'In no country, perhaps, do popular errors and prejudices prevail so much [as] in China'.[82] From conversations with those whom they met, the British found that the Chinese had scarcely any idea of there being any other country of importance other than their own. They believed themselves 'the only enlightened people, and that all other nations are barbarous; that China is situated in the middle of the earth, and all other countries scattered round it'.[83] Staunton once heard that Holland was considered by the ministers of China as bearing a political weight in proportion only to its size, and the same rule was applied to Britain. He was also informed that, in the opinion of the Qing court, a key criterion for judging the relative importance of other nations was the degree to which they accepted the superiority of the Chinese sovereign. It was due to this, Staunton inferred, that Britain, as a small island country whose ambassadors did not even know how to perform kowtow, failed to establish equal diplomatic relations with the Chinese empire.[84]

With respect to science, Macartney was convinced that 'the Chinese are certainly far behind the European world'.[85] Staunton discovered that no branch of natural philosophy underwent serious study in China, because 'as soon as the product of any art or manufacture has appeared to answer the general purpose for which it was intended, it seldom happens that the Chinese ... endeavour to make any further progress'.[86] For instance, as Dinwiddie found, although Chinese superstition attached much importance to astrology, 'not a single Chinese, nor a Tartar, ... were possessed of the slightest knowledge of astronomy, nor one who could explain any of the various phenomena of the heavenly bodies'.[87] The devoted scientist added, 'of pneumatics, hydrostatics, electricity, and magnetism, they may be said to have little or no knowledge'.[88] In the art of navigation, the Chinese had no means of ascertaining the latitude or the longitude of any place. Instead, 'The present system of Chinese navigation is to keep as near the shore as possible; and never to lose sight of land, unless in voyages that absolutely require it'.[89]

With regard to the military and civil infrastructures of China, members of the Macartney embassy also obtained rather negative impressions. Although the Qing court was keen to impress (or perhaps to scare) the British with military displays wherever the embassy visited, Dinwiddie found military men in China 'always unsoldierlike, and their march tumultuous. Bows, sabres, and matchlocks, were the only distinguishable weapons'.[90] Holmes depicted guns in China as 'nothing more than a piece of hollowed wood'.[91] Throughout the journey, the embassy had never spotted proper cannons except for a few ill-maintained pieces in Beijing, Hangzhou and on the frontiers of Canton. Moreover, there were basically no inland roads in China, insomuch that 'there is scarcely a road in the whole country that can be ranked beyond a foot-path'.[92] Chinese carriages, even though they were the best ones the Qing government could provide for the use of the embassy, were found to be extremely uncomfortable. Holmes even maintained that they were 'the most uneasy vehicles that can be imagined'.[93] As for the imperial palace in which the British stayed in Beijing, Anderson commented that 'I could see nothing that disposed me to believe the extraordinary accounts which I had heard and read of the wonders of the imperial residence of Pekin'.[94] He thought that the architecture of that palace was 'not only destitute of elegance, but in a wretched state of repair', and generally 'unworthy the residence of the representative of a great monarch'.[95] Even the dwelling of the emperor and the grand hall in which he held audiences, in Barrow's opinion, 'when divested of the gilding and the gaudy colours with which they are daubed, are little superior, and much less solid, than the barns of a substantial English farmer'.[96] In comparing Beijing with cities in Britain, Barrow noted that the Chinese capital had no such conveniences as common sewers to carry off the dirt, dregs and effluents that must necessarily accumulate in large cities. Hence, 'a constant disgusting odour remains in and about all the houses the whole day long, from the fermentation of the heterogeneous mixtures kept above ground, which, in our great cities, are carried off in drains'.[97] In the rural areas, contrary to the notion that the Chinese excelled in agricultural techniques, Barrow found that the Chinese approach to farming was in fact 'incapable of performing the operations of husbandry to the greatest advantage'.[98] Not only were some of the implements which they made use of the same as those employed two thousand years ago, but 'they have no knowledge of the modes of improvement practised in the various breeds of cattle; no instruments for breaking up and preparing waste lands; no system for draining and reclaiming swamps and morasses'.[99]

With respect to Chinese arts and literature, Barrow found that Chinese painters were 'unable to pencil out a correct outline of many objects, to give body to the same by the application of proper lights and shadows, and to lay on the nice shades of colour, so as to resemble the tints of nature'.[100] Even with regard to the paintings in the imperial collection, 'none of the rules of perspective were observed, nor any attempt to throw the objects to their proper distances'.[101] The Chinese mode of education, Barrow went on to claim, focused too much on the classical works of Confucius. As a result, 'little improvement seems to have been made in the last two thousand years'[102] in Chinese literature. Since the examinations to be passed for the attainment of government office were principally confined to the knowledge of the language, no progress in science was likely to be fostered in such a system. Even with respect to the high civility of the Chinese, which was well-known to European readers, Dinwiddie asserted that the previous authors on China must 'have made out their description from Confutzee what ought to be, rather than what is',[103] because, throughout their journey, the British travellers failed to form such an impression. Instead, 'we have experienced ... the most violent fermentation of passions, throwing stones, boxing on the highway, frequent wrangling in the palace, and impudent boys'.[104]

The accounts published by members of the Macartney embassy presented a very different image of China from those which readers might have previously found in the works of the Jesuits and other earlier commentators. These British observers more or less agreed that, no matter the degree of civilisation the Chinese had reached in the distant past, they had both failed to develop in recent times and had even taken some retrograde steps. With regard to the progress of science and technology, Britain had clearly leaped far ahead of China. Staunton and Macartney, for example, claimed that

> when China was visited by Marco Polo, the natives of it had already reached their highest pitch of civilization, in which they were certainly much superior to their conquerors, as well as to their European contemporaries[105]

> but not having improved and advanced forward, or having rather gone back, at least for these one hundred and fifty years past, since the last conquest by the northern or Manchu Tartars; whilst we have been everyday rising in arts and sciences, they are actually become a semi-barbarous people in comparison with the present nations of Europe.[106]

To account for the underdevelopment of China, members of the Macartney embassy developed a key perception which explained why the Chinese had failed to keep pace with the West. They maintained that the fundamental reason for this lay in the fact that the Chinese government had embedded a range of societal values that had retarded the development of its people. In particular, the principle of filial piety had gained such a deep rootedness that a system of universal obedience towards superiors pervaded every branch of China's public service. According to Barrow, for example, this system of patriarchal authority had led to a series of problems for China. First, there did not exist in China a middle class of people whose independent ideas gave them weight and influence in their country. Nor was there an enlarged sphere of public life or any voluntary associations in which the transactions of government could be freely and openly discussed as in Britain. On the contrary, there were 'no other than the governors and the governed'[107] in the entire empire of China. Second, as everything was at the instant command of the state, the fatherly affection that the government was supposed to show, in reality, turned out to be exercises in tyranny and oppression. The officers of government became the oppressors of the people and the latter rarely had any means to seek redress, or of declaring their sentiments on the conduct of their rulers. Particularly, through the operation of this paternal authority, the maxims of the government commanded, and the opinions of the people accepted, that every officer of the government was entitled to inflict corporal punishment on the people. This created in the latter a natural dread of the former and established a system of universal servility in Chinese society. Barrow remarked that 'The condition itself of being dependent upon, and subject to, the caprice of another, without the privilege of appeal, is such a degraded state of the human species, that those who are unfortunately reduced to it have no further ignominy or sense of shame to undergo'.[108]

Furthermore, the British travellers analysed how the arbitrary nature of this system had considerably eroded mutual confidence between people in China. Consequently, caution and suspicion became an integral part of Chinese national character. These British observers commented that, unlike in Britain, where laws afforded security for the possession of private property and hence stimulated individuals to amass a fortune by all legal means, the Chinese government failed to provide such security. As a result, everyone in China was extremely reserved and suspicious of their neighbours, because:

> If a man, by trade, or industry in his profession, has accumulated riches, he can enjoy them only in private. He dares not, by having a grander house, or finer clothes, to let his neighbour perceive that he is richer than himself, lest he should betray him to the commanding-officer of the district, who would find no difficulty in bringing him within the pale of the sumptuary laws, and in laying his property under confiscation.[109]

For this reason, Staunton found that 'the characteristic disposition of the Chinese merchants is that of timidity and caution',[110] and normal social intercourse within Chinese society was restricted within narrow boundaries. This lack of communication among Chinese people, as well as the absence of any stimulus to build up personal wealth, made it impossible to promote innovation in China. Instead, over the centuries, as Barrow wrote, 'the talent of invention is there seldom exercised beyond suggesting the means of providing for the first necessities and the most pressing wants'.[111]

Members of the Macartney embassy were also informed that mutual distrust and sense of insecurity were not confined to the common people, but were experienced by every officer in the government. According to Chinese law, mandarins from the ninth degree upwards to the fourth could administer a gentle 'correction' to their inferiors at any time. The emperor ordered punishments to his ministers, as well as to the other four classes, whenever he might think it necessary. Meanwhile, spies were often dispatched from the imperial court into the provinces to watch over the actions of the local mandarins. Other magistrates also kept a steady eye upon each other. They, particularly, 'let no opportunity slip of making unfavourable reports to their superiors',[112] because 'it frequently happens that the informer is rewarded by the office of the man he has been the instrument of removing'.[113] As a result of such policies, mutual suspicion among officials in the Chinese government was even more intense than among the common people. These qualities and failings, therefore, not only became a natural characteristic of all Chinese but produced a culture that was extremely cautious of accepting anything new or foreign and hence proved 'greatly detrimental to the progress of the arts and manufactures'.[114]

After having obtained this first-hand knowledge about China's conditions at the time as well as about its problems, Macartney realised that the breakup of the Qing empire was a possibility. He wrote that 'Scarcely a year now passes without an insurrection in some of the provinces. It is true that they are usually soon suppressed, but their frequency is a strong symptom of the fever within.'[115] Even though, Macartney added, 'it is possible ... that the momentum impressed on the machine by the vigour and wisdom of the present Emperor may keep it steady and entire in its orbit for a considerable time longer ... I should not be surprised if its dislocation or dismemberment were to take place before my own dissolution'.[116] Once such an event occurred, Macartney predicted that it would cause 'a complete subversion of the commerce, not only of Asia, but a very sensible change in the other quarters of the world'.[117] Since entry into the Chinese market would certainly be attempted by all major trading nations, it would probably induce much rivalry among these countries as well as severe disorder in China. Given Britain's political, commercial and military strength, however, Macartney firmly believed that Britain would 'prove the greatest gainer' in the end and 'rise superior over every competitor' in any case.[118]

It has been explained earlier in this chapter that the two leaders' suggestions on Britain's future policy in China are inherently associated with their intention to justify their decisions and conduct. When concluding their accounts of the mission, Macartney and Staunton re-emphasised their views that Britain should not initiate a change in Sino-British relations in the near future. On the basis of the assertion that the embassy had created favourable sentiments among the Chinese, Macartney maintained that, for the time being, priority should be given to preserving 'the ground we have lately gained'.[119] He insisted that there was nothing wrong in Britain's present means of engagement with the Chinese empire. Since the emperor 'entertained kind intensions [sic] with regard to us',[120] Staunton added that favourable relations with China would eventually be established 'by time and management'.[121] In particular, having been told to adopt such a policy by Father Amiot, Macartney stressed that patience and perseverance were extremely important in obtaining beneficial results in China over the next few decades. Given the unique character of the Qing government, he wrote, 'it would certainly require in us great skill, caution, temper and perseverance ... no shorter way will do it'.[122]

Despite proffering this advice, Macartney is well known for his reference to the potential use of violence against China should it become necessary. Macartney did claim that, in the event of a breakdown in Sino-British relations, 'we certainly have the means easy enough of revenging ourselves, for a few frigates could in a few weeks destroy all their coast navigation and intercourse from the island of Hainan to the Gulf of Pei-chili [Bei-zhili]'.[123] Despite this seemingly belligerent statement, however, Macartney was by no means an advocate of war against China. Neither does it mean that from this time on 'the era of the Opium War was imminent'.[124] In fact, in the same place where he made this statement, Macartney also solemnly reminded his readers of the devastating effects that a Sino-British war would have on Britain and its empire in the East. He wrote:

> Our settlements in India would suffer most severely by any interruption of their China traffic which is infinitely valuable to them, whether considered singly as a market for cotton and opium, or as connected with their adventures to the Philippines and Malaya.
>
> To Great Britain the blow would be immediate and heavy. Our great woollen manufacture, the ancient staple of England, would feel such a sudden convulsion as scarcely any vigilance or vigour in Government could for a long time remedy or alleviate. ... We should lose the other growing branches of export to China of tin, lead, copper, hardware, and of clocks and watches, and similar articles of ingenious mechanism. We should lose the import from China not only of its raw silk, an indispensable ingredient in our silk fabrics, but of another luxury, or rather an absolute necessary of life: tea.[125]

It was because of these considerations that Macartney reaffirmed the absolute necessity of avoiding an aggressive line of action – 'our present interests, our reason, and our humanity equally forbid the thoughts of any offensive measures with regard to the Chinese, whilst a ray of hope remains for succeeding by gentle ones'.[126] From this, we can see that Macartney deemed military aggression against China to be inadvisable and likely to be very harmful to Britain's interests. Although it is possible that some of his comments on Chinese affairs may have had an impact on those who later suggested a violent line of action against China, it is clear that Macartney himself was strongly opposed to any hostile measures. Macartney should be properly considered as an advocate of peaceful relations with China, rather than being an early agitator for a war against China.

It has been shown in this chapter that the Macartney embassy provided the British with an unprecedented opportunity to have direct contact with the Chinese government and people, as well as to observe China's conditions at this time. This chapter also reveals that, well before the

British commentators at home helped 'create' new cultural representations of China on the basis of the Macartney embassy's findings, the two leaders of the mission who encountered China in the 'contact zone' had already intervened in the knowledge production about China at first hand. To interpret the experience and the result of the mission in a light most favourable to themselves, Macartney and Staunton had to gloss over or withhold certain aspects of the embassy while, at the same time, to exaggerate the good relationship they had allegedly built up with the Qing court. These carefully constructed images, together with the omission of some ungracious treatments that they had received, certainly helped glorify the embassy's 'achievements', which in turn shaped and justified their suggestions on Britain's future policy towards China. We do not know whether it was due to their lack of ability or willingness (or a combination of both) that the two leaders failed to ascertain the true behind-the-scene motives on the Chinese side. It is, however, worth remembering that both of them were eager to demonstrate that a good job had been done by the embassy, probably to prepare for the blame they might face after their return to Britain. It was in this context that Macartney and Staunton produced and edited their narratives of the embassy. They suggested that the original goals of the mission had not been achieved because they were essentially unrealistic – under the current circumstances, the hostility of a few Qing ministers and the nation's habitual caution against sudden change were insurmountable obstacles. Yet, on the positive side, the embassy had resulted in the improvement of Britain's image in China. Particularly, the emperor had shown kindness to the British and was ready to protect Britain's trade with China. On the basis of these justifications, the two leaders of the embassy proposed that, even though the Qing government did not seem to be well liked by its Han Chinese subjects, no measure should be taken by Britain to challenge this authority. To preserve a peaceful relationship and to maintain the previous means of engagement with the Qing court was their advice to policy-makers back in Britain. It was under the influence of these ideas and interpretations that the second British embassy to China became possible in the early nineteenth century.

Notes

1 It should be noted that Warren Hastings, Governor-general of Bengal, organised a British mission to approach China in 1774. He appointed George Bogle to travel to Qing-controlled Tibet, wishing to establish a backdoor trade relationship with China. The goal was not fulfilled, but Bogle managed to build a good relationship with the sixth Panchen Lama.

2 For example, Zhang Shunhong, 'Historical Anachronism: The Qing Court's Perception of and Reaction to the Macartney Embassy', in *Ritual and Diplomacy: The Macartney Mission to China, 1792–1794*, ed. Robert A. Bickers (London: Wellsweep, 1993); Zhu Yong, *Buyuan Dakai De Zhongguo Damen* (The Chinese Gate Unwilling to Open) (Nanchang: Jiangxi Renmin Chubanshe, 1989).
3 Alain Peyrefitte, *The Collision of Two Civilisations: The British Expedition to China in 1792–4* (London: Harvill, 1993); James L. Hevia, *Cherishing Men from Afar: Qing Guest Ritual and the Macartney Embassy of 1793* (Durham, NC: Duke University Press, 1995).
4 Hevia, *Cherishing Men from Afar*; Joseph W. Esherick, 'Cherishing Sources from Afar', *Modern China*, 24 (1998), 135–61; James L. Hevia, 'Postpolemical History: A Response to Joseph W. Esherick', *Modern China*, 24 (1998), 319–27; Joseph W. Esherick, 'Tradutore, Traditore: A Reply to James Hevia', *Modern China*, 24 (1998), 328–32. See also *Ritual and Diplomacy*, ed. Bickers; Huang Yinong, 'Yinxiang yu Zhenxiang: Qingchao Zhongying Liangguo de Guanli Zhizheng' (Impressions v. Reality: A Study on the Guest Ritual Controversy between Qing China and Britain), *Zhongyang Yanjiuyuan Lishi Yuyan Yanjiusuo Jikan* (Bulletin of the Institute of History and Philology Academia Sinica), 78:1 (2007), 35–106.
5 Joanna Waley-Cohen, 'China and Western Technology in the Late Eighteenth Century', *American Historical Review*, 98 (1993), 1525–44; Joanna Waley-Cohen, *The Sextants of Beijing: Global Currents in Chinese History* (New York; London: Norton, 1999), pp. 92–128.
6 Maxine Berg, 'Britain, Industry and Perceptions of China: Matthew Boulton, "useful knowledge" and the Macartney Embassy to China, 1792–94', *Journal of Global History*, 1 (2006), 269–88. Henrietta Harrison has recently explored the cultures of gift-giving in Britain and China at the time of the Macartney embassy. See Henrietta Harrison, 'Chinese and British Diplomatic Gifts in the Macartney Embassy of 1793', *English Historical Review*, 560 (2018), 65–97.
7 William Christie, 'China in Early Romantic Periodicals', *European Romantic Review*, 1 (2016), 25–38; Logan P. Collins, 'British Periodical Representations of China: 1793–1830' (University of Houston M.A. thesis, 2014).
8 Henrietta Harrison, 'The Qianlong Emperor's Letter to George III and the Early-Twentieth-Century Origins of the Ideas about Traditional China's Foreign Relations', *American Historical Review*, 3 (2017), 680–701.
9 Hevia has also studied how the European discourse of humiliation and abasement influenced Macartney's (mis)understanding of the kowtow ceremony. See James L. Hevia, '"The Ultimate Gesture of Deference and Debasement": Kowtowing in China', *Past and Present*, 203 (2009), 212–34.
10 Song-Chuan Chen, *Merchants of War and Peace: British Knowledge of China in the Making of the Opium War* (Hong Kong: Hong Kong University Press, 2017), pp. 3, 119, 142.
11 Peter J. Kitson, *Forging Romantic China: Sino-British Cultural Exchange 1760–1840* (Cambridge: Cambridge University Press, 2013), p. 7.
12 Waley-Cohen, 'China and Western Technology'.
13 Li Chen, 'Law, Empire, and Historiography of Modern Sino-Western Relations: A Case Study of the *Lady Hughes* Controversy in 1784', *Law and History Review*, 1 (2009), 5.
14 Robert Swanson has recently made an attempt to locate the surviving documents of the Macartney embassy, which are now scattered across the world. See Robert Swanson, 'On the (Paper) Trail of Lord Macartney', *East Asian History*, 40 (2016), 19–25.
15 John Barrow also published part of Macartney's journal in 1807. See John Barrow, *Some Account of the Public Life and a Selection from the Unpublished Writings of the Earl of Macartney* (London: T. Cadell, 1807).
16 John Barrow, *Travels in China* (Philadelphia: W. E. M'Laughlin, 1805), p. 393.
17 J.L. Cranmer-Byng (ed.), *An Embassy to China: Being the Journal Kept by Lord Macartney during His Embassy to the Emperor Ch'ien-lung 1793–1794* (London:

Longmans, Green and Co., 1962), p. 346. In addition to the works mentioned, there are a few unpublished manuscript journals kept by those in the retinue of Macartney's embassy. They are: Stephen Else, *Journal of a Voyage to the East Indies and an Historical Narrative of Lord Macartney's Embassy to the Court of Pekin* (London: Royal Geographical Society, 1793), B.K.S. case 260 H; William Alexander, *Journal of Lord Macartney's Embassy to China, 1792–1794* (London: British Museum), Add 35, 174 (I. 9); Edward Winder, *Account of a Journey in China in 1793 in Lord Macartney's Mission* (Dublin: National Library of Ireland), MS 8799 (1). These materials are not preserved very well and some parts are missing.
18 Cranmer-Byng, *An Embassy to China*, p. 226.
19 Christie, 'China in Early Romantic Periodicals', 25.
20 Barrow, *Travels in China*, p. 18.
21 *Ibid.*, p. 21.
22 William Jardine Proudfoot, *Biographical Memoir of James Dinwiddie: Embracing Some Account of His Travel in China and Residence in India* (Liverpool: E. Howell, 1868), p. 27.
23 George L. Staunton, *An Authentic Account of an Embassy from the King of Great Britain to the Emperor of China* (2 vols, London: W. Bulmer, 1798), II, 104.
24 Proudfoot, *Biographical Memoir of James Dinwiddie*, p. 55.
25 Aeneas Anderson, *A Narrative of the British Embassy to China, in the Years of 1792, 1793 and 1794* (London: J. Debrett, 1795), p. 270. Italics added.
26 *Ibid.*, pp. 266–7.
27 Cranmer-Byng, *An Embassy to China*, p. 150.
28 Staunton, *An Authentic Account*, II, 337–8.
29 Both Song Yun and Chang Lin were men of very high rank. The former was one of the six grand councillors of the Qianlong court, the latter a relation of the emperor and the next governor-general of Guangdong and Guangxi provinces.
30 Staunton, *An Authentic Account*, II, 337.
31 Harrison, 'The Qianlong Emperor's Letter'.
32 Cranmer-Byng, *An Embassy to China*, p. 215.
33 *Ibid.*, p. 213.
34 Staunton, *An Authentic Account*, II, 514.
35 *Ibid.*, II, 534.
36 *Ibid.*, II, 214.
37 Cranmer-Byng, *An Embassy to China*, p. 236. 'Tartar', technically, is a general term denoting peoples of central Asia. At this time, however, it was a term used by many Britons to refer to 'Manchu', inhabitants of Manchuria who conquered China and founded the Qing dynasty (1644–1912).
38 *Ibid.*, p. 153.
39 Staunton, *An Authentic Account*, II, 274.
40 *Ibid.*, II, 210–11.
41 Cranmer-Byng, *An Embassy to China*, p. 163.
42 *Ibid.*, p. 236.
43 Staunton, *An Authentic Account*, II, 413–14.
44 *Ibid.*, II, 219.
45 *Ibid.*, II, 134.
46 Cranmer-Byng, *An Embassy to China*, p. 153.
47 *Ibid.*
48 Staunton, *An Authentic Account*, II, 335.
49 *Ibid.*, II, 334.
50 *Ibid.*, II, 335–6.
51 Proudfoot, *Biographical Memoir of James Dinwiddie*, p. 70.
52 *Ibid.*, p. 87.
53 *Ibid.*, p. 86.
54 *Ibid.*, p. 78.
55 *Ibid.*, p. 70.
56 *Ibid.*, p. 78.

57 *Ibid.*, p. 78.
58 *Ibid.*, p. 71.
59 Samuel Holmes, *The Journal of Mr Samuel Holmes, Serjeant-Major of the Sixth Light Dragoons, during His Attendance, as One of the Guard on Lord Macartney's Embassy to China and Tartary, 1792–3* (London: W. Bulmer, 1798), p. 150.
60 *Ibid.*, p. 138.
61 *Ibid.*, p. 139.
62 Harrison, 'The Qianlong Emperor's Letter', 684–7.
63 Anderson, *A Narrative of the British Embassy*, p. 208.
64 *Ibid.*, p. 211.
65 Some accounts of the return journey can be found in Aubrey Singer, *The Lion and the Dragon: The Story of the First British Embassy to the Court of the Emperor Qianlong in Peking 1792–1794* (London: Barrie and Jenkins, 1992); and Peyrefitte, *The Collision of Two Civilisations*.
66 Barrow, *Travels in China*, p. 125.
67 Cranmer-Byng, *An Embassy to China*, p. 237.
68 *Ibid.*, p. 227.
69 *Ibid.*, pp. 237–8.
70 *Ibid.*, pp. 222.
71 Barrow, *Travels in China*, p. 280.
72 Cranmer-Byng, *An Embassy to China*, pp. 87–8.
73 Holmes, *The Journal of Mr Samuel Holmes*, p. 139.
74 Cranmer-Byng, *An Embassy to China*, p. 155.
75 Staunton, *An Authentic Account*, II, 36.
76 Cranmer-Byng, *An Embassy to China*, p. 275.
77 *Ibid.*, p. 226.
78 See, for example, Waley-Cohen, 'China and Western Technology in the Late Eighteenth Century'; Waley-Cohen, *The Sextants of Beijing*; and Mark C. Elliott, *Emperor Qianlong: Son of Heaven, Man of the World* (New York: Longman, 2009).
79 Proudfoot, *Biographical Memoir of James Dinwiddie*, p. 74.
80 Cranmer-Byng, *An Embassy to China*, p. 80.
81 Holmes, *The Journal of Mr Samuel Holmes*, p. 158.
82 Proudfoot, *Biographical Memoir of James Dinwiddie*, p. 83.
83 *Ibid.*
84 Staunton, *An Authentic Account*, II, 131–2.
85 Cranmer-Byng, *An Embassy to China*, p. 264.
86 Staunton, *An Authentic Account*, II, 539.
87 Proudfoot, *Biographical Memoir of James Dinwiddie*, p. 194.
88 *Ibid.*, p. 228.
89 *Ibid.*
90 *Ibid.*, p. 41.
91 Holmes, *The Journal of Mr Samuel Holmes*, p. 157.
92 *Ibid.*, p. 347.
93 *Ibid.*, p. 61.
94 Anderson, *A Narrative of the British Embassy*, p. 259.
95 *Ibid.*, pp. 166–7.
96 Barrow, *Travels in China*, p. 84.
97 *Ibid.*, p. 67.
98 *Ibid.*, p. 383.
99 *Ibid.*, p. 384.
100 *Ibid.*, p. 216.
101 *Ibid.*
102 *Ibid.*, p. 182.
103 Proudfoot, *Biographical Memoir of James Dinwiddie*, p. 50.
104 *Ibid.*
105 Staunton, *An Authentic Account*, II, 514.

106 *An Embassy to China*, p. 222. Similar views can also be found in Barrow, *Travels in China*, p. 238.
107 Barrow, *Travels in China*, p. 261.
108 *Ibid.*, p. 120.
109 *Ibid.*, p. 261.
110 Staunton, *An Authentic Account*, II, 566.
111 Barrow, *Travels in China*, p. 119.
112 *Ibid.*, p. 262.
113 Proudfoot, *Biographical Memoir of James Dinwiddie*, p. 52.
114 Barrow, *Travels in China*, p. 204.
115 Cranmer-Byng, *An Embassy to China*, p. 191.
116 *Ibid.*, p. 239.
117 *Ibid.*, p. 213.
118 *Ibid.*
119 *Ibid.*, p. 214.
120 *Ibid.*, p. 166.
121 Staunton, *An Authentic Account*, II, 334.
122 Cranmer-Byng, *An Embassy to China*, p. 210.
123 *Ibid.*, pp. 210–11.
124 Adrian Hsia, 'Introduction', in *The Vision of China in the English Literature of the Seventeenth and Eighteenth Centuries*, ed. Adrian Hsia (Hong Kong: The Chinese University Press, 1998), p. 18. There was a common belief among Chinese historians that Britain had a plan to attack China long before 1840. See, for example, Zhang Ming, *Kaiguo Zhihuo* (Founding the Nation: A Puzzle) (Chongqing: Chongqing Chubanshe, 2016), p. 65; *Zhongguo Tongshi* (General History of China), ed. Bai Shouyi and Gong Shuduo (12 vols, Shanghai: Shanghai Renmin Chubanshe, 2013), XI, 106; Chen Qin, Li Gang and Qi Peifang, *Zhongguo Xiandaihua Shigang* (A Brief History of Modernisation in China) (2 vols, Nanning: Guangxi Renmin Chubanshe, 1998), I, 40–1.
125 Cranmer-Byng, *An Embassy to China*, p. 212.
126 *Ibid.*, p. 213.

CHAPTER TWO

The Amherst embassy

The Amherst embassy to China (1816–17) is a critical but under-researched event in the history of British–Chinese relations. Dispatched twenty-two years after the Macartney embassy, it was Britain's second formal attempt to improve its commercial and diplomatic relations with China. Compared to Macartney's embassy, which was at least given the opportunity to meet the Qianlong emperor, the Amherst mission is traditionally regarded as more fruitless than the former. This is mainly because Lord Amherst did not even achieve an audience with the Jiaqing emperor, the Qianlong emperor's fifteenth son and successor. Largely for this reason, unlike Macartney's embassy that has attracted much scholarly attention, the Amherst embassy has received very little analysis, although several works have provided brief descriptions of the mission.[1] It was not until recently that Peter Kitson, Robert Markley and I started to point out that the Amherst mission is worthy of closer study – and that the failure to investigate the complexity of this event has left much valuable information unexplored.[2] In particular, because of the neglect of the Amherst embassy, the Macartney embassy and the Opium War, the two events on which the historiography of early Sino-British relations primarily focuses, have tended to be regarded as two distinct and largely unrelated events. Since leaders of the Macartney embassy had considered it inappropriate to abandon the policy of currying favour with the Chinese emperor, historians analysing the origins of the Opium War have found no strong links between the views of leading war agitators in the late 1830s and the attitude held by members of the early British embassies to China. To explain why the Opium War broke out, they have had to emphasise the 'irreconcilable' economic or cultural conflicts between the two countries or have had to concentrate on the opium trade and so on. The Amherst embassy, in any case, has been considered insignificant according to these narratives.

Although an in-depth investigation into the Amherst embassy can offer new insights into Sino-British relations in the pre-Opium War era, little effort has occurred to explore precisely what happened during the mission. Two doctoral dissertations, by Jodi Eastberg and Zhang Shunhong, have attempted to examine the Amherst embassy from a perceptional point of view,[3] but neither has explored how these British perceptions of China related to the later mode of engagement between the two powers. Patrick Tuck's substantial introduction to the reprint of George Thomas Staunton's *Notes of Proceedings* has offered useful background information of the embassy, but the work was conducted mainly from Staunton's standpoint.[4] Moreover, because Amherst's refusal to kowtow to the Jiaqing emperor has emerged as the main reason for the embassy's failure, Wu Xiaojun and Eun Kyung Min have studied the Sino-British dispute about performing the kowtow ceremony from the Chinese perspective.[5] Important inner workings of the Amherst embassy, however, remain under-researched. In their recently edited book on the Amherst embassy and Sino-British cultural relations, Kitson and Markley have explored the wider economic, cultural and environmental contexts of the Amherst embassy. Kitson has investigated how the ritual of present exchange and the kowtow ceremonial served to disguise the material reality of the vastly expanding opium trade.[6] Markley has suggested that the eruption of Mount Tambora, the largest volcanic eruption in modern history, in Indonesia in April 1815, had a range of knock-on effects on the ecology and economy in China. These conditions were misread by the Amherst embassy as signs of China's stagnation when they were crossing China in 1816 and, hence, reinforced their negative views of the Qing regime and Chinese culture.[7] This body of new scholarship has shed new light on the Amherst mission, but two crucial aspects of the embassy need to reach a wider readership before this field expands further – how was the issue of kowtow debated within the embassy's leadership? What new about China did members of the Amherst embassy discover as a result of their journey? By concentrating on these two fundamentally important themes, this chapter suggests that the Amherst embassy should not be viewed as an insignificant diplomatic failure. On the contrary, it not only promoted new developments in British imperial attitudes towards China but laid the foundations for the deterioration of Sino-British relations in the run-up to the Opium War.

Inner kowtow controversy

The neglect of the Amherst embassy cannot be attributed to a lack of source materials. The number of available primary sources for Amherst's mission is in fact greater than those for Macartney's. Eleven members of the Amherst embassy left more than fifteen accounts of their visit to China. Although Amherst's diary was lost because of the shipwreck of the embassy's main ship, the *Alceste*, on its return voyage, some of Amherst's observations on China exist in the India Office Library and Records held in the British Library. George Thomas Staunton, Macartney's page on the first mission and the son of George Leonard Staunton, served as the second commissioner of the Amherst embassy. As an eminent 'China expert', Staunton produced several works that relate to the Amherst mission.[8] Henry Ellis, the third commissioner, published his *Journal of the Proceedings of the Late Embassy to China* shortly after his return to Britain.[9] This book was widely considered to be the most official account of the Amherst mission. Robert Morrison, who had entered China in 1807 as the pioneer Protestant missionary, was the chief translator for Amherst's embassy. With his remarkable knowledge of Chinese culture and language, Morrison was able to publish *A View of China*[10] as well as his memoir of the Amherst mission.[11] After Morrison died, his wife compiled the two-volume *Memoirs of the Life and Labours of Robert Morrison, D.D.*, which complements Morrison's observations on China published in his earlier works.[12] John Francis Davis, who also had a good command of the Chinese language and later became the second governor of Hong Kong, authored a number of books on China and its peoples, such as *Sketches of China* which includes his journal of the embassy.[13] Apart from these individuals, other members of the Amherst embassy who also kept or published journals of their visit to China include: Clarke Abel, the chief medical officer and naturalist; John Macleod, a surgeon aboard the *Alceste*; Basil Hall, the commander of HMS *Lyra*; and Henry Hayne, Amherst's private secretary.[14]

Despite the existence of these materials, historians have not revealed the complex reasons for launching the Amherst embassy. The prevailing explanation for the genesis of this mission is clear and straightforward. Christopher Hibbert maintains, 'neither the merchants at Canton nor the British government were content to let matters rest where the failure of Lord Macartney's mission had left them; and on the death of the old Emperor Ch'ien-lung [Qianlong] in 1799 hope was revived that a satisfactory trade agreement might be negotiated'.[15] Alain Peyrefitte claims, 'the British, having vanquished Napoleon, now had the means – and the need – to try one last diplomatic approach',[16] to place Britain's commercial and political relations with China on a secure footing. These arguments have indicated the consistency between the two British missions, but they have overlooked the different expectations entertained by the East India Company and the British government.

In the two decades after the Macartney embassy, according to Staunton, British citizens in Canton were 'neither protected by the physical force of armies, nor by that moral security which is derived from the plighted faith of treaties'.[17] The 'highly jealous, despotic, and arbitrary' government of Canton oversaw their trade.[18] The EIC's trade monopoly in India, except for the tea trade and trade with China, terminated in 1813. As a result, its commerce with China became more important than ever. Given the perceived character of the local Chinese authorities, the EIC's Select Committee at Canton believed that to maintain its China trade, there was a serious need to appeal directly to the emperor in Beijing. Under such circumstances, the EIC's Court of Directors in London pleaded with the British government for sending another royal ambassador to the Qing court. The result was the Amherst embassy formed at the request and expense of the EIC.

Accordingly, the Amherst mission resulted primarily by the EIC's anxiety about the preservation of its China trade, rather than because of any broader design of the British government to develop further its relations with the Chinese court. For the EIC, the trade in Canton was its only concern because experience had shown it that nothing more seemed possible under the current circumstances. According to the Secret Commercial Committee of the Company, the most immediate cause of this embassy was very specific. They stated that, 'the insolent, capricious, vexatious proceedings which the local Government of Canton has for some time past held towards the Company's Representatives there ... have obstructed, and embarrassed the conduct of the Company's commerce'.[19] Staunton even maintained that the embassy was sent out 'for the single purpose of settling the Canton disputes and re-establishing the trade'.[20] This sentiment, however, did not entirely coincide with the expectations of the British government. In addition to the EIC's objective to defend its commerce in Canton, the government wished that 'every opportunity should be taken to enquire how the purchase of British manufactured goods in China could be *increased*'.[21] John Francis Davis, in this respect, noted in his journal that:

> It was curious to observe the difference between the instructions received from the government and the recommendations emanating from the Court of Directors. The former implied that we went simply in search of whatever we could pick up ... The Company said, 'Have most regard to the effect that the embassy is to produce at Canton; complain of the conduct of the local authorities to our trade ...'[22]

This difference between the objectives of the British government and the EIC did not seem remarkable at the beginning, but it turned out to be increasingly significant as the Amherst mission proceeded.

THE AMHERST EMBASSY

In July 1816, when Lord Amherst reached the China coast, he was joined by a group of EIC employees in Canton. This resulted in a major difference between the Amherst and the Macartney embassies. When Macartney visited China, no one in his mission had had prior experience of that country. Unassisted by any 'local inside knowledge', Macartney had to make most of the decisions himself. Amherst, however, had an advisory team consisting of these EIC's employees. George Thomas Staunton, then president of the Select Committee at Canton, received appointment as the second commissioner and minister plenipotentiary of the embassy. Other persons such as Robert Morrison, John Francis Davis, Francis Toone, Thomas Manning and Alexander Pearson all had a command of the Chinese language and had lived in Canton and Macao for extended periods. Since these EIC staff members had had experience dealing with the Chinese authorities at Canton, Amherst, instead of relying entirely on his own judgement, sometimes felt obliged to solicit opinions from these so-called 'China experts'. Although there was little disagreement between Amherst and these EIC employees on most of the proceedings of the mission, on some occasions they did entertain different aspirations and held contrasting attitudes. Although Tuck's introductory essay briefly mentions these subtle but critical differences of opinion, as well as the impact of these EIC staff members on the proceedings of the embassy,[23] no historian has seriously researched them. In particular, previous scholars have failed to examine the 'inner kowtow controversy' by adopting a similar approach to that which James Polachek used in his book *The Inner Opium War*,[24] which explores the behind-the-scenes political struggles within the Qing court that shaped China's foreign policy in the 1830s and 1840s. This important disagreement within the Amherst embassy on whether or not to kowtow before the Jiaqing emperor was in fact an early example of the collision between the appeasing and the hard-line diplomatic attitudes in Britain's approach to China. Amherst's decision to assume an uncompromising stance, as strongly demanded by Staunton, not only directly resulted in the rejection of the embassy from Beijing but it also encouraged many Britons thereafter to dispute the necessity of persisting in the deferential posture towards China that had been advocated by Macartney. In this sense, therefore, the Amherst embassy provides a vital link connecting the Macartney embassy and the Opium War in the development of Sino-British relations by laying the foundations for Britain's increasingly belligerent attitude towards China in the lead-up to the Opium War.

To understand the 'inner kowtow controversy', we should first note that Staunton, unlike his father, was keen to stress that his advice was pivotal to the embassy. Although he had never been to the interior of

China again following the Macartney embassy (when he was only twelve), Staunton had been employed by the EIC to work in Canton and Macao since 1798. This made him believe that, 'from my local experience, and from habits of long and deep reflection upon it, I ought to be fully prepared to offer a well-grounded opinion'.[25] In his *Miscellaneous Notices*, Staunton even implied that Amherst's opinion was in no way superior to his, while all decisions ought to be collective. He wrote:

> the *principle* upon which this embassy was constituted, was extremely judicious. – The appointment of a commission in which a nobleman was to preside, with two members of the Select Committee for his assessors, combined two very essential requisites upon the occasion, which it was impossible to find centred in any one individual, in an equal degree.[26]

Moreover, because the principal motive for the dispatch of this mission was for the wellbeing of the EIC's merchants in Canton, Staunton argued that the opinions of other EIC representatives required serious attention. To justify this standpoint, he asserted:

> It [the embassy] grew so entirely out of the measures which had been adopted by the Company's authorities there, to that end, and was so especially designed to strengthen their hands, and to obtain, if possible, the emperor's confirmation of the provincial adjustment which they had already obtained, that any scheme of an embassy which had not included persons who were locally, and in the fullest manner acquainted, both with what had been done, and with what was still required, would, however complete in other respects, have been obviously worse than useless.[27]

The reason Staunton attached so much importance to his own advice and that of other EIC staff was that he did not think the Amherst embassy had arrived at a propitious time. Staunton maintained that the Company had requested an embassy be dispatched 'when the alarm for the safety of the trade was at its highest'.[28] This situation had changed considerably, however, by the time that the Select Committee at Canton learned that an embassy was on its way. For this reason, Staunton claimed that 'had the measure however been postponed for six months, it very probably would never have been adopted at all; for it would have become evident ... that the peculiar ground for attempting to re-open a diplomatic intercourse with the court of Pekin ... no longer existed'.[29] Because of these concerns, Staunton maintained that the main purpose of the Amherst mission was 'not to propose any innovation, but merely to secure and consolidate, and to restore, in the event of its being found to have been again suspended, the ordinary commercial intercourse between the two countries'.[30] In particular, Staunton deemed it inappropriate to undertake the embassy 'with any special view towards the attainment of additional privileges, such as the opening of a new port for the extension of our commerce, or any other of the wild and visionary projects'.[31] Since, at least according to his view, those with local knowledge all agreed that the embassy was unlikely to obtain any additional benefits from the Qing court, Staunton explained the embassy's paramount objective. 'If it were found, that no *good* could be done; at least, to take especial care to do no *harm* – Not to *lose* any of the ground that the Select Committee had gained – not to *frustrate* the success of the line of policy they had adopted.'[32]

There is no evidence that Amherst or any member of the embassy raised a straightforward objection to Staunton's view. Nevertheless, although some of them showed respect for the advice of the 'China experts', they were neither as committed to the instructions of the EIC nor convinced that no positive good was achievable. Compared to the EIC representatives in the embassy, Amherst was less prepared for the difficulties he might encounter. A favourable impression of the Chinese emperor reinforced his relative optimism. By 1816, both the British government and the EIC's employees at Canton still entertained a perception of a somewhat enlightened Chinese sovereign. This impression apparently derived from the opinions of early Catholic missionaries in China as well as from the views of some members of the Macartney embassy.[33] On the basis of these positive views of the emperor's character, the British, including the EIC's employees at Canton, attributed the difficulties in Canton entirely to the misconduct of the local authorities. They believed that these authorities concealed their transgressions from the emperor and, hence, once they had communicated these oppressive actions against foreign merchants to His Imperial Majesty, the grievances in Canton would find quick redress. Based on this belief, the EIC's instructions to Amherst clearly stated that the anticipated outcome of the mission was 'the establishment of the Company's trade upon a secure, solid, equitable footing, free from the capricious arbitrary aggressions of the local Authorities, and under the protection of the Emperor, and the sanction of Regulations to be appointed by himself'.[34] Thus, at this stage, a favourable response from the Chinese sovereign seemed almost taken for granted. This confidence placed upon the Jiaqing emperor, however, underwent considerable revision as the Amherst mission progressed.

The Amherst embassy travelled to and from Beijing on the Chinese mainland for approximately four months, but the most significant intercourse with the Qing government lasted only about twenty days. It is worth noting that, in the years before the Amherst embassy, it had become clear that the Qing dynasty was in decline and its rulers were beginning to lose control over their vast empire. The early decades of the nineteenth century saw a rash of rebellions and secret societies across many parts of China. As these movements were often associated with persistent Ming loyalism whose political objective was to 'overthrow the Qing and restore the Ming (*fanqing fuming*)', the Qing government was extremely anxious to guard against threats from these difficult-to-control societies. Especially after the Eight Trigrams uprising of 1813, when a contingent of the Heavenly Principle Society (*Tianli jiao*) penetrated into the Forbidden City, the Jiaqing court became seriously alarmed at any potential disturbance which might be excited in the country. According to Wensheng Wang's revisionist study on the Jiaqing reign,[35] however, the Qing court at this time was actually not as 'degenerate and corrupt'[36] as H.B. Morse had believed. Instead, the Jiaqing emperor was a thoughtful, self-critical ruler who was capable of reacting pragmatically to the complex political circumstances that confronted him. The monarch was keenly aware of and concerned about Britain's naval ambitions in the China Seas. Particularly in 1802 and 1808, the British made two attempts to occupy Macao.[37] Although unsuccessful, these events led the Guangdong provincial government to represent the British as 'the most harsh and cruel barbarians'[38] who 'live[d] by plunder'[39] in its correspondence with the Jiaqing emperor. In his instructions to the authorities in Canton, the emperor described the British as 'proud, tyrannical and generally obnoxious', and 'always unreasonable and dishonest'.[40] In the case that the British might 'dare to occupy the strategic spots of our frontier', he added, 'we must not show the least sign of weakness or cowardice'.[41]

Kitson's recent articles also confirm that 'the Jiaqing Emperor understood something of the threat the British might pose'.[42] Apart from their invasions of Macao, the British were known to have chased an American schooner in Chinese waters in 1814 (to carry out a blockade against American merchants) and to have refused to send their ship HMS *Doris* away when requested by the Canton government.[43] In 1816, the Rajah of Nepal also warned the Jiaqing emperor of Britain's possible designs on Tibet when petitioning for help against the British in Bengal.[44] All this evidence has shown that before the arrival of the Amherst embassy the British had built a reputation among the Qing court for being trouble-makers who were potentially dangerous. In addition, as soon as Amherst and his party came ashore in Dagu and embarked on the overland journey to Beijing, the British ships sailed back to Canton to await the embassy there. This act of sending away ships without first notifying the Chinese officials became an insult to the Jiaqing emperor. It not only entailed the embassy being escorted back to Canton through another route, which caused additional trouble and expense to the Qing court, but it gave the British ships an opportunity to survey the Chinese coast, thus making the Jiaqing government more sensitive to the issue of British naval presence in Chinese waters. Perhaps for these reasons, compared to his father, the Jiaqing emperor seemed more determined to demonstrate his imperial strength to the British embassy. As early as 1809, after he successfully forced the British to withdraw from Macao, the Jiaqing emperor had commented, 'we have been too lenient with them [the British]. From now on, we must make amends and be more severe.'[45] This mindset certainly contributed to the emperor's inflexible attitude in 1816 that Amherst should perform the kowtow ceremony. For Amherst and his fellow Britons, it meant renewal of the kowtow controversy as soon as their contact with the Chinese began.

Unlike what the Macartney embassy had experienced, before Amherst's embassy was conducted to Beijing, the Qing court organised two rounds of negotiations to test Amherst's willingness to perform kowtow. As a result, the kowtow issue became not only a central cause of dispute between Britain and China but a highly controversial subject within the Amherst embassy. The first negotiation took place in Tianjin on 13 August 1816, four days after Amherst's mission set foot on Chinese soil. At the command of the Jiaqing emperor, two royal legates, Soo (Su Leng'e) and Kwang (Guang Hui), prepared an imperial banquet to provide the British with an opportunity to rehearse the kowtow ceremony. For this purpose, there was a symbol of the Imperial Majesty's presence – a table covered with yellow silk. The two legates expected the British delegation to pay *sangui jiukou*[46] before it. Although the instructions given by the British government gave much latitude to the ambassador's discretion with regard to the observation of Chinese court ritual, Amherst was determined not to prostrate himself before any representative of the sovereign. Instead, he paid some reverential low bows without clarifying whether he was going to perform kowtow before the emperor himself.

The second test of Amherst's readiness to kowtow was conducted in Tongzhou, twelve miles from the capital. The emperor deputed two mandarins of very high rank, Duke Ho (He Shitai) and Duke Moo (Muke Deng'e),[47] to meet the British delegation. According to the accounts of the Amherst embassy, in the first of the two meetings, the dukes adopted a haughty manner. They maintained that under no circumstances would the Qing court dispense with its established usages. When Amherst referred to Macartney's example, Ho asserted that, for one thing, the present emperor had declared that he himself had witnessed Macartney's performance of *sangui jiukou* in 1793; for another, no matter what form of respect Macartney had paid to the previous emperor, that precedent was not to govern proceedings on the present occasion. Five days later, however, when the two parties met for the second time, the dukes' attitude had become much more courteous. Ho first asked what the British side expected from this mission. After Amherst informed him of the various wishes entertained by the EIC and the British government, Ho suggested that all these expectations might be satisfied if the British envoys agreed to perform kowtow. In this context, Amherst replied about needing some deliberations before he could provide a final answer. When he solicited opinions from Staunton and Ellis, an internal kowtow controversy took place. Ellis, as well as Amherst, was more inclined to go ahead with the ceremony to secure Chinese trade concessions. Staunton insisted that the Chinese would respect the British only if the British stuck to what they had said and done in the past.

The leaders of the Amherst embassy advanced such conflicting views because of their different perceptions of the mission's ultimate objectives. Since the British government clearly stated that it was inadvisable to 'let any trifling punctilio stand in the way of the important benefits which may be obtained by engaging the favourable disposition of the Emperor and his Ministers',[48] Amherst's and Ellis's attitudes towards kowtow were more flexible. In particular, with Ho's hint of a favourable response in mind, they were of the opinion that too much emphasis on the ceremonial details would be injurious to the overall aims of the embassy. For this reason, a compromise on formality was not entirely unacceptable. Ellis maintained:

> the sole chance of success to the ulterior objects of the embassy exists in producing a favourable impression upon the mind of the Emperor; and this can only be effected by complying with the particular usages of the court and nation, as far as a due sense of our own dignity, combined with considerations of policy, will permit.[49]

Although Ellis admitted that the kowtow ceremony was certainly disagreeable to the sense of honour and propriety of every British visitor, 'it could scarcely be deemed inadvisable to sacrifice the more important objects of the embassy to any supposed maintenance of dignity by insisting upon such a point of etiquette, in such a scene'.[50]

As head of the mission, Amherst essentially concurred with Ellis. He pointed out that, once the Qing court was offended, it was possible that 'not only former grievances would not have been removed, but new misunderstandings would have arisen; and new evils would have been incurred', whereas 'a prospect was held out to us of positive good by a compliance with the Emperor's wishes'.[51] With such statements, it can be suggested that Amherst was in some sense attempting to show that he was not biased against either the EIC's or the British government's vision of the embassy's ultimate objectives. On the one hand, he worried that any insistence on not performing kowtow might induce the emperor to treat the EIC's trade ungraciously in future. On the other, to achieve the 'positive good' that the government desired, he deemed it worthwhile to keep that prospect alive by making a reasonable concession to the Chinese emperor.

Ellis's contention on the propriety of performing kowtow, as well as Amherst's efforts to support this opinion, however, was not acceptable to Staunton. In opposing the Amherst–Ellis view, Staunton asserted that, 'judging from my general knowledge and experience of the Chinese character', compromise on the court ritual 'would not be likely to promote the attainment of any of the objects we have in view'.[52] Basing his views on the example of the Dutch embassy, which performed kowtow in 1795 but was still treated badly,[53] Staunton was convinced that the performance of kowtow would not do Britain any favour. With respect to Amherst's apprehensions about EIC interests at Canton, he believed that refusal to kowtow would not cause any serious trouble to British interests in China. Again, from his knowledge, Staunton maintained that 'It is not agreeable to the Chinese character to have recourse to violent measures, or to push matters to extremities unnecessarily, especially when they have (as I may safely say, in this case) no colour or ground for proceeding'.[54] To prove this, he referred to a Russian embassy in 1806. Although the Russian ambassador refused to kowtow and the Jiaqing emperor rejected him, this action did not cause any interruption of trade between China and Russia. Moreover, with regard to the aim of achieving certain 'positive good' beyond Canton, Staunton alleged that it was an unrealistic assumption that favourable actions would result from such a concession on ceremonies. He stated:

> I am fully sensible of the importance of the objects of the present mission; but I cannot bring myself to believe that their attainment would in the smallest degree be promoted by the compliance in question; and the mere reception (it could hardly be termed honorable reception) of the Embassy, would, I think, be too dearly purchased by such a sacrifice.[55]

Becuase of these considerations, Staunton's conclusion was to avoid kowtow by all means, even though it might result in the rejection of the embassy. 'Under such very singular circumstances', he later wrote, 'the mere ceremonies of a court reception, had they taken place, would have been nothing compared to the moral effect which the judiciously sustained proceedings of the British Mission would be calculated to produce.'[56]

Apart from these arguments based on his 'local' knowledge, it is interesting to observe how Staunton, in the minority of the embassy's three-man leadership, managed to convince the other two of his viewpoint. When the answer to the kowtow question was shortly to be confirmed in Tongzhou, Staunton stressed that, because the embassy was sent out to China 'solely and entirely for the sake of the local interests of the Company', it was 'not unnatural that the opinion of the persons connected with that interest should preponderate'.[57] Since this was a subject of extreme importance, not only were the attitudes of the envoys important but the advice of the five other EIC representatives should also be seriously considered, especially given that they too 'possessed such acknowledged talents, judgment, and local experience, as must necessarily entitle their opinions to considerable weight'.[58] On these grounds, Staunton had permission to consult with these men individually. Unsurprisingly, all of them, either firmly or conditionally, agreed with Staunton that it was unwise to comply with the kowtow ceremony.[59] In this way, Staunton artfully turned his minority position in the dispute with Ellis and Amherst into a six-to-two advantage. As a result, Amherst abandoned the idea of performing kowtow and, probably with it, of winning the chance of achieving any 'positive good'.

Although it seems as if it was the embassy's collective decision to proceed according to Staunton's advice, deeper analysis into primary sources shows that, in fact, Staunton's arguments did not convince everyone in the mission. In particular, an underlying debate between Ellis and Staunton existed after reaching the resolution not to perform kowtow. Staunton's accounts demonstrate that he was anxious to prove that he had helped the embassy to make a correct decision in 1816. Even four decades later, he was still referring to various sources in his and others' memoirs to support this view. In particular, he highlighted some passages from one of Ellis's books, in which Ellis had stated: 'I do not in the least blame myself for having surrendered my opinion to the experience of Sir George Staunton ... I must confess that I could not have found another person to whose character and acquirements I would have preferred yielding the guidance of my actions.'[60] Staunton took this statement as proof that Ellis had willingly yielded his opinion to Staunton's considerable local knowledge, but a wider and closer examination of their two accounts suggests that Ellis never really accepted Staunton's assertions.

First, although Ellis did indeed mention that he did not feel regret for complying with Staunton's suggestion, his account conveyed a quite different tone to that which appeared in Staunton's memoirs. Ellis, in fact, wrote in his official journal:

> I have naturally felt deep regret at the prospect of being denied reception [at the Chinese court] from a continued refusal to comply with the wishes

of the Chinese, and yet I do not in the least blame myself for having surrendered my opinion to the experience of Sir George Staunton. I am ready, when called upon to act, to yield crude notions to experienced opinion, but regarding the question as matter of speculation, my sentiments remain unchanged.[61]

To elaborate on this point, Ellis questioned 'whether a contrary result would have been too dearly bought by sacrificing the distinction between nine prostrations of the head to the ground upon two knees, and nine profound bows upon one knee'.[62] He maintained that, even without regard to the major objectives of the embassy, 'I shall still be inclined to believe, that the irritation produced by protracted contest has been, in some measure, an obstacle to their favourable consideration'.[63]

Second, as seen from the evidence above, Ellis suggested that the inflexible stance that the British envoys decided to adopt in their negotiations was harmful to the success of the mission. This view produced another underlying debate between the second and third commissioners. In contrast to what Ellis stated, Staunton remained convinced (or at least he insisted) that, when dealing with the Chinese court in the past, the British had been not overly inflexible but, rather, resolute. Staunton maintained that, despite the fact that many people were in favour of the policy that questions relating to Chinese court ceremony should be determined on the spot, 'the delay, which ensued in consequence, was fatal'.[64] Ellis, in his journal, made it very clear that he was opposed to this view. He claimed, 'I cannot but regret this inevitable multiplication of subjects of ceremonial discussion, for I consider every victory upon these points as a diminution of the chances of success upon the more material objects of the embassy'.[65] His opinion did not find basis in any prior knowledge or experience concerning the kowtow question. Rather, he always believed 'the time employed in contending for the manner in which the embassy is to be received, and the temper generated by even successful inflexibility, are not calculated to dispose the mind of the Emperor ... to listen favourably to propositions in which they do not see any reciprocal advantage'.[66] Moreover, Ellis added, 'the dismissal of the embassy, without access being obtained to the imperial presence, would be a confirmation to the present and future Viceroys of Canton, that their own interest is the only check to their extortion and injustice'.[67] Because of these considerations, Staunton's efforts at persuasion never influenced Ellis's personal opinion on this issue. In concluding his explanation, Ellis stated, 'should the reception or rejection of the embassy depend upon an adherence, on the present occasion, to the mode observed in the case of all former European embassadors admitted to an audience, except Lord Macartney,

I should have no hesitation in giving up the maintenance of the single exception as a precedent'.⁶⁸

Furthermore, Ellis cast a great deal of doubt on the value of the local knowledge which Staunton was so proud of possessing. The third commissioner was also sceptical about the allegedly 'extensive acquaintance with the language'⁶⁹ of the other 'China experts', who were simply, in Ellis's opinion, '*more or less* acquainted with the Chinese language'.⁷⁰ Most important, Ellis argued that this local knowledge was obtained only from Canton. Since the situation in Beijing was vastly different, experiences gained in Canton might not necessarily be applicable elsewhere in China. For these reasons, Ellis claimed that he was '*uninfluenced* and unaided by local knowledge',⁷¹ a statement which probably implies that, in his view, the so-called 'local' knowledge, if insufficient, might rather mislead than assist the possessor's judgement. To support further his perspective, Ellis took every opportunity to note the instances when Staunton failed to deliver the right interpretation. For example, Ellis recorded that, in Tongzhou, the Chinese side once unofficially informed the embassy that the emperor had already dispensed with the kowtow. On hearing the news, 'Sir George had no doubt that the point was conceded, and that we might be perfectly satisfied'.⁷² This belief soon proved to be utterly erroneous.

As for Staunton's interpretation that the kowtow implied political submission, Ellis was also suspicious. Instead, he was more inclined to perceive the kowtow as a mere formality and as part of the Chinese court's normal conventions. Ellis noted that a Chinese official informed him that 'His Majesty ... was not greater, nor we [the British] lower, by the performance; that the ko-tou did not constitute us tributaries'.⁷³ In another conversation, Ellis reported that the embassy's conducting officer, Chang (Zhang Wuwei), observed:

> he was aware our resistance arose from a belief that the ko-tou [kowtow] was an admission of political dependence, but in this we were mistaken; that if he met a friend of superior rank, he went upon his knees to salute him; that however he neither considered himself a servant, nor did his friend pretend to be his master; the ko-tou was merely a court ceremony, and the Emperor considered it rude in the Embassador to refuse compliance.⁷⁴

Although these statements might well be untruthful comments made by the Chinese authorities, it is interesting to note that Staunton and other EIC representatives never attempted to disprove them but chose to ignore them. Because of his lack of understanding of Chinese customs, Ellis was certainly unable to provide a more definite interpretation of the implications of performing or not performing the kowtow. His efforts to challenge Staunton's 'local inside knowledge' shown in this internal kowtow controversy, however, offered valuable perspectives on the existing degree of understanding of Chinese customs and practices by the Amherst embassy.

Because of Staunton's strong and skilful opposition to the suggestion of complying with the kowtow ceremony, Amherst eventually decided to 'shew deference to an opinion [advanced by Staunton and] founded on long observation and on local experience'.[75] This course of events when the kowtow question arose greatly magnified the slight difference between the expectations of the EIC and those of the British government for the Amherst embassy. The outcome of this 'inner kowtow controversy', however, signified that the balance between Britain's appeasing and its uncompromising attitude towards China was shifting away from the former and towards the latter. In consequence, a disappointing outcome of the embassy became almost inevitable.

'A capricious despot'

Despite his decision not to perform kowtow, Amherst and his embassy were still allowed to proceed to Beijing. As soon as he arrived in Yuan-ming-yuan, the palace in which the imperial audience was supposed to be held, Amherst received information that the Jiaqing emperor would receive him almost immediately. Exhausted from the overland journey from Tongzhou and unaccompanied with his credentials and costumes,[76] Amherst pleaded for another time. Unable to produce Amherst, Ho falsely reported that Amherst was sick. Suspecting the British envoy of fabrication, the emperor sent his own surgeon to attend him. After the surgeon's report about Amherst shamming illness and hearing the fact that he had been determined not to kowtow, the emperor issued an order for the embassy's immediate departure from his court. He terminated the official proceedings of the Amherst mission.

As with Macartney and George Leonard Staunton, leaders of the Amherst embassy had to explain why their mission had failed to achieve its goals. This made it necessary to gloss over their own possible faults, just as their predecessors did in 1793. In their accounts of the embassy, we can find that Amherst and others kept off the subject of whether they had made an appropriate decision as a result of the 'inner kowtow controversy'. Instead, they held the Jiaqing emperor responsible for the unsatisfactory outcome of the mission (again, they tried to avoid the term 'failure'). This argument somewhat contradicts what Macartney had claimed. Macartney met the Qianlong emperor and his encounters in China allowed leaders of that mission to create a positive image of the Chinese emperor, who they maintained to be benevolent and concerned about the welfare of the British merchants trading with China. Since the Amherst embassy was not granted an imperial audience and there was no sign at all showing the Jiaqing emperor's kindness towards the British, Amherst and George Thomas Staunton were not able to sustain that favourable image of the Chinese monarch presented by the previous mission. Regardless of their different views about the kowtow ceremony, Amherst and Staunton agreed that 'the personal character of the monarch'[77] was the primary reason for the failure of their embassy. In this respect, Staunton maintained that, 'the emperor's violence and precipitation must ... be considered as the main cause of what has happened. ... his conduct throughout has certainly been ungracious in the extreme, and totally unlike that of his predecessor, upon the occasion of the former embassy.'[78] In a similar vein, Amherst argued in his correspondence with Canning, 'my want or success is not to be attributed to want either of zeal or discretion in the performance of my duty'.[79] The real reason for the mission's failure was, Amherst claimed, the Jiaqing emperor. His 'reign has been frequently and very lately disturbed by insurrections'; he was less ready to 'dispense with outward fame of respect than his Father, whose reign was long and victorious, ... [and so] might attach less consequence to any shew of external homage'.[80]

Apart from the kowtow issue, members of the Amherst embassy were also greatly exasperated by the way they were treated by the Jiaqing emperor. To explain some strange and unexpected occurrences during the visit, they represented the monarch as a capricious despot. In Tianjin, for example, when the British delegation was fully prepared to proceed to Beijing, Amherst was suddenly told that his musical band was not allowed to enter the capital and that these musicians had to be left behind at once. This unexpected command from the emperor created much anxiety among the embassy. Its members did not want to separate from each other at such a late stage, especially since no clear explanation was given on why they had to do so. While the leaders of the embassy were hesitating about whether to make a protest, this order was swiftly countermanded for no reason. On this occasion, Ellis commented that 'The objection made by the Emperor to the band is only so far important as it marks the capricious weakness of his character, and shews that he may be expected to adopt measures without any apparent or indeed assignable reason'.[81] What was more hurtful to the British delegation was the emperor's ejection of the embassy from Beijing, immediately after an exhausting overnight journey. It ignited so much indignation across the entire British delegation that no one was willing to suppress his anger. Davis claimed, 'This certainly was a barbarous, not to say brutal, measure, considering that we had only just arrived from a most fatiguing night journey. ... The insult offered had been so gross.'[82] Finding it impossible to explain what had occurred 'in any probable chain of cause and effect,' Abel wrote, 'We could only conjecture that we had been hurried to and from Yuen-min-yuen, and subjected to all kinds of indignity and inconvenience, to suit the will of a capricious despot'.[83]

Moreover, by contrast with the Macartney mission, the Amherst embassy's criticism of the Qing court centred mostly on the emperor himself rather than on any of his key ministers. These British travellers believed that Jiaqing emperor manipulated every transaction between the embassy and the Chinese government, whereas all his mandarins were simply fulfilling the duties imposed upon them. Hayne noted in this regard that 'We all felt much for the situation of the Mandarins attached to us, having had great reason to be perfectly satisfied with their whole conduct toward us, and at the same time extremely zealous in the cause of their Emperor'.[84] Ellis concurred with Hayne. He maintained, 'we must consider ourselves fortunate in the Mandarins with whom we had to transact business ... the rupture must be attributed to the personal character of the Emperor, who is capricious, weak, and timid, and the combined effect of these feelings will account for his pertinacity'.[85]

This production of an unfavourable image of the Chinese sovereign did not cease with the dismissal of Amherst's mission. At the beginning of the embassy's return journey from Beijing to Canton, Amherst was concerned that the emperor's displeasure would result in much inconvenience for his embassy. Yet, upon his return to Tongzhou, Amherst received a visit from Soo and Kwang, who informed him of the emperor's proposal for a partial exchange of presents. The Jiaqing emperor decided to accept three items from the British – the portraits of the King and Queen, a case of maps and a collection of prints and drawings. In return, he wished to present the British ambassador with a white agate sceptre, a string of sapphire beads and a box of embroidered purses.[86] Amherst considered this attempt to keep on good terms with the British, together with the kind treatment of the mission received during the rest of its return journey, as 'a sort of reparation for its abrupt dismissal from Yuen-min-yuen'.[87] Nevertheless, since neither an explanation for the rejection nor a clearly stated willingness to preserve good relations with Britain was communicated, the belated graciousness of the Chinese sovereign did not generate much good will on the part of the British. On the contrary, the Jiaqing emperor's quick change of mind appeared as proof of both his caprice and his weakness, as well as an example of his inconsistent mode of government. Ellis, for instance, stressed:

> This weak and capricious monarch, soon after the flagrant outrage had been committed under the impulse of angry disappointment, may be supposed to have become alarmed at the consequences of his own violence, and the habitual notions of decorum belonging to Chinese character and usage resuming their influence, produced the partial reparation.[88]

Although not founded on solid evidence, this interpretation was to the British the most credible explanation for what had transpired on the Chinese side.

The negative image of the Jiaqing emperor was further 'confirmed' by the contradictory accounts he provided to explain the dismissal of Amherst's embassy. Although the sovereign had never clarified to the British what induced him to reject their mission, he did issue a few accounts to different readerships in China on this subject. On 4 September 1816, the *Pekin Gazette* (*Jing Bao*), a bulletin for officers of the Qing government, released an imperial edict, in which the emperor attributed the dismissal of the British embassy to the false reports of his ministers, especially Ho. The Jiaqing emperor lamented, 'If, at that time, Ho-she-tay [Ho] had addressed to me a true report, I, the Emperor, would certainly have issued my commands, and have changed the period of the audience, in order to correspond with their intentions, in thus coming ten thousand lees to my court'.[89] In another edict, addressed to the viceroy of Jiangsu, Anhui and Jiangxi provinces, the emperor not only enjoined government officers in this area to treat the British with attention and civility but offered a more detailed explanation for his decision to reject the embassy. Although, in this document, the emperor dwelt less on the culpability of his ministers, his general sentiments on this issue did not seem to have changed – the blame was still placed on the misconduct of a few individuals when they received the British mission.

Members of the Amherst embassy were by and large satisfied with these two edicts, which they obtained through unofficial channels. Amherst claimed, 'He [the Jiaqing emperor] at least absolves me and those who were associated with me from having been instrumental to our own dismissal'.[90] Davis added that, 'inasmuch as it was a public notification that the emperor was sorry for what had passed, [it] was a very good supplement to the exchange of presents at Tung-chow, and placed our affairs on the best footing that they now admitted of'.[91] These optimistic views, however, were considerably changed when the British envoys later discovered that there was another imperial interpretation for what had occurred. Upon his arrival at Canton, Amherst received from a source in Macao a copy of the emperor's edict to the viceroy of Guangdong and Guangxi. This edict was dispatched only two days after the one which had appeared in the *Pekin Gazette*, but it contained an entirely different account of the incident. In contrast to what he wrote in the previous two edicts, the Jiaqing emperor was completely silent about the conduct of his ministers. Instead, he pointed out that the British ambassador's refusal to perform kowtow was the reason for the dismissal of the embassy. This edict greatly surprised the British envoys, especially because the two contradictory explanations had been produced by the sovereign's own hand within such a short period. Although it could be speculated that the latter account was created to prevent any voice for change being expressed by the foreign residents in Canton, the inconsistency between the two explanations strengthened the belief that the present Chinese emperor possessed a capricious and arbitrary character. Ellis conjectured, 'either at the suggestion of ministers adverse to the semblance of concession to foreigners, or from the returning haughtiness of national feeling and personal character, it was determined by the Emperor to justify his violence by a false statement'.[92] Since these edicts were not addressed, nor were they supposed to have come to the knowledge of the British, Ellis maintained that 'they are therefore only important as evidences of the general disposition of the Chinese government, or as instances of fluctuation in a mind known to be at once timid and capricious'.[93]

It can be observed from the above that, in explaining the failure of the mission, leaders of the Amherst embassy spoke little about the 'inner kowtow controversy'. Instead, they changed the subject and created a vastly different image of the Chinese sovereign from that which had developed as a result of the Macartney mission. Unlike the Qianlong emperor, about whom Macartney generally spoke positively, members of the Amherst embassy represented the Jiaqing emperor as a capricious despot. They held him as the very reason why the mission was not successful. Despite the dishonourable treatment it received in Beijing, Amherst's embassy had greater freedom of movement during its return journey through the interior of China than Macartney's embassy had received. As a result, these British travellers were able to explore the country as never before.

New discoveries in China

In comparison with the Macartney mission, members of the Amherst embassy were provided with much greater opportunities to explore the real state of Chinese society. During the return journey from Beijing to Canton, the experience of Amherst's mission differed markedly from that of the previous embassy. The Qing government under the Qianlong emperor strictly constrained the Macartney embassy's freedom of movement. In Macartney's own words, throughout the embassy's stay in China, 'we have indeed been very narrowly watched, and all our customs, habits and proceedings, even of the most trivial nature, observed with an inquisitiveness and jealousy which surpassed all that we had read of in the history of China'.[94] The Chinese authorities also took particular care to prevent the Macartney embassy from making contact with the common people of China. When the British requested permission to make some excursions from their boats into the nearby towns or countryside, 'our wishes were seldom gratified'.[95] In sharp contrast, the Amherst embassy was not subject to the same restrictions during most of its stay in China. After its members were compelled to leave Beijing, the Amherst mission quite unexpectedly enjoyed 'a greater degree of liberty than had been granted to any former embassy'.[96] During their prolonged return journey across mainland China, members of the Amherst mission were not only allowed to wander about various Chinese cities, towns and rural areas but were also able to have contact with different ranks of Chinese people, including artisans, merchants and others in the middle and lower ranks of Chinese society. This unprecedented liberty of movement enabled these travellers to observe the Chinese empire more closely than any previous British visitors. In consequence, Britain's limited first-hand knowledge on China was greatly expanded, when members of the embassy reported on their experiences after their return to Britain.

Moreover, the Amherst embassy's return journey covered new areas and lasted a longer time. Unlike the Macartney mission, which travelled to the southern end of the Grand Canal, the Amherst embassy transferred from Guazhou to the renowned Yangtze River. Its members then sailed 285 miles along the Yangtze to join the Poyang Lake, from whence the embassy travelled on smaller inland waterways to Canton. The Jiaqing emperor ordered the British to be conducted along this route, because he believed it to be the quickest route from Beijing to Canton. Nevertheless, because of adverse weather conditions, the journey took considerably longer than expected. It resulted in 'the fortunate occasion'[97] which allowed members of the Amherst embassy not only to spend more time in the interior of China but also to visit some parts of the lower Yangtze delta, the most prosperous region of the Chinese empire that had hitherto not been explored by any Europeans.

Before we start examining the Amherst embassy's discoveries in China, it should be noted that, under the influence of Edward Said's *Orientalism*,[98] historians have been paying much attention to the patronising attitudes which Westerners often adopted towards 'the Orient' during their encounters with it. David Porter and Jeng-Guo

Chen, for example, have studied the emerging discourses of political liberty, free trade and class differentiation in the context of an ascendant Britain. Their works have shown how economic and social advances in the eighteenth century gave rise to the increasingly critical British understandings of China.[99] Elizabeth Hope Chang has also revealed that, instead of showing China as it really was, the vision of China in nineteenth-century Europe was 'in fact a reflection mirrored back to the European reader by a representation made by a Western writer'.[100] Such views are unquestionably useful correctives for our previous understanding of early Western attitudes towards China, but, in the case of the Amherst embassy, it would be equally erroneous to ignore the worsening state of the Qing dynasty after Macartney's embassy. When Macartney was visiting the Qing court, China was at the very end of the so-called '*Kang-Qian shengshi* (prosperous age of the Kangxi until the Qianlong reigns, 1662–1795)'. Even though Macartney described China as 'an old, crazy, first-rate Man of War',[101] he was in fact comparing the Chinese empire with a glorious past that was the product of many Westerners' imagination. When Amherst reached China in the later 1810s, as explained earlier in this chapter, signs of the Qing dynasty's decline had become increasingly evident. Overpopulation, land shortage and unceasing rebellions were major developments during this period.[102] The Jiaqing court, moreover, was facing serious fiscal troubles. The enormous cost of the Qianlong emperor's military campaigns, as well as the luxury of official lives, seriously depleted the Chinese treasury's once healthy finances. In order to slow the drain of revenues, the Jiaqing emperor extolled frugality through personal example. He initiated a publicised campaign to reduce spending by curbing waste and unnecessary consumption at court.[103] Most notably, he gave up the extravagant tradition of southern tours along the Grand Canal to the lower Yangtze delta. Since the numerous lavishly decorated buildings on this route, many of which had been built expressly for these imperial tours, remained unattended after the Qianglong emperor's last visit in 1784, their dilapidation, when they were seen by members of Amherst's embassy, became a clear and visible indicator of China's decline under the present emperor. On the basis of this discovery, the widely circulated image in Britain of a backward and declining Chinese empire could be supported for the first time by an abundance of reliable first-hand evidence.

In the various accounts of China produced by members of the Amherst embassy, there was a general impression that China was in decay during the reign of Jiaqing. Staunton, as the only person who had travelled with both embassies, maintained that 'there can be little doubt that the prosperity of this empire has been on the decline under the government of the present emperor, that is, since the period at which it was visited by Lord Macartney's embassy'.[104] Staunton wrote that 'in most points, our present views and estimation of the country and inhabitants, seem to differ from those which were formed by the former party, for the worse',[105] and he believed that it could be attributed to the different state of the imperial finances at the two periods. Having read in the *Pekin Gazette* that the Jiaqing emperor was compelled to abandon even the refurbishment of his own garden for want of available funds, Staunton became convinced that the Chinese empire was indeed declining under its present ruler. To prove this, Staunton recorded every sign of poverty and dilapidation that he discovered throughout the long journey from Beijing. As a result, terms such as 'decay', 'decline' and 'ruinous' can be frequently found in his journal. Staunton even claimed that 'almost every public building we have seen in our route, has exhibited to us more or less evidence of the poverty or negligence of the government'.[106] In order to illustrate the destitution common in the Chinese countryside, Staunton wrote:

> These hills are perfectly barren, and destitute even of trees – no signs whatever of cultivation or inhabitants, except at their feet near the river, or in the lowest parts of the intervening vallies [sic]. At one, we passed on our left a ruined pagoda of nine stories [sic] – It seemed wholly abandoned, and had no house or religious establishment of any kind in its vicinity. ... Some spots had very much the appearance of the entrance of mines which, being no longer worked, had been neglected, and closed up.[107]

With regard to an average city in Jiangxi province, he recorded that:

> Within the walls we found no improvement in the style of the houses, or any shops that attracted our attention – the walls were low and ruinous ... a range of buildings ... in the style of a large joss-house, but at present in a ruinous state, and wholly untenanted ... the tribunals of the Nan-gan-foo or governor, ... it is certainly at present the poorest and most ruinous ... The governor's tribunal and residence, was a lofty and extensive, but neglected pile of building. The tribunal of the Hien ... appeared in so ruinous a state as to be scarcely habitable ... several stone pailoos ... seemed to denote that this city had once existed in a state of comparative splendor, from which it had latterly declined.[108]

Other members of the embassy joined with Staunton in providing their readers with an image of a declining China, even though they had not visited China two decades before. Ellis, when passing Tsing-heen [Qing xian], noted that 'the walls and the town itself are falling to decay'.[109] In viewing a pagoda near the city of Nanchang, Ellis commented that it was 'in exceedingly bad proportions' and 'evinced the decay of architecture among the Chinese'.[110] Davis, subsequent to his visit to Wu-yuan, an imperial residence of the Qianlong emperor, could not conceal his disappointment at what he saw. He entered into his *Sketches of China* that, 'Like almost everything of the kind that we had seen in the country, this once decorated abode was in a sad state of dilapidation and ruin and calculated to produce no other emotions than those of melancholy'.[111] After Abel paid a visit to the celebrated city of Guazhou, he recorded similar scenes in his narrative. He wrote that:

> The city of Qua-tchow [Guazhou] did not answer the expectations raised by its advantageous situation. Its streets exhibited no characters of opulence, and its walls were in ruins. In the days of Kien-Lung [Qianlong], it flourished under imperial favour; ... Since these golden days in the history of Qua-tchow, as its governor informed Mr Morrison, the Fung-shway [Feng-shui], or 'fortune of the place,' had gradually declined.[112]

On the basis of their conviction that China was in decay, these British travellers became increasingly disenchanted with the state of Chinese civilisation. At the beginning of the Amherst mission, members of the embassy were still divided into 'those who landed with an impression that the Chinese were to be classed with the civilised nations of Europe' and others who 'ranged them with the other nations of Asia'.[113] By the end of the mission, however, a general consensus on the backwardness of China had emerged. This unfavourable perception of the Chinese empire was based, first of all, on the perceived image of the Chinese being an unrefined people. Upon their arrival on the China coast, members of the Amherst embassy were soon 'astonished to find the fishermen in their boats as naked as savages, without appearing conscious of shame. Sometimes they wore a jacket over their shoulders, but had no clothing for the lower part of the body.'[114] It was also a commonly held view that 'poor boys to the age of twelve or thirteen were generally naked, standing, running about in promiscuous crowds'.[115] In light of these impressions, the Chinese were more and more presented to readers of these accounts as a barbaric people or some kind of subhuman, who were frequently compared with animals rather than with human beings from elsewhere. For instance, when Hall gave the local shipmen some dollars as presents, he noted, 'The captain and his crew assembled in a ring, and turned over the pieces from hand to hand, just as I have seen a group of monkeys do when puzzled with some new object'.[116] The residences of ordinary Chinese people, in Abel's opinion, were 'miserable beyond anything which England can exemplify' and 'more like the dens of beasts than the habitations of men'.[117]

In light of these discoveries, Abel, the embassy's naturalist, identified the 'leading characteristics' of ordinary Chinese people as 'dirt, squalidness, and extreme poverty'.[118] He particularly highlighted the Chinese people's unhygienic living conditions. Abel found that, in addition to the shortage of clean water and the ubiquity of mosquitoes in many parts of China,[119] 'The Chinese are less fastidious than perhaps any other people in the choice of their food'.[120] Whenever dead pigs or rotting vegetables were thrown overboard from the British ships, there were always some Chinese people rushing to pick them up and eat them afterwards. Abel and other members of the embassy also presented the Chinese as a people 'utterly insensible to bad smells'.[121] When surrounded by curious crowds in Tianjin, Ellis recalled, 'there literally prevails a compound of villainous stenches, and this constitutes one of the principal inconveniences of the crowd that gather round us'.[122] On a visit to the famous 'Bath of Fragrant Water' near Nanjing, the empire's second city, Ellis claimed that 'the stench is excessive; altogether I thought it the most disgusting cleansing apparatus I had ever seen and worthy of this nasty nation'.[123] On the same occasion, Abel noted that 'There appeared no intention of renewing the water [which] thus become saturated with dirt ... The steam arising from it, however fragrant to the senses of the Chinese, was to mine really intolerable, and drove me away before I could ascertain in what manner the baths were heated.'[124] By such multi-sensory examinations, the Chinese people's want of cleanliness, as well as the general image of them as an unrefined people, were further confirmed.

The British travellers' disenchantment with Chinese civilisation was intensified by the poor condition of the public infrastructure in China. According to Ellis, the majority of the streets in Chinese cities were 'imperfectly paved, narrow, and saturated with bad smells'.[125] The roads Amherst took in Tongzhou, Morrison noted, were so 'dirty and slippery' that 'the poor creatures who carried the chairs were up to the knees in water'.[126] The express way, which the Chinese promised to be of superior construction, turned out to be simply 'a broad road of hewn granite, which was evidently very old, and in so ruined a state that it might have been referred to [in] the days of *Yaou* and *Shun*'.[127] Even the Grand Canal, which was renowned as an example of the immense power of human labour, was considered by Davis to be much overrated, because most of it was 'only a natural river, modified and regulated by sluices and embankments'.[128] In a similar way, members of the Amherst embassy complained about the vehicles provided by the Qing government. Staunton described the Chinese boats as 'ill constructed for comfort in cold weather'.[129] Abel believed the junks for conveying supplies 'the most clumsy looking vessels imaginable'.[130] He also deemed the Chinese carts 'the most execrable machines imaginable'.[131] Riding in these carriages, Morrison noted that, 'without constant effort to hold by the sides of the carriage, a person's head was thrown first on one side and then on the other'.[132] During the exhausting overnight journey from Tongzhou to Beijing, Davis expressed his regret at having exchanged his horse for one of these Chinese carts, because 'the convulsive throes of this primitive machine, without springs, on the ruined granite road, produced an effect little short of lingering death; and the only remedy was to get out as often as possible and walk'.[133] By contrast, Morrison observed that it was probably due to the poor transport available in China that Amherst's British-made carriage attracted so much admiration from the Chinese and was recognised by them as 'proper for the Emperor'.[134]

In addition to such observations on the facilities and infrastructure in China, the British visitors commented on the state of the Chinese military. Many military posts in China, as with other public buildings, were considered to be in urgent need of repair. In particular, the British observers found it amusing and absurd that some watch-towers in Shandong province, formed entirely of mats, were painted to imitate brick or stone. Davis regarded it as 'a most unequivocal proof of the unwarlike habits of the nation'.[135] Members of the Amherst embassy also concluded that 'the art of war must be in a very low state'[136] in China. Through contacts with various Chinese soldiers and mandarins, they found that the Chinese still saw bodily strength and courage as the only qualities that were required for military advancement. The most frequently used weapons of Chinese military men were bows and arrows. According to Davis, most of the matchlocks that he saw in China were 'truly wretched and appeared rusted through, so as not to be fired without danger'.[137] When Chinese soldiers were using these weapons, Ellis noted, 'they immediately retreat upon applying the match, squatting down at a short distance with their backs turned; the iron tube is always placed upright, so that every possibility of danger from the wadding is guarded against'.[138] All these findings led members of the Amherst embassy to confirm Macartney's impression that the Chinese were indeed a militarily weak nation.

The British observers' discoveries about the knowledge and characteristics of the Chinese people reinforced their unfavourable perception of Chinese civilisation. As with the Macartney mission, members of Amherst's embassy were convinced by their experiences that the Chinese were indeed so ignorant that the Europeans 'can learn nothing from China'.[139] Shortly after the embassy landed in China, Morrison realised that, although he had marked all the baggage in Chinese characters, the boatmen and porters were unable to read.[140] Davis also noticed that the military mandarin attached to his boat could not even write in Chinese as well as he could and that this man's 'general ignorance on every subject ... made it vain to hope for any information from him'.[141]

When Abel was collecting plants or examining stones during the journey, he was often laughed at by the natives and the escorting soldiers, as if he did so only to satisfy his peculiar curiosity. When Abel spoke to some of these people, he found the British to them were like 'inhabitants of another world', because 'our features, dress, and habits, were so opposed to theirs, as to induce them to infer that our country, in all its natural characters, must equally differ from their own. "Have you a moon, and rain, and rivers in your country?" were their occasional questions.'[142]

Despite their profound ignorance, the British observers discovered that the Chinese still had a deep conviction of China's superiority over all other nations. In the vicinity of Shandong's northern frontier, the British envoys met the judge of Beizhili, a loquacious man who had a certain amount of knowledge about the world beyond China. Although he was better informed of the geography and history of European states than perhaps any other Chinese whom the embassy had met, this gentleman spoke of Britain as a country 'depending altogether on commerce ... great by sea, but weak by land'.[143] He also asserted that, in contrast to the inferior position and status of Britain, 'the Chinese empire was in the center of the universe and was the supreme head of all nations'.[144] For this reason, the British ambassador should pay homage to the emperor of China in order to win concessions for British merchants who traded at Canton. Otherwise, the judge was afraid that it might cause the ruin of the British nation. To Davis, this understanding of Britain as well as of Sino-British trade was so poor that 'ignorance and conceit were perhaps never more strongly combined'.[145] He found that, because of their unique sense of self-importance, the Chinese were very reluctant to recognise anything foreign that appeared to be superior to their own designs. In terms of the different attitudes that the Chinese and the British adopted towards science and technology, Davis maintained:

> they are too proud to learn anything about us, while we foreigners of course never lose an opportunity of studying them in every relation of life, and have availed ourselves to some purpose of the opportunities (scanty as these may have comparatively been,) which years of intercourse afforded us. That 'power' which consists in 'knowledge', therefore, preponderates on our side.[146]

Apart from their investigations into the Chinese people's knowledge, members of the Amherst embassy also attempted to examine the spiritual state of the Chinese people. Ellis, for example, discovered that, compared to the serious and exalted religious beliefs in Europe, religion in China 'has all the looseness and vanity with less of the solemnity and decency of ancient Polytheism'.[147] According to the observations of these British travellers, there were no particular dates set aside for public worship, nor did the Chinese attend temples congregationally. The majority of the Chinese population were unselective in the deities to which they paid respect, so long as they believed that the practice would help avert mischief befalling them. Most of the priests in China were found to be uninstructed themselves, as well as largely illiterate. As mere performers of ceremonies, they neither preached like their counterparts did in Europe, nor were they treated by their followers with the reverence that was 'justly and reasonably due to the respectable ministers of religion in all countries'.[148] In view of these facts, Morrison claimed that:

> The general principles of our religion give a tone of elevation and dignity to the human mind which is not felt here. ... They do not associate under something approaching equality for the worship of their gods. ... The multitudes of people in this country are truly, in a moral and religious view, as 'sheep without a shepherd'.[149]

On the basis of such images, Morrison described the main characteristics of the Chinese people as being 'selfish, cold-blooded and inhumane'.[150] He discovered that the professed moral maxims of the Chinese were actually ineffectual in regulating their minds and conduct. Since the Chinese were never 'nice about a strict adherence to the truth',[151] they could, in fact, be 'complaisant and servile, or insolent and domineering, according to circumstances'.[152] For instance, 'When interest or fear do not dictate a different course, they are to the strangers, haughty, insolent, fraudulent and inhospitable'. Moreover, 'A merchant will flatter a foreign devil (as they express it), when he has something to gain from him; then he can be servile enough; particularly if he is not seen by his own countrymen'.[153] Abel, in this regard, pointed out that, particularly in the Chinese mercantile community, 'the principle of cheating is so legitimated amongst them by the general practice and toleration of their countrymen, as to be considered rather as a necessary qualification to the successful practice of their calling, as an immoral quality'.[154] Because of what constantly occurred to the Amherst embassy, Abel added that, 'giving false weight, charging centuple prices, and substituting bad articles for good, ... is [are] not only tolerated but applauded, especially when foreigners are its victims'.[155] On the basis of all these findings and experiences, when it came to the general character of the Chinese, Ellis contended that they were 'half civilized, prejudiced'[156] and, 'without exaggeration', a 'nefarious' people.[157] As for China's ranking in comparison to other civilisations in the world, Ellis concluded that, although it was 'superior to the other countries of Asia in the arts of government and the general aspects of society', China was undoubtedly 'inferior by many degrees to civilised Europe in all that constitutes the real greatness of a nation'.¹⁵⁸ On the question of whether the Chinese could justifiably be described as barbarians, Morrison produced the following statement:

> If 'barbarity' or being 'barbarous' expresses something savage, rude and cruel, the present inhabitants of China do not deserve the epithet; if it expresses a cunning selfish policy, endeavouring to deceive, to intimidate, or to brow beat, as occasion may require, connected with an arrogant assumption of superiority on all occasions, instead of cultivating a liberal, candid, friendly intercourse with men of other nations, they are barbarians.¹⁵⁹

These arguments put forward by Ellis and Morrison fairly represent the common opinions of the members of Amherst's embassy by the end of their visit to China. We can see that the disagreements previously expressed on this subject had changed significantly. A consensus on the half-civilised image of China was reached by the British observers who participated in the Amherst embassy and subsequently recorded their opinions on China.

No more embassies

In seeking an explanation for the backwardness of Chinese civilisation, members of the Amherst embassy concluded that the Qing government was the primary cause. Since, during the return journey, they were given many opportunities to visit Chinese cities and villages as well as to communicate with various Chinese people, these British travellers were able to gather much more first-hand evidence than their predecessors on the real conditions in China. In particular, they were convinced that the suspicious government of China had deliberately designed its policies to suppress the natural sentiments and pursuits of its subjects. First of all, these British observers believed that, although the leading characteristics of the Chinese appeared to be prejudiced and inhuman, these qualities were more the consequence of the government's narrow policies than the natural disposition of the Chinese people. They maintained that the Qing government attached a great deal of importance to restricting contacts between foreigners and the Chinese people, and hence the country's foreign trade was restricted only to the port of Canton.¹⁶⁰ Although the Macartney embassy had been permitted to pass through the interior of China, its members had not been allowed to make extensive contact with the local inhabitants. Because of such restrictions, the previous Western impressions of the Chinese people and of the state of Chinese society were drawn mainly from evidence gained at Canton. This allowed Hall to admit that 'it is obviously as unfair to judge of the Chinese by such data, as it would be to estimate the character of the English from such materials as Rotherhithe and Wapping might afford'.[161]

The Qing authorities were also found to have promoted a belief in the inferiority of foreign nations and a distrust of their good intentions in regions where frequent engagements with foreign people had taken place. In consequence, a deep prejudice against, as well as a serious contempt for, all foreigners had been inculcated in the minds of these Chinese people. Despite this, Hall discovered that, 'in places remote from Canton, and where it is not the policy of the local authorities to discourage all inquiry, there is no jealousy or apprehension of strangers'.[162] When the Amherst embassy travelled to some places which had probably never been visited by any Westerners before, its members often discerned and benefited from the cheerful disposition and hospitality of the local inhabitants. Many examples can support this claim. Abel noted that:

> I was often enabled to get amongst them apart from my friends and usual attendant soldiers, and always found them mild, forbearing, and humane.[163]
> ... especially when they were peasants, [they] afforded a pleasing contrast in their simple manners and civil treatment of strangers, to the cunning designs of the salesmen of Tung-Chow, and the brutal importunity of the courtiers of Yuen-Ming-Yuen.[164]

Ellis added that, when he entered the dwellings of some local residents, 'No dislike is shewn by the people in general to natural inquisitiveness; on the contrary, our momentary intrusions have been met by invitations to sit down'.[165] In contrast with the prevailing impression that the Chinese were guarded in their relations with foreigners, these friendly natives either pressed them to partake of their meals or supplied them with tea, or even invited these visiting strangers to examine the yards and outer apartments of their houses.[166] As a result of these experiences, members of the Amherst mission were further convinced that it was the deliberate policies of the Qing government that considerably altered the genuine disposition of the Chinese people.

These British observers also learned that, in addition to its efforts to restrict the nation's contact with foreigners, the Chinese government also promoted tensions and difficulties within the country's hierarchical society. On the one hand, the Chinese people were in awe of the government, because, under the powerful hand of that authority, government officials 'have the knack of rendering life very miserable, and assume the power of bambooing, torturing, fining (or squeezing), and every species of oppression short of death'.[167] Throughout their journey, the British travellers witnessed a number of cases where Chinese men and women were bambooed or face-slapped for making trifling mistakes. They also found that the embassy's attendant officials sometimes forced some poor people to work for the fleet without pay. Influenced by these experiences, Morrison believed that 'China does not enjoy *liberty*. Her government is a military despotism. ... The strong arm of power intimidates them.'[168] In consequence, the Chinese people were seriously discouraged from discussing affairs of state or forming any societies which might seek to influence or oppose the government. Moreover, since according to the criminal code of China, 'an ineffectual attempt to save the life of another, under the slightest shade of suspicion, is followed by the punishment of death',[169] Abel found that the Chinese were unwilling to give assistance when they saw someone's life was in danger. Instead of taking this as an example of the Chinese people's inhumane character, Staunton attributed it to the 'absurd and unjust principles upon which the Chinese laws are administered by the mandarins'.[170] Macleod also clearly stated that 'It is lamentable to observe that the institutions of any nation should have the effect of deadening every feeling of sympathy, and of exciting, instead of discouraging, "man's inhumanity to man;" but such is the case in this country'.[171]

On the other hand, these British observers found that the mandarins themselves were also not free from concerns about their own self-preservation. Their offices and lives were totally subject to the will of the emperor, inasmuch as 'not only the more important measures of government, but the most trifling details of office, depend for their execution upon the supposed irresistibility of the imperial power'.[172] In particular, Davis was informed that, 'in the event of any suspicion of a collusion with foreigners', the emperor's 'single word was sufficient to consign them [the mandarins] to death'.[173] For the members of the Amherst embassy, this explained the sharp contrast between the attendant officers' extremely reserved manner in the vicinity of Beijing and the good temper they manifested during the rest of their time with the embassy. In the early stages of the return journey, Amherst believed that, 'Being now at so short a distance from the Capital, it appeared probable that most questions would be decided by an immediate appeal to the Emperor himself'.[174] Probably for this reason, the mandarins appeared quite cautious about entering into any formal conversation with the British envoys and nothing could induce them to accept any presents. Nevertheless, Davis and others observed that 'as we receded from the neighbourhood of Peking, the mandarins had become more frequent and less reserved in their visits, very readily accepting any presents that were made them'.[175] In light of these discoveries, the British observers were led to believe that, just as with the Chinese populace, the government officials in China were entirely at the mercy of their sovereign. The power and caution of the Chinese emperor greatly constrained their liberty and natural sentiments.

Last, but not least, members of the Amherst embassy consolidated the idea that the government of China was the chief obstacle to the Chinese people's pursuit of knowledge and wellbeing, as well as to the progress of Chinese civilisation. To justify this conclusion, Macleod maintained that the Chinese government not only made its people believe themselves 'at the summit of perfection' but established 'the absurd tyranny of fettering the human understanding, by forbidding all innovation and improvement'.[176] For instance, although some Chinese people did exhibit interest in astronomy, the study of the human frame, Western medical practices and so on,[177] the government prohibited the masses from undertaking such studies. It narrowed their ideas 'by compelling their attention, and attaching importance, entirely to the observance of useless forms and ceremonies', and 'by admitting of no deviation from one contracted path, even in the simplest transactions of life'.[178] In particular, Davis maintained that the Chinese government habitually inculcated a respectful demeanour on the part of young people towards their elders. He believed that such practices had apparent effects, because 'in no country of the world does a quiet, easy subordination so extensively prevail as in China', where the 'inexperience and headstrong passion of youth' were repressed without inspiring resistance.[179] Furthermore, these British commentators contended that many measures adopted by the Chinese government were inimical to the welfare of the people and also restricted the development of China's civilisation. For example, they maintained that although China's foreign trade was restricted to Canton, there was actually much interest in trading with foreigners among the Chinese people.[180] In those places where greater engagement with Westerners took place, particularly in Canton, the British travellers claimed that they could discern a distinct air of opulence that was hard to see in the rest of China. Ellis noted in this regard that

> Canton, from the number and size of the vessels, the variety and decorations of the boats, the superior architecture of the European factories, and the general buzz and diffusion of a busy population, had, on approaching, a more imposing appearance than any Chinese city visited by the present embassy; nor do I believe, that in the wealth of the inhabitants at large, the skill of the artificers, and the variety of the manufactures, it yields, with the exception of the capital, to any city in the empire. ... The whole effect of foreign commerce is here concentrated and displayed, and the employment which the European trade affords to all classes of the inhabitants diffuses an air of general prosperity, not to be expected where this powerful stimulus does not operate.[181]

With regard to this phenomenon, Davis believed that it was 'owing greatly to hints furnished by our examples'[182] rather than being due to any positive influence exerted by the local government. To prove this, Abel provided evidence to demonstrate that modern technology introduced by the British had benefited the communities around Canton remarkably. He noted:

> The small pox, which for centuries has at different periods made dreadful havock all over the empire, is likely soon to be extirpated by the benign influence of vaccination establishing under the auspices of Mr Pierson the principal surgeon of the British factory. ... Native vaccinators have been appointed and educated under the eye of Mr Pierson, and are taking from him the labour of inoculating the lowest class of Chinese. I witnessed their operations in a temple near the British factory, on some of the children of the hundreds of anxious parents who flocked to procure the preservation of their offspring from the small pox, at that time prevalent at Canton. If the paternal government of China can free itself from national prejudices, it will erect a monument of gratitude to the discovery of Jenner, and the services of Pierson.[183]

In contrast to such positive benefits arising from contact with Britain, the British observers lamented that similar changes had been impossible in the rest of China because of the Qing government's policies. For this reason, the common belief within the embassy was further strengthened that the Chinese 'have had for some thousand years a dawn of civilisation', but, 'from the operation of the most narrow-minded principles', it 'has never brightened into day'.[184] Accordingly, the suspicious Qing government, as the designer of such restrictive policies, was seen as the primary cause of China's backwardness and the country's stagnant civilisation.

In light of these unfavourable images of the Chinese government, as well as some experiences they gained during the return journey from Beijing to Canton, members of the Amherst mission analysed the lessons they had learned in China. As a result, some key ideas left by the Macartney embassy regarding how to improve Britain's relations with China faced revision. First, seriously challenged were the grounds for sending another complimentary embassy to China. Amherst suggested that China's current financial circumstances, combined with the character of the Jiaqing emperor, rendered such a mission unwelcome to the Chinese. He maintained:

> The disordered state of the Imperial Finances would make it an object to save the expense attending the transport of a numerous company of persons from one extremity of the Empire to the other; and the same reason added, I believe, to the personal fears and jealousies of the Emperor would probably retrench a great part of the train of any future Embassador.[185]

Pointing out that it was actually not sensible to attempt to strengthen Britain's commercial links with China by dispatching another embassy. Ellis contended:

> Royal embassies, avowedly complimentary, but really directed to commercial objects, are perhaps, in themselves, somewhat anomalous, and are certainly very opposite, not only to Chinese feelings, but even to those of all Eastern nations; among whom trade, although fostered as a source of revenue, is never reputed honourable.[186]

In light of such advice given by the ambassador and the third commissioner, it is understandable why the Amherst embassy did indeed become the last mission of its kind that Britain sent out to China.

Second, from their daily contacts with officials of the Chinese government, members of the Amherst embassy accumulated some useful knowledge on how to deal with the Chinese authorities in practice. In particular, under most circumstances to achieve an objective, the best way was simply to ignore government authorities and not request formal approval before proceeding to business. For example, as had frequently happened on their return voyage from Beijing to Canton, Hall noted that, 'whenever we began by soliciting leave to walk into the country or to look at anything, our request was almost invariably refused'; however, when '[we] go straight ... by seeming to imagine any permission [un]necessary', a Chinese official would rarely come to stop them.[187] For this reason, Hayne was convinced that 'by experience we have found beyond a doubt, that to obtain an end in China, is to ask no question, and if there is no real objection, it will pass unnoticed'.[188] Experience had also shown that on the occasions when British interests confronted neglect, such as when daily supplies were deficient, it was important for the British to make their voices heard and, if necessary, to express their demands in a resolute manner. Davis maintained in this regard that it was a well-proven fact that, every time the British remonstrated strongly, their grievances were not only soon redressed but, in most cases, handled with great care. Hence, to produce a favourable response, a 'determined step was the more requisite'.[189]

Finally, these different interpretations of the situation in China, together with the conclusions reached about the character of the Chinese emperor and his people, seemed to have influenced some of the tactics that British observers proposed should be adopted in future Sino-British relations. According to the suggestions coming from members of the Amherst embassy, most significant was the advice to promote a more powerful and steadfast image of Britain in the imperial court of China. Ellis, for example, suggested that if 'it still be deemed advisable to assist our commerce by political intercourse',[190] the British authorities should look to their 'possessions in Hindostan and Nepaul', and use 'the supreme government of Bengal as the medium of that intercourse'.[191] By this means, he expected that

> there the representative of armed power will encounter its fellow; and if ever impression is to be produced at Pekin, it must be from an intimate knowledge of our political and military strength, rather than from the gratification produced in the Emperor's mind by the reception of an embassy on Chinese terms, or the moral effect of justifiable resistance terminating in rejection.[192]

Macleod advocated measures that were even more coercive. He wrote with assurance that, because 'so feeble is their naval force ... the appearance of a few of our lightest cruisers on their coasts, would throw the whole of this *celestial* empire into confusion'.[193] Although there is some similarity between this statement and Macartney's famous aggressive comments, it is worth noting that, unlike Macartney, Macleod did not prefer a policy of forbearance. On the contrary, next to the above passage, Macleod quoted a remark by Krusenstern, a Russian navigator who had experienced similar vexation in China and who had alleged that 'the forbearance and mistaken lenity of the greater civilised powers have emboldened these savages [the Chinese], not only to consider as barbarians all Europeans, but actually to treat them as such'.[194] With reference to this statement, it can be observed that not only was China being viewed as an isolated 'other' from the civilised European countries, but Macleod was implying that a wrong approach had been adopted by Western nations in their relations with China. Although Macleod was not a leading member of the Amherst embassy and plans to demonstrate British power and resolution were not yet under serious consideration at this stage, the previous effort to curry favour with the Chinese emperor had proved to be ineffective.

In conclusion, although the Amherst mission failed to achieve its original objectives just like Macartney's mission in 1793, this embassy was by no means an unimportant event in the course of Sino-British relations. Neither was the result of the embassy a mere repetition of the fate of Macartney's mission. In the complexity of its launch and its proceedings, as well as the reflections left by its participants, the Amherst embassy actually encountered a range of new situations which did not exist in the case of the first embassy. In particular, the variance between the expectations of the EIC and the British government for the mission did not seem to be a notable factor in the beginning, but its significance considerably enlarged as the Sino-British kowtow dispute re-emerged. In this context, Staunton, the leading EIC representative whose 'local inside knowledge' was supposed to assist Amherst in achieving the diplomatic goals of the embassy, set off an 'inner kowtow controversy' that proved critical to the outcome of the mission. Because of this internal struggle, conducted mainly between Staunton and the rest of the embassy's leadership, Amherst had to yield to Staunton's 'experience-based' assessment of the situation and adopt an unbending stance that resulted in the dismissal of the mission. To explain this unpleasant outcome, however, both sides significantly – perhaps also deliberately – downplayed the importance of the 'inner kowtow controversy' to the failure of the embassy. Instead of suggesting that it might have been their faults, these men, who were either primarily or partly responsible for this collective decision, chose to focus on the personal character of the Jiaqing emperor, whom they maintained to be extremely capricious and arbitrary. On the basis of this largely invented image, leading members of the Amherst embassy were able to justify the idea that the means of dispatching complimentary embassies to China was problematic *per se*, while a demonstration of British power and firmness would be a better way to conduct Britain's future relations with China.

Moreover, the unprecedented freedom of movement afforded the members of the Amherst embassy during their return journey through China allowed these British observers to explore the interior of China and to communicate more fully with the Chinese government and people than ever before. As a result of the considerable first-hand evidence gathered and subsequently published by these men, a consensus was reached about the backward image of China. Some unfavourable perceptions of Chinese civilisation, which had already been circulating in Britain, were rendered more credible than ever before. To explain China's backwardness, these British visitors blamed the Qing government for placing obstacles in the way of the progress of Chinese civilisation as well as damaging the general welfare of the Chinese people. This view of the Qing government, to a great extent, laid the foundations for the mounting hostile attitude in Britain towards the government of China. For these reasons, the Amherst mission's significance to the development of Sino-British relations was undoubtedly profound. As subsequent events showed in consequence of this mission, no royal embassy went to the Qing court again, and the British government ceased to pursue the policy of appeasing the Chinese emperor as suggested by Macartney. Britain's previously deferential posture in its relations with China was beginning to give way to a more hard-line approach in the decades to come.

THE EMBASSIES
Notes

1. For example, Hosea Ballou Morse, *The Chronicles of the East India Company Trading to China, 1635–1834* (5 vols, Oxford: Clarendon Press, 1926; reprinted, London: Routledge, 2000), III, 256–306; Li Chien-nung, *The Political History of China, 1840–1928* (Princeton, NJ: Van Nostrand, 1956), pp. 17–18; A.E. Grantham, *A Manchu Monarch: An Interpretation of Chia Ching* (Arlington, VA: University Publications of America, 1976), pp. 154–201; Christopher Hibbert, *The Dragon Wakes: China and the West, 1793–1911* (New York: Penguin, 1984), pp. 54–69; and Alain Peyrefitte, *The Collision of Two Civilisations: The British Expedition to China in 1792–4* (London: Harvill, 1993), pp. 504–11.
2. Peter J. Kitson and Robert Markley (eds), *Writing China: Essays on the Amherst Embassy (1816) and Sino-British Cultural Relations* (Woodbridge: Boydell & Brewer, 2016); Hao Gao, 'The Amherst Embassy and British Discoveries in China', *History*, 337 (2014), 568–87; Hao Gao, 'The Inner Kowtow Controversy during the Amherst Embassy to China, 1816–1817', *Diplomacy & Statecraft*, 4 (2016), 595–614.
3. Jodi Eastberg, 'West Meets East: British Perceptions of China through the Life and Works of Sir George Thomas Staunton, 1781–1859' (Marquette University Ph.D. thesis, 2009); Zhang Shunhong, 'British Views on China during the Time of the Embassies of Lord Macartney and Lord Amherst (1790–1820)' (Birkbeck College, University of London Ph.D. thesis, 1990). The latter has recently appeared as a monograph; see Zhang Shunhong, *British Views on China at the Dawn of the 19th Century* (Reading: Paths International Ltd, 2013).
4. Patrick Tuck, 'Introduction: Sir George Thomas Staunton and the Failure of the Amherst Embassy of 1816', in *Britain and the China Trade 1635–1842*, ed. Tuck (10 vols, London: Routledge, 2000), X, vii–xlii.
5. See Wu Xiaojun, 'A'meishide Shijietuan Tanxi: Yi Tianchao Guan zhi Shijian Wei Zhongxin (On the Amherst Mission: with Its Focus on the Practice of the World View of the Celestial Empire)' (National Tsinghua University M.A. thesis, 2008); Eun Kyung Min, 'Narrating the Far East: Commercial Civility and Ceremony in the Amherst Embassy to China (1816–1817)', in *Interpreting Colonialism*, ed. B. Wells and P. Steward (Oxford: Voltaire Foundation, 2004) pp. 160–80. Kitson also has an article which partly discusses the kowtow controversy. See Peter J. Kitson, 'The "Catastrophe of This New Chinese Mission": The Amherst Embassy to China of 1816', in *Early Encounters between East Asia and Europe: Telling Failures*, ed. Ralf Hertel and Michael Keevak (London; New York: Routledge, 2017), pp. 67–83.
6. Peter J. Kitson, 'The Dark Gift: Opium, John Francis Davis, Thomas De Quincey, and the Amherst Embassy to China of 1816', in *Writing China*, ed. Kitson and Markley, pp. 56–82.
7. Robert Markley, 'The Amherst Embassy in the Shadow of Tambora: Climate and Culture, 1816', in *ibid.*, pp. 83–104.
8. These works include: George T. Staunton, *Notes of Proceedings and Occurrences during the British Embassy to Pekin in 1816* (London: Habant, 1824; reprinted, with an introduction by Patrick Tuck, London: Routledge, 2000); George T. Staunton, *Miscellaneous Notices Relating to China, and our Commercial Intercourse with that Country* (London: John Murray, 1822); and George T. Staunton, *Memoirs of the Chief Incidents of the Public Life of Sir George T. Staunton* (London: L. Booth, 1856).
9. Henry Ellis, *Journal of the Proceedings of the Late Embassy to China* (London: John Murray, 1817).
10. Robert Morrison, *A View of China, for Philological Purposes: Containing a Sketch of Chinese Chronology, Geography, Government, Religion and Customs* (London: Black, Parbury, and Allen, 1817).
11. Robert Morrison, *A Memoir of the Principal Occurrences during an Embassy from the British Government to the Court of China in the Year 1816* (London: Hatchard & Son, 1820).

12 Eliza Morrison (ed.), *Memoirs of the Life and Labours of Robert Morrison, D.D.* (2 vols, London: Longman, 1839).
13 John Francis Davis, *Sketches of China; Partly during an Inland Journey of Four Months between Peking, Nanking, and Canton* (2 vols, London: Charles Knight, 1841).
14 Clarke Abel, *Narrative of a Journey in the Interior of China in the Years 1816–1817* (London: Longman and Hurst, 1818); John Macleod, *Narrative of a Voyage in His Majesty's Late Ship Alceste to the Yellow Sea, along the Coast of Corea, and through Its Numerous Hitherto Undiscovered Islands, to the Island of Lewchew* (London: John Murray, 1817); Basil Hall, *Narrative of a Voyage to Java, China and the great Loo-Choo Island* (London: Edward Moxon, 1840); and Henry Hayne, *Henry Hayne Diary 1816–1817* (4 vols), *China through Western Eyes: Manuscript Records of Traders, Travellers, Missionaries and Diplomats, 1792–1942* (London: Adam Matthew 1996).
15 Hibbert, *The Dragon Wakes*, pp. 55–6.
16 Peyrefitte, *The Collision of Two Civilisations*, p. 506.
17 Staunton, *Miscellaneous Notices*, p. 192.
18 Ibid.
19 Letter from the Secret Commercial Committee to the Right Honble Lord Amherst, 17 Jan. 1816, in Morse, *The Chronicles*, III, 284.
20 Staunton, *Memoirs*, p. 65.
21 British Library, London: India Office Library and Records [hereafter IOLR]: India Office Amherst Correspondence, Lord Amherst's Embassy, 1815–17, G/12/196. Letter from Lord Castlereagh to Amherst, 1 Jan. 1816. Italics added. Castlereagh was then the Foreign Secretary.
22 Davis, *Sketches of China*, I, 55–6.
23 Tuck, 'Introduction', xxii–xxiv.
24 James M. Polachek, *The Inner Opium War* (Cambridge, MA: Harvard University Press, 1992).
25 Staunton, *Notes of Proceedings*, p. 31. It should be noted that Canton and Macao are further from Beijing than Naples is from Hamburg.
26 Staunton, *Miscellaneous Notices*, pp. 232–3. Italics in the original. The initial arrangement was that John Elphinstone and Staunton, both members of the EIC's factory at Canton, would serve as the second and third commissioners. By the time the embassy arrived, however, Elphinstone had resigned as president of the Select Committee at Canton and decided to withdraw from the mission. As a result, Staunton moved to second place. The original secretary to the embassy and a former Bengal Company servant, Ellis succeeded to the vacancy as third commissioner.
27 Ibid., p. 233.
28 Ibid., p. vii.
29 Ibid.
30 Ibid., p. 239.
31 Ibid., pp. 237–8.
32 Ibid., p. 240. Italics in the original.
33 In 1793, when Staunton met the Qianlong emperor as Macartney's page, the emperor showed much favour to him. Perhaps for this reason, Staunton also had a favourable impression of the Qianlong emperor.
34 Letter from the Secret Commercial Committee to the Right Honble Lord Amherst, 17 Jan. 1816, in Morse, *The Chronicles*, III, 285.
35 Wensheng Wang, *White Lotus Rebels and South China Pirates: Crisis and Reform in the Qing Empire* (Cambridge, MA: Harvard University Press, 2014).
36 Morse, *The Chronicles*, III, 285.
37 The British merchants in Canton had long wanted an island, or a port, of their own on the China coast. The two British attempts to occupy Macao were made in the contexts of British–French rivalry, before and during the Napoleonic Wars. See Song-Chuan Chen, *Merchants of War and Peace: British Knowledge of China*

in the Making of the Opium War (Hong Kong: Hong Kong University Press, 2017), pp. 48, 107–9; Dong Wang, 'Between Tribute and Unequal Treaties: How China Saw the Sea World in the Early Nineteenth Century', *History*, 355 (2018), 277–9.

38 Letter from the viceroy of Guangdong and Guangxi to the Jiaqing emperor on Britain's intrusion into Macao and the stoppage of Britain's trade, 4 September (lunar calendar), the thirteenth year of the Jiaqing reign (1808), in Palace Museum (ed.), *Qingdai Waijiao Shiliao (Jiaqing Chao)* (Qing Dynasty Diplomatic Documents (the Jiaqing period)) (6 vols, Taipei: Chengwen Press, 1968), II, 23.
39 Report from the viceroy of Guangdong and Guangxi to the Jiaqing emperor on the mission to drive out the British barbarians, 27 October (lunar calendar), the thirteenth year of the Jiaqing reign (1808), in *ibid.*, II, 35.
40 Lo-shu Fu, *A Documentary Chronicle of Sino-Western Relations 1644–1820* (Tucson, AZ: University of Arizona Press, 1966), pp. 371, 377.
41 *Ibid.*, 371.
42 Kitson, 'The Dark Gift', p. 66.
43 John Francis Davis, *The Chinese: A General Description of the Empire of China and Its Inhabitants* (2 vols, London: Charles Knight, 1836), I, 88.
44 The Jiaqing emperor refused to aid, but secretly strengthened defences on the Tibetan and Nepalese border in response. See Kitson, 'The "Catastrophe of This New Chinese Mission"', p. 73. It remains unclear to what extent the Qing court at this point was aware that Britain was behind the opium trade. Kitson suggests that the Jiaqing emperor might know something, but there is very little mention of the opium trade in the British accounts of the Amherst embassy. Mao Haijian's research on Chinese sources shows that until as late as 1838 the Qing court had not connected the opium problem with Sino-British relations. The upper echelons of the Qing bureaucracy at the time saw opium mainly as a domestic problem. See Mao Haijian, *The Qing Empire and the Opium War: The Collapse of the Heavenly Dynasty*, trans. Joseph Lawson, Craig Smith and Peter Lavelle (Cambridge: Cambridge University Press, 2016), pp. 78–9.
45 Fu, *A Documentary Chronicle*, p. 377.
46 Technically, 'kowtow' only denotes the performance of three simple genuflexions, a mode of greeting which was widely practised in China on both public and private occasions. The court ritual that gave rise to the dispute, strictly speaking, was called *sangui jiukou*. It was the utmost form of ceremony in China and implied thrice kneeling and nine times bowing the head to the ground.
47 He Shitai was the brother of the empress and president of the Board for Foreign Affairs. Muke Deng'e was president of the Tribunal of Ceremonies. They were not actually 'dukes'. It was simply the title that the British used for them, for lack of anything better.
48 Letter from the Right Honble Lord Castlereagh to the Right Honble Lord Amherst, Jan. 1816, in Morse, *The Chronicles*, III, 281.
49 Ellis, *Journal of the Proceedings*, pp. 52–3.
50 *Ibid.*, pp. 50–1.
51 IOLR, G/12/197/269. Letter from Amherst to George Canning, 28 Feb. 1817. Canning was then the president of the Board of Control, the chief official in the British government who oversaw the EIC and Indian affairs.
52 Staunton, *Notes of Proceedings*, pp. 31–2.
53 In January 1795, a Dutch embassy led by Isaac Titsingh (1745–1812) arrived in Beijing. Unlike the Macartney mission, members of the Dutch embassy did not refuse to perform kowtow. It, however, did not help the Dutch achieve any of their commercial or diplomatic objectives. On the contrary, this embassy was treated in a more disgraceful manner than the Qing court's reception of Macartney's mission. More details about Titsingh's embassy can be found in André Everard Van Braam, *An Authentic Account of the Embassy of the Dutch East-India Company, to the Court of the Emperor of China, in the Years 1794 and 1795* (London: R. Phillips,

1798); and in J.J.L. Duyvendak, *The Last Dutch Embassy to the Chinese Court, 1794–1795* (Leiden: Brill, 1938).
54 Staunton, *Notes of Proceedings*, p. 100.
55 *Ibid.*, p. 32.
56 Staunton, *Memoirs*, p. 67. Davis also shared this view; see Davis, *Sketches of China*, I, 56–7.
57 Staunton, *Miscellaneous Notices*, p. 211.
58 Staunton, *Notes of Proceedings*, p. 102.
59 *Ibid.*, pp. 102–3.
60 Cited by Staunton, in Staunton, *Memoirs*, pp. 68–9. Staunton did not give the exact name of the account from which he quoted. He only noted that these passages were from 'Vol. i. p. 233' and 'Vol. ii. p. 195' of Ellis's 'published narrative'. Although Ellis's *Journal of the Proceedings* was reprinted in two volumes in 1818, these passages cannot be found on these pages.
61 Ellis, *Journal of the Proceedings*, p. 151.
62 *Ibid.*, p. 153.
63 *Ibid.*
64 Staunton, *Miscellaneous Notices*, p. 233.
65 Ellis, *Journal of the Proceedings*, p. 108.
66 *Ibid.*, p. 109.
67 *Ibid.*, p. 53.
68 *Ibid.*
69 Staunton, *Miscellaneous Notices*, p. 242.
70 Ellis, *Journal of the Proceedings*, p. 58. Italics added.
71 *Ibid.*, p. 151. Italics added.
72 *Ibid.*, p. 173.
73 *Ibid.*, p. 228.
74 *Ibid.*, p. 155.
75 IOLR, G/12/197/271. Amherst to Canning, 28 Feb. 1817.
76 After Tongzhou, the terminus of the Grand Canal, the embassy had to leave behind their comfortable barges and travel the final leg of the journey overland.
77 IOLR, G/12/197/295. Amherst to Canning, 8 Mar. 1817.
78 Staunton, *Notes of Proceedings*, p. 144.
79 IOLR, G/12/197/381. Amherst to Canning, 21 Apr. 1817.
80 IOLR, G/12/197/387. Amherst to Canning, 8 Mar. 1817.
81 Ellis, *Journal of the Proceedings*, p. 115.
82 Davis, *Sketches of China*, I, 155.
83 Abel, *Narrative of a Journey*, p. 11.
84 Hayne, *Henry Hayne Diary*, pp. 44–5.
85 Ellis, *Journal of the Proceedings*, p. 122.
86 The selection of these items was supposed to be an observance of the maxim of Confucius, 'give much, but receive little'.
87 IOLR, G/12/197/305–6. Amherst to Canning, 22 Mar. 1817.
88 Ellis, *Journal of the Proceedings*, p. 425.
89 Extract from 'the *Pekin Gazette* on the 13th Day of the 7th Moon of the 21st year of Kea-king [Jiaqing], September 4, 1816', quoted in *ibid.*, p. 501.
90 IOLR, G/12/197/310–11. Amherst to Canning, 22 Mar. 1817.
91 Davis, *Sketches of China*, I, 205.
92 Ellis, *Journal of the Proceedings*, p. 425.
93 *Ibid.*, p. 426.
94 J.L. Cranmer-Byng (ed.), *An Embassy to China: Being the Journal Kept by Lord Macartney during His Embassy to the Emperor Ch'ien-lung 1793–1794* (London: Longmans, Green and Co., 1962), p. 87.
95 *Ibid.*, p. 88.
96 IOLR, G/12/197/281. Amherst to Canning, 8 Mar. 1817.
97 Davis, *Sketches of China*, II, 29.

98 Edward W. Said, *Orientalism* (London: Penguin, 1995).
99 David Porter, 'A Peculiar but Uninteresting Nation: China and the Discourse of Commerce in Eighteenth-Century England', *Eighteenth-Century Studies*, 2 (2000), 181-99; Jeng-Guo Chen, 'The British Views of Chinese Civilization and the Emergence of Class Consciousness', *The Eighteenth Century*, 2 (2004), 193-205.
100 Elizabeth Hope Chang, *Britain's Chinese Eye: Literature, Empire and Aesthetics in Nineteenth-Century Britain* (Stanford, CA: Stanford University Press, 2010), p. 22.
101 *An Embassy to China*, p. 212.
102 See Susan M. Jones and Philip A. Kuhn, 'Dynastic Decline and the Roots of Rebellion', in *The Cambridge History of China*, ed. John K. Fairbank, et al. (15 vols, Cambridge: Cambridge University Press, 1978), X, 107-62.
103 Rumours had it that even his imperial robes were repeatedly patched. The Jiaqing emperor's financial concern might well be another reason why he did not welcome the Amherst embassy and wished the unsolicited British guests to leave as soon as possible.
104 Staunton, *Notes of Proceedings*, p. 157.
105 *Ibid.*, p. 205. It is now common knowledge among historians that the decline of the Qing dynasty indeed commenced in the late Qianlong (1735-95) and Jiaqing (1796-1820) reigns. See Philip A. Kuhn, *Origins of the Modern Chinese State* (Stanford, CA: Stanford University Press, 2002), pp. 2-8.
106 Staunton, *Notes of Proceedings*, p. 157.
107 *Ibid.*, p. 380.
108 *Ibid.*, pp. 435-7. A pailoo is a monumental gateway.
109 Ellis, *Journal of the Proceedings*, p. 218.
110 *Ibid.*, p. 364.
111 Davis, *Sketches of China*, II, 2-3.
112 Abel, *Narrative of a Journey*, p. 11.
113 Ellis, *Journal of the Proceedings*, p. 197.
114 Morrison, *A Memoir*, p. 8.
115 *Ibid.*, p. 9.
116 Hall, *Narrative of a Voyage*, p. 8.
117 Abel, *Narrative of a Journey*, p. 87.
118 *Ibid.*
119 *Ibid.*, pp. 75, 128.
120 *Ibid.*, p. 230.
121 *Ibid.*, p. 232.
122 Ellis, *Journal of the Proceedings*, p. 205.
123 *Ibid.*, p. 301.
124 Abel, *Narrative of a Journey*, p. 159.
125 Ellis, *Journal of the Proceedings*, p. 157.
126 Morrison, *A Memoir*, pp. 31-2.
127 Davis, *Sketches of China*, I, 144. Italics in the original. Emperors Yao and Shun are semi-mythological rulers in ancient Chinese history.
128 Davis, *Sketches of China*, I, 249.
129 Staunton, *Notes of Proceedings*, p. 143.
130 Abel, *Narrative of a Journey*, p. 71.
131 *Ibid.*, p. 94.
132 Morrison, *A Memoir*, p. 38.
133 Davis, *Sketches of China*, I, 148-9.
134 Morrison, *A Memoir*, p. 38.
135 Davis, *Sketches of China*, I, 248.
136 Ellis, *Journal of the Proceedings*, p. 253.
137 Davis, *Sketches of China*, I, 90.
138 Ellis, *Journal of the Proceedings*, p. 202.
139 Morrison, *A View of China*, p. 121.
140 Morrison, *A Memoir*, p. 13.
141 Davis, *Sketches of China*, I, 186.

142 Abel, *Narrative of a Journey*, p. 141.
143 Staunton, *Notes of Proceedings*, p. 141.
144 Ibid., p. 163.
145 Davis, *Sketches of China*, I, 179.
146 Ibid., 109.
147 Ellis, *Journal of the Proceedings*, p. 438.
148 Macleod, *Narrative of a Voyage*, p. 151.
149 *Memoirs of Robert Morrison*, I, 447–8.
150 Morrison, *A View of China*, p. 125.
151 Ibid., p. 122.
152 Morrison, *A Memoir*, p. 67.
153 Morrison, *A View of China*, p. 125.
154 Abel, *Narrative of a Journey*, p. 232.
155 Ibid., p. 113.
156 Ellis, *Journal of the Proceedings*, p. 388.
157 Ibid., p. 384.
158 Ibid., p. 429.
159 Morrison, *A Memoir*, p. 67.
160 Before 1757, China's external trade was open to three more ports: Ningbo, Quanzhou and Songjiang.
161 Hall, *Narrative of a Voyage*, p. 10.
162 Ibid., p. 14.
163 Abel, *Narrative of a Journey*, p. 232.
164 Ibid., p. 130.
165 Ellis, *Journal of the Proceedings*, pp. 163–4.
166 Abel, *Narrative of a Journey*, pp. 119–20; Ellis, *Journal of the Proceedings*, pp. 164, 283; and Hall, *Narrative of a Voyage*, pp. 10, 12, 14, etc.
167 Macleod, *Narrative of a Voyage*, p. 153.
168 Morrison, *A Memoir*, p. 67. Italics in the original.
169 Abel, *Narrative of a Journey*, p. 236.
170 Staunton, *Notes of Proceedings*, p. 182.
171 Macleod, *Narrative of a Voyage*, p. 156.
172 Ellis, *Journal of the Proceedings*, p. 241.
173 Davis, *Sketches of China*, I, 168.
174 IOLR, G/12/197/256–7. Amherst to Canning, 28 Feb. 1817.
175 Davis, *Sketches of China*, I, 248–9. See also Ellis, *Journal of the Proceedings*, p. 247; IOLR, G/12/197/317–8. Amherst to Canning, 22 Mar. 1817.
176 Macleod, *Narrative of a Voyage*, p. 159.
177 Examples can be found in Abel, *Narrative of a Journey*, pp. 216–17.
178 Macleod, *Narrative of a Voyage*, p. 160. In this respect, Davis noted that even the Chinese emperor was subject to various forms of court ritual, so that in some ways the monarch himself was also 'a slave to ceremony'. See Davis, *Sketches of China*, II, 23.
179 Davis, *Sketches of China*, I, 38.
180 Examples can be found in Staunton, *Notes of Proceedings*, p. 40; Ellis, *Journal of the Proceedings*, p. 14; Abel, *Narrative of a Journey*, p. 6, etc.
181 Ellis, *Journal of the Proceedings*, p. 408. Ellis also suggested herein that 'The traveller who only sees Canton will be liable to form an exaggerated opinion of the population and wealth of China'.
182 Davis, *Sketches of China*, II, 149.
183 Abel, *Narrative of a Journey*, pp. 218–19. The 'Mr Pierson' here should be Dr Alexander Pearson, who introduced smallpox vaccination to Macao and Canton in 1805.
184 Macleod, *Narrative of a Voyage*, p. 158.
185 IOLR, G/12/197/378–9. Amherst to Canning, 21 Apr. 1817.
186 Ellis, *Journal of the Proceedings*, pp. 437–8.
187 Hall, *Narrative of a Voyage*, p. 11.
188 Hayne, *Henry Hayne Diary*, p. 68.

189 Davis, *Sketches of China*, II, 143.
190 Ellis, *Journal of the Proceedings*, p. 438.
191 *Ibid.*
192 *Ibid.*
193 Macleod, *Narrative of a Voyage*, p. 142. Italics in the original.
194 *Ibid.*

PART II

Prelude to the Opium War

CHAPTER THREE

The EIC versus free traders

The East India Company Act of 1813 not only led to the dispatch of the Amherst embassy but initiated significant changes in Britain's contacts with Asia. Although the Act renewed the EIC's charter for another twenty years, it ended the Company's commercial monopoly in India but not the tea trade and trade with China. This partial opening of the Indian trade led an increasing number of British private merchants to establish themselves in India. Unprecedentedly close to the Chinese market, many of them were keen to have access to the China trade. Although, in theory, non-EIC merchants were still prohibited from trading with the Chinese, a lot of them had succeeded in approaching the Chinese market by different means. Claiming themselves to be 'free traders', these British men either purchased an expensive licence from the EIC to conduct the so-called 'country trade'[1] or bypassed the Company's control by signing up with foreign companies to trade in Canton under other flags. Since, following the failure of the Amherst mission, Britain sent no more embassies to the Qing court, the main 'contact zone' between the British and the Chinese was moving from the imperial capital Beijing to China's south-east coast, particularly Canton. The expanding body of British merchants, including the 'free traders' and those worked for the EIC, also began to replace diplomatic visitors as the main interpreters of Chinese affairs from the 1820s onwards.

The relationship between the EIC and the 'free traders' was complicated. It also varied from time to time. In the beginning, the private merchants were unable to challenge seriously the EIC at Canton. Nevertheless, the rapid increase in the volume of their trade, which nearly doubled between 1817 and 1830, changed the situation. This was because, in parallel with the Company's commerce with the Qing-government-authorised

Hong merchants, these British 'free traders' developed a lucrative trade with unlicensed Chinese dealers who clandestinely engaged in foreign trade, especially in opium smuggling. Instead of using the term 'illegal trade', they often referred to it as the 'unauthorised trade'. From the EIC's point of view, this trade was a mixed blessing, because it both created troubles and solved problems. On the one hand, the EIC had been generally law-abiding in its trade with China. Over the years, the Company established a reasonably good relationship with its Chinese partners, who had some degree of trust in the EIC's employees. These EIC's representatives knew that the Qing court would be unhappy with the private merchants' trade if it continued to grow. On the other hand, the EIC needed that trade, particularly in opium. For decades, the Company had been struggling to find a market for British goods in China so as to defray the cost of its ever-increasing import of Chinese tea, which became Britain's favourite drink by the end of the eighteenth century. It was opium that offered a solution to this long-lasting problem. Although the EIC kept its hands clean from the opium trade in Canton, it developed opium production on a huge scale in its colony in Bengal. The private merchants bought the company's opium on credit, sold it to the Chinese and then paid the EIC's representatives in Canton, who used the money to purchase tea. According to Michael Greenberg, because of 'its vital role as the indispensable means of providing funds at Canton for the tea investment and furnishing a channel of remittance from India to England',[2] the opium trade gave the British private merchants growing influence in China.

From the perspective of the 'free traders', they had many reasons to dislike the EIC's monopoly. These newcomers to the Asian markets neither wished to pay for the expensive licence, nor were entitled to the financial and administrative support that the Company provided for its factory in Canton. Since their trade was not safeguarded by the government of either side, or by the EIC's representatives at Canton, their position in China was never secure. Also, although very few of them were entirely pro-free-trade, these self-proclaimed 'free traders' believed that the EIC's monopoly had posed significant obstacles to the extension of their trade. It had long been their desire that the British government could remove these constraints for them. In the late 1810s and early 1820s, however, it still seemed unrealistic for the private merchants to expect a change in the structure of Britain's China trade. For one thing, after two unsuccessful embassies, the British government adopted a 'hands-off' policy which allowed the EIC freedom to conduct its Chinese affairs as it saw fit. For another, even though its supremacy was being challenged, the Company at this time still had much influence over Britain's commerce with China. An establishment of supercargoes and writers, about twenty in all, managed the Company's trade at Canton. Three or four of the senior supercargoes were annually formed into a Select Committee, who conducted the EIC's affairs in China under the orders of the Company's Court of Directors in London.[3] The EIC's trade, through the medium of Hong merchants, was the only legal form of commerce between Britain and China. The Select Committee also possessed certain powers over British subjects and ships when in China. For this reason, the Chinese authorities expected the EIC's representatives to be responsible for the behaviour of all British subjects trading with China. Believing the EIC to be well connected with both sides, in the event of a dispute, the Chinese government as well as the British private merchants could only rely on the Company to represent each of them against the other, although the Select Committee had no effective power to place a check on either side.

A serious dispute of this kind did not develop until the late 1820s. For a short period following the Amherst embassy, the EIC's employees in Canton held a relatively firm stance towards the Guangdong authorities. After the news reached London, the Court of Directors strongly criticised this line of action. They announced that their representatives at Canton should not remonstrate with the Chinese government on their own initiative, unless they received clear instructions from London. For the EIC's directors, the primary concern was to secure its tea trade with China. They deemed it necessary to preserve a policy of conciliation in the Company's intercourse with the Chinese. In their letters to Canton, the Court of Directors affirmed that the Select Committee should do everything it could to avoid disputes with the Chinese government, while any deviation from this guidance would cause the court's serious displeasure. As a result, the EIC's representatives at Canton were obliged to restrain their personal irritation with the local government. Twelve years of relative harmony followed in the Company's trade with China. Despite the conciliatory policy laid down for the EIC's employees, the private merchants were under no such restraint. As the 'unauthorised trade' continued to develop, private merchants gradually realised that, as well as the EIC, the Chinese government was another great obstacle to the expansion of their commerce. They believed that nothing was to be gained by obedience to the Chinese. Because of this attitude, the private merchants wished the EIC to act aggressively on their behalf against the local authorities. Although some of the Company's staff in Canton were personally sympathetic to this idea, the plea was apparently in conflict with the instructions emanating from London. Since the Select Committee was unable to offer such assistance, the private merchants' dissatisfaction with the EIC increased over the 1820s. With the rapid growth of their trade, their attitudes towards the Company increasingly 'gave place to one of rivalry if not of hostility'.[4]

In 1829, the Sino-British trade reached a turning point when a number of Chinese Hong merchants went bankrupt. They were unable to pay off their debts to the foreign merchants and the situation resulted in serious friction between the EIC and Chinese commercial communities. The majority of the Select Committee now tended to agree with the private merchants that British dissatisfaction with the Canton authorities could no longer be endured. Believing that a change had to be made, the Company's employees at Canton acted on their own again. In 1829 and 1831, they strongly petitioned the local government, demanding a reform of China's commercial system. When the Court of Directors was notified of these actions, it strongly rebuked the Committee for its non-compliance with the standing order. The court decided to demote those responsible and to reaffirm the importance of sticking to the conciliatory policy. Despite this clear instruction, there was, at this time, a real possibility that the future of Britain's China trade would no longer depend on the attitudes of the EIC. This was because, once again, the charter of the Company was on the point of expiring and, after twenty years of continued growth in the 'unauthorised trade', the call for the termination of EIC's China monopoly became overwhelming both at Canton and in Britain. The private merchants, along with their supporters back home, not only petitioned Parliament for full commercial freedom with China but waged a pamphlet war against the EIC. This debate on the EIC's monopoly and Britain's future China policy went hand-in-hand with a controversy over the images of China. To defend their respective standpoints, the campaigners for the EIC and for its critics constructed vastly different images of the China trade, the Chinese government and its people. Although historians such as Hosea Ballou Morse, Michael Greenberg, C.H. Philips, Anthony Webster and Yukihisa Kumagai have studied the termination of the EIC's China monopoly in great detail,[5] this underlying debate about China remains little researched.

The EIC's views

With the rise of the private merchants' trade, the EIC was no longer the only actor in Canton who directly encountered the Chinese. Their employees ceased being the only voices 'on the spot' that put forward images of China and the China trade. From 1829 to 1833, the private merchants and their supporters in Britain, including merchants and industrialists in Liverpool, Glasgow, Manchester and other provincial cities, as well as their allies in London, mounted a free trade movement against the EIC. They challenged the Company in a variety of ways, particularly its remaining trading monopoly of China trade. It should be noted that the EIC was not a homogeneous group. At this time, some London East India agency houses began to see advantage in the opening of the China trade as they developed links with manufacturers in British industrial cities. The emergence of these interest groups means that there was no complete unity within the EIC's leadership in London. Also, as shown in the crises of 1829 and 1831, the Select Committee at Canton did not always abide by the instructions given by the Court of Directors, partly because of the long time needed for information to travel between China and Britain, usually four to five months. There were officials of the EIC who became 'free traders'. A prominent example is Hugh Hamilton Lindsay, who challenged the Company's China policies and later set up his own business.[6] There were also those who were outside the Company such as R. Montgomery Martin, an Irishman who later became the Colonial Treasurer of Hong Kong (from 1844 to 1845), or had not worked in China such as Thomas Fisher, but were in favour of the continuance of the EIC's monopoly. Therefore, 'the EIC and its supporters' can be understood only in general terms in the rest of this chapter. It does not mean that the Company produced only one voice about China and the China trade. It is the *general* attitudes that these campaigners held to defend the EIC's monopoly in China that this chapter concentrates on.

According to Webster, the 'defenders of the Company's privileges did little or nothing to lobby in their defence'.[7] Philips has also maintained that the directors of the EIC 'made no effort … to controvert the arguments of the merchants of the outports' and '[t]he Court of Proprietors sleepily, unquestioningly awaited its fate'.[8] A wider reading of historical sources, however, shows that, although the Company's leadership itself did not do much to defend the EIC's position in China, a lot of the Company's supporters did attempt to campaign for the continuance of the EIC's monopoly. They, first and foremost, endeavoured to justify the economic importance of its monopoly. In the free trade movement, campaigners against the Company's China monopoly sought to promote a view that, since the India trade had started in 1813 on the principle of free trade, it was unreasonable to preserve the EIC's trading privileges in China. Opposed to this argument, the pro-monopoly commentators' main justification was that, however compelling this theory sounded in principle, 'the peculiar circumstances' of the China trade rendered the principles of international commerce 'wholly inapplicable' to the case of China.[9] To support this claim, they pointed out that it was actually unrealistic to expect that the opening of China trade from the British side alone could produce any material effect, because, as long as the institution of the Chinese monopoly remained, no significant change could happen. In this respect, Henry Ellis, who served in the civil service of the EIC for six years and the third commissioner of the Amherst mission, maintained that 'The peculiar circumstances under which the trade of foreigners is placed by the laws of China, ... have led me to reject, as fallacious, the anticipations of those who consider the surprising effects produced in India by unrestricted intercourse, as indicative of equal results in China'.[10] For this reason, Ellis believed that, under the present circumstances, it would be wrong to open the China trade only from the British side. 'Until some change takes place in both these respects', he wrote, 'the extension of the British trade contemplated by the merchants and manufacturers who have petitioned parliament on the subject, is hopeless'.[11]

On the basis of this assertion, others in favour of maintaining the EIC's trading privileges in China such as Martin maintained that, since, under the current system, the China trade was carried on with profit and with a certain degree of security, there was an 'absolute necessity for an undisturbed continuance of the Company's factory at Canton'.[12] George Thomas Staunton added that, through its lawful and extensive commercial activities, the EIC had, over the decades, developed a wholesome system that

> diffuses the profits and advantages of a great and well-regulated commerce, in equitable proportions, directly or indirectly, over the whole of the British community; first, by its regular and secure contributions to the revenue ... secondly, by its satisfactory abundant supply of an universally desired article of daily, consumption; thirdly, by its distinguished success in extending the sales and maintaining the credit of British manufactures and productions.[13]

Because of their long-lasting commercial relations with the Hong merchants, the Company's representatives were said to have developed considerable power in Canton. An anonymous writer in *The Asiatic Journal* stressed that 'by the extent of their dealings, the unerring regularity of their transactions, their proverbial probity, and the duration of their connections with China', the EIC's representatives gained a high character and an augmented influence in the minds of the Chinese.[14] Agreeing with this viewpoint, Staunton argued, the Company not only managed to secure the best supply of its merchandise at the cheapest rate but acquired the legitimate means of 'either favouring or counteracting the views of the Chinese government', and of 'influencing the proceedings of the licensed Chinese merchants'.[15] For instance, in the tea trade, the Company not only unified the price but had the right of selection before the tea was brought to market. Moreover, according to the 'Report of the Select Committee of the House of Commons in 1831', all forms of foreign trade had more or less benefited from this positive influence of the British EIC. Even the private merchants' trade was not an exception, because 'by the influence of the Company, searches of country ships had been prevented, and difficulties in the prosecution of their transactions removed'.[16]

In addition to these statements, the Company's supporters emphasised that the EIC was the only party that could guarantee the present prosperity and comparative security of the China trade. In opposition to the view that it was now time to throw the China trade open, Staunton insisted that, given the uniqueness of this trade, nothing could prevent 'the exercise of arbitrary and dictatorial powers over the trade, on the part of the Chinese merchants, but the present system'.[17] To prove this, others created a fearful image that the whole international trade in China would be in danger if the EIC system ceased to operate. Ellis, for example, asserted that:

> There can be no doubt that, in the first instance, the announcement that the East India Company were no longer the representatives of the British nation, and were no longer responsible for the conduct of persons trading to China, would shake the confidence of the Chinese; and that no consul, with the usual powers attached to the office, could establish for himself the confidence and influence now attached to the Company's factory. All that might be lost in these respects by the supercargoes, would be turned to the advantage of the local government and of the Hong merchants, and consequently to the injury of the foreign trade in general.[18]

Martin, who visited India in the 1820s and later became an India expert, added that the termination of the EIC's China monopoly might cause even greater detrimental effects across the British Empire. He wrote: 'that instant change would, most probably, be productive of ruin to the Indian, as well as to the English, Chinese commerce; and that with a diminishing government revenue, increasing public burthens, a possibility of general war, and a variety of taxes pressing on the industry and comfort of the people'.[19]

To justify further the claim that any alternative mode of commerce in China was not going to benefit the British, the experience of American merchants was used to show that 'though exclusive privileges may be prejudicial, *to throw open the English China trade might prove still worse in its consequence*'.[20] Ellis shared this view. He commented that, although American traders in China were not restricted by any kind of monopoly on the American side, they were unable to 'maintain either their pretensions as traders, or to protect the life of an American subject through the official authority of a consul'.[21] For this reason, these Americans were at the mercy of the Hong merchants. They were even 'very jealous of the superior influence possessed by the Company's factory'.[22] To the EIC's supporters, the predicament of American traders confirmed their opinion that, while the system of the Chinese monopoly remained, the principle of free trade would never work in China. This allowed Martin to argue that the Company actually acted as 'a most valuable protection to all British interests',[23] rather than as an obstacle to the extension of British–Chinese commerce. Since 'by the present constitution and instrumentality of the East India Company, a vast empire is administered ... without charge on the national resources; a trade with a government remarkable for jealousy of foreigners, and for indifference to foreign commerce, is conducted with certainty and advantage', Ellis stressed that it would be 'most unwise to deal hastily with the system by which they are secured'.[24]

Nevertheless, in an era when criticism of the EIC's administration in India and of its negative impact on the economy was considerable, the Company's supporters knew that their arguments in favour of the monopoly would sound more convincing with the 'local inside knowledge' about China possessed by the EIC's employees. To win support from Parliament as well as the British public, they highlighted that China was a culturally 'peculiar' nation. Since China's commercial and political culture was so different, it would be wrong to assume that the doctrine of free trade could be applied in China. These key differences, or 'peculiarities', include the following. First, the long history of China's self-contained economy had led the Chinese to believe that they stood in no need of trade with other countries. The Chinese, hence, did not value external trade as much as the Europeans did. Since the Chinese government had, from the earliest ages, directed its attention to render the intercourse between the different provinces of the empire easy and secure, China had long been 'enjoying within its own territories all the necessaries and conveniences, and most of the luxuries of life'.[25] As a result, throughout Chinese history, neither the necessities of the people nor the policy of the government had looked to foreign trade as a principal source of individual wealth or of imperial revenue. Second, China's unique history and its geographical position had resulted in the country's political isolation, as well as the government's suspicious attitude towards foreigners. Fisher, for example, claimed that, since 'the Chinese had acquired the art of living in a state of high mental cultivation and social enjoyment ... long before they could have the remote idea of intercourse' with foreign nations, their government had proclaimed its independence of every nation in the world during much of its history.[26] For this reason, the benefits of international communication had never been cultivated in China. On the contrary, the Chinese authorities believed that the safety of the state rested upon insulating the nation from outside influences. In this context, Ellis pointed out that having contact with foreigners, unlike in European countries, was considered in China as 'having a positive tendency to corrupt the morals and derange the harmony of those institutions, political and domestic'.[27] To restrict contact with foreigners hence quite naturally became the maxim of state policy in China.

Furthermore, because the culture of China was so different from that of Britain, the British were unable to appreciate some of the Chinese institutions. British observers, for example, had often regarded the principle of strict control and subordination in the Chinese government as signs of China's backwardness. In opposition to this view, Staunton pointed out that, 'however despotic and oppressive the operation of this principle may appear in our eyes, in those of the Chinese it has invariably been considered as one of the first requisites of a good government, and one of the surest tests of a civilised people'.[28] Speaking from his long experience of living in China, Staunton explained that the principle pervaded not only the government of China but the domestic lives of the Chinese people. 'In the same manner as the magistrate controls and is responsible for the conduct of the inhabitants of his district', he wrote, 'the master of each family is supposed to control, and [is] required to be responsible for, his relations, connections, and dependents'.[29] By pointing out these facts about the Chinese context, it seems that Staunton, as someone who had considerable first-hand knowledge about China, was suggesting that it was China's cultural *difference*, rather than its backwardness, that distinguished the Chinese from the British. Since the Chinese had governed their vast empire by their own means so efficiently for so long, the British criticism against Chinese institutions deserved reconsideration.

The reason why the EIC's campaigners stressed the cultural difference or 'peculiarity' of China was that, compared to the private merchants, they had advocated a higher degree of reverence towards Chinese laws and usages. Instead of promoting a rather barbaric image of the Chinese, some pro-monopoly commentators tended to see the Chinese as 'highly civilised',[30] or 'semi-civilised',[31] people who had a right to regulate their own affairs. The EIC's Court of Directors also clearly stated in its instructions to the Select Committee: 'We cannot, in fairness, deny to China the right which our own nation exercises as she sees fit, either by prohibiting, restraining, or subjecting to certain laws and regulations its commercial dealings with other countries. China must be considered free in the exercise of her affairs, without being accountable to any other nation.'[32] In terms of the applying the so-called 'natural' law of free trade to the China, the EIC and its supporters stressed that private merchants had no right to demand of China that it must open its markets. Martin, for example, claimed that the principle of free trade, in the first place, should depend on 'the disposition, wants, or reciprocal feelings of a separate, and perhaps, rival or hostile state'.[33] Moreover, 'freedom in *politics*, and freedom in *commerce*, are two distinct things; that they are not ... at every period called for by all countries; and that, although political liberty is essentially requisite in domestic commerce, and highly advantageous in foreign trade, particularly for a manufacturing community such as that of England, yet, that it is not considered *paramountly* necessary by every nation'.[34]

In line with these principles, campaigners for the EIC's China monopoly proclaimed that Britain should not employ a coercive line of action in its future relations with China. To justify that the conciliatory policy should be maintained, Fisher insisted that, on the one hand, 'any attempts to force upon this singular people an unacceptable intercourse with us, by outraging their laws or institutions, would ... only render profitable intercourse with them more difficult'.[35] On the other hand, the Chinese should be regarded as a reasonable people. He stated, 'the educational bias of the Chinese disposes them on all occasions to appeal to reason'. Hence, the Chinese developed a disposition towards 'mildness and urbanity, with a wish to show that their conduct is reasonable, and generally a willingness to yield to what appears to be so'.[36] Even the government of China, which was often believed to be arbitrary and despotic, was keen 'to make it appear to the people that its conduct is reasonable and benevolent on all occasions'.[37] This interpretation of the Chinese people's natural willingness to appeal to reason corresponded with the EIC's view that a forceful course of action was harmful to British trade with China. It gave the EIC's Court of Directors another reason to contend that Britain's commercial intercourse with the Chinese could be improved only 'by evincing a disposition to respect their regulations',[38] rather than by challenging that authority.

As defenders of the Company's privileges were presenting a seemingly objective and genuine perception of China, it should be noted that, in the meantime, they were suggesting that the cultural difference of China was beyond the comprehension of anyone else but the EIC's representatives. An anonymous writer summarised the attitudes of the EIC as: 'We [The Company] alone are acquainted with the Chinese people; We alone have established any relations with the Chinese government. That people is incomprehensible by any but our servants; that government hates and despises all foreigners, except only our supercargoes of the factory at Canton.'[39] This statement clearly shows that the EIC and its campaigners were attempting to portray the Company as the exclusive authority in understanding China and in dealing with Britain's relations with that country. In sum, in the debate on the EIC's China monopoly, we have seen that the Company's supporters endeavoured to promote a twofold image of China. First, in spite of its various differences from Britain, China, as a sovereign state, was by no means too depraved to be respected. Second, China's 'peculiarities' were not inexplicable if one had a deep understanding of Chinese history and culture. For these reasons, commercial and diplomatic relations with China should and indeed must be conducted by professionals who were equipped with profound local experience. Since, over past decades, the EIC had accumulated such abundant knowledge of this unique nation and had established positive relations with the local authorities in Canton, it would be most unwise to abolish such advantages that had proved 'so safe and so efficacious'.[40] As Staunton confidently affirmed, although there seemed no immediate danger to British–Chinese trade in the early 1830s, past experience had indicated that 'the means by which it has been averted are excellent' and, on this ground, the current EIC system should by all means 'be diligently traced, and carefully adhered to'.[41]

Views of the 'free traders'

While the East India Company and its campaigners were sparing no effort to justify its trade monopoly in China, the private merchants' call for the removal of this monopoly grew even stronger. The so-called 'free traders', together with their friends in both provincial Britain and London, launched an anti-EIC campaign aiming to completely abolish the Company's privileges in China. They claimed that it had been unfair to deprive the private merchants of the rights to participate in the China trade, while the removal of the EIC's monopoly, according to an anonymous author, 'would be an undoubted advantage to the commerce and manufactures of Britain'.[42] To strengthen these opinions, some British merchants in Calcutta employed John Crawfurd, one of Britain's leading 'oriental' experts at this time, to write articles to support their disputes with the EIC. Crawfurd, a Scot and a life-time free trade advocate, paid multiple visits to South-east Asia, but actually he had never been to China. To form his ideas about Chinese affairs, Crawfurd had to rely on interviews with and reports from those who traded with the Chinese. The fact that he was regarded as a specialist on China also shows that the British at this point did not make too much effort to understand the 'Orient' – not so many of them even bothered to distinguish China from the rest of Asia. Webster has stated that 'in many ways Crawfurd epitomised Said's notion of the influence of the orientalist intellectual. Not only did his writings ... shape western thinking about India, south-east Asia and China, but he was also an active political campaigner on a range of issues related to Britain's Asian empire.'[43] Hence, Crawfurd proved vital to the victory of the 'free traders'. He used his reputation and knowledge of the East in many ways to persuade the British government to free up the China trade.

To challenge the EIC's views, Crawfurd contested a range of ideas about China and the China trade presented by the Company as if he really understood the country. First, Crawfurd accused the EIC and its supporters of misleading the public by presenting untruthful views of the China trade. Against the EIC's statements about its positive impacts on the China trade, Crawfurd produced a number of works to argue that the Company's actual records, 'so far from showing what they assert, show the very reverse of it'.[44] Crawfurd maintained that, unlike what the EIC's supporters had claimed, the Company's trade in China in fact afforded no satisfactory prospect for either the merchants or the British state. Taking the tea trade for example, because of the EIC's monopoly, not only had the tea price been greatly increased, but the teas imported into Britain were in no respect superior in quality to those imported into America or the European continent.[45] With regard to the EIC's performance over the past two decades, Crawfurd wrote that:

> They show that the supply of tea is, in proportion to the population of the United Kingdom, considerably less than it was twenty years ago. They show that within the same time the exports of British produce and manufactures to China have fallen off from a million sterling per annum to much less than one-half of that amount. ... the same records show that the nation has been taxed during the currency of the present charter to the extent of 40,000,000*l*, sterling, in consideration of this monopoly which by the Company is modestly stated to have been exercised not for its own exclusive interest 'but likewise for the benefit and advantage of England and of India'. [46]

In addition to this direct attack on the Company's economic influence, Crawfurd criticised the EIC for exaggerating the problems caused by the Chinese monopoly, in order to show that the idea of free trade was unrealistic in China. From interviews he conducted with the private merchants, Crawfurd concluded that the so-called 'restrictions' set by the Chinese government were actually not as significant as defenders of the EIC had described. Although in theory the private merchants' commerce in China was not sanctioned by the Qing government, in practice the 'unauthorised trade' had been openly conducted on the China coast to such an extent that a substantially 'free' trade on the Chinese side had already been established.[47] In contrast to the images of the Chinese monopoly presented by the pro-EIC commentators, Crawfurd's interviewees denied that the Canton system posed an insurmountable obstacle to the application of the free trade principle. For example, one of them pointed out: 'Individuals are ... at perfect liberty to deal with any Hong merchant ... or with any *outside merchant*, that is, with any Chinese merchant not belonging to the Hong ... though there are only eight or ten Hong merchants at Canton, there is, notwithstanding, quite as extensive a choice of merchants with whom to deal in that city as in Liverpool or New York'.[48] Apart from this considerable freedom in trading with the Chinese, Crawfurd discovered that the scale of the 'unauthorised trade' had greatly exceeded the EIC's regular trade. According to his statistics, its total volume in the early 1830s reached nearly three times that of the Company's trade.[49] Largely for this reason, an anonymous writer condemned the EIC's attempts to fix public attention only on the Company's trade and to overstate the strictness of the Canton system. Once the scale and importance of the 'unauthorised trade' were communicated to the public, he believed, 'the Company's monopoly of the British market would be considered doubly unjust and injurious to the nation'.[50]

Furthermore, against the EIC's contention that the private merchants' lack of understanding of China or experience trading with the Chinese was likely to cause disputes between the two countries, Crawfurd asserted that this claim was utterly 'futile and visionary'.[51] To challenge the EIC's views, those who were interviewed by Crawfurd stressed that the 'unauthorised trade' had actually been operating with great order and mutual confidence for a long time. The American merchant Joshua Bates, another key figure in influencing the British government's decision, even told him that the facilities and efficiency that Canton provided foreign traders were 'decidedly superior in both these respects to London'.[52] Moreover, Crawfurd learned, in the past few decades the British private merchants had not experienced any inconvenience in contacting the Chinese. Nor had other Western traders, such as the Americans and the Dutch who were already 'free traders', ever met 'any interruption or obstacle of any sort'[53] when they traded with the Chinese. This information about the China trade allowed Crawfurd to demonstrate that the EIC's campaigners had exaggerated the difficulties on the Chinese side. He made a rather convincing case that the company was indeed trying to hide some 'truths' with regard to the China trade. The EIC's monopoly, rather than the Canton system, hence seemed more likely to be the primary constraint on the application of *laissez-faire* principles in China.

Advocates of 'free trade' in China also challenged other images of China presented by the Company, especially on China's cultural 'peculiarity' and the need to respect the Qing government and its laws. A notable source of information came from a clandestine reconnaissance of the southern and eastern ports of China in 1832. It was led by Hugh Hamilton Lindsay, who was still an EIC employee at the time but managed to persuade the Select Committee in Canton to dispatch the voyage in defiance of the Chinese prohibition and the instructions of the Company's leadership in London.[54] Perhaps having formed the idea of trading on his own account in the presumably forthcoming 'free trade' era, Lindsay took this initiative to scout out business opportunities beyond Canton, especially in the ports of Amoy (Xiamen), Fuzhou, Ningbo and Shanghai – all of which later became the 'treaty ports' according to the Treaty of Nanjing, 1842. This voyage also provided the 'free trade' advocates a great opportunity to gather so-called 'first-hand' knowledge about China, so that they could contest the EIC's claim that only its servants in Canton knew the real state of the country. The 'free trade' advocates, it should be noted, were an amorphous group. Supported by the industrial and commercial interests in Britain, they were not necessarily the private merchants who had been conducting the 'unauthorised trade'. Lindsay, although still not a 'free trader' at this point, clearly agreed with the private merchants on the need to challenge the existing system of the China trade. Another key figure, Karl Gützlaff, who served as the interpreter and physician during the voyage of 1832, was neither British nor a merchant. A Lutheran missionary from Prussia, Gützlaff was keen to spread the word of God among the Chinese. Hence he shared the same interests with the British private merchants in 'opening' China. Often referring to the British as 'us' in his writings, Gützlaff played an important role in Britain's intercourse with China in the 1830s and 1840s. He commanded a good knowledge of the Chinese language, which allowed him to interpret for Jardine, Matheson & Co. during its smuggling of opium and to assist in the Sino-British negotiations during the Opium War.[55] Both Gützlaff and Lindsay published their reports of the reconnaissance shortly after the voyage. Together with articles written by Crawfurd and others, these publications, which were arguably results of a first-hand investigation, greatly challenged the EIC's assertion that China was so culturally different from Britain that the free trade principle was inapplicable in China. This point of view was bolstered by the following claims.

First, the Chinese were *'a highly commercial people'*[56] just as with the British. According to Crawfurd, the ordinary Chinese people were not only 'able and willing to trade' but 'desirous of an extended intercourse with foreigners'.[57] During the voyage up the China coast, Gützlaff accumulated much evidence showing that the natives whom he met appeared 'anxious to gain a livelihood and accumulate riches',[58] and they sometimes 'complained bitterly of the system of exclusion'.[59] In addition, even some of the government officials, who were supposed to suppress contacts between foreigners and the Chinese, had acknowledged in private that vast advantage could be drawn from international trade. In this respect, Gützlaff noted a remarkable case that occurred in the vicinity of Amoy, where the admiral of a local station asked to purchase opium. When he was told that no opium was carried on board the ships, the admiral appeared 'much disappointed when we [the British] had none to sell'.[60] Reports on such first-hand experiences in China enabled Crawfurd to claim with confidence that 'It appears quite certain that the Chinese, a money-making and money-loving people, are as much addicted to trade, and as anxious as any nation on earth to court a commercial intercourse with strangers. The government and its officers perhaps not less anxious for foreign commerce than the people themselves, could they see their way to admit it without danger.'[61]

Second, the Chinese, instead of being a nation that did not value international communications, were a friendly and 'kind-hearted race of people'[62] who were keen to have free intercourse with foreigners. In his journal of the voyage, Gützlaff carefully recorded the kindness with which the common Chinese people received him. For example, he wrote, although some natives lived 'in the most wretched hovels imaginable', their hospitality 'formed a striking contrast to their extreme poverty'.[63] They not only invited Gützlaff and other foreign visitors into their houses but shared with them their scanty meal. Particularly, as one of the few quotations cited from conversations with the Chinese, the following statement was minutely noted down by the Prussian missionary: 'How gladly ... would we, if permitted, [have] cultivated amicable intercourse with you! But we are always forbidden to obey the impulse of our hearts!'[64] With the assistance of these vivid images, Gützlaff concluded that 'the Chinese character in its true light' was 'that of friendliness and kindness towards foreigners'.[65] This opinion confirmed Crawfurd's belief that 'Whatever peculiarities may attach to the Chinese ... an antipathy to strangers is not one of them'.[66]

Third, the Chinese held an open attitude towards knowledge about the external world. In particular, they were eager to possess information about Christianity and the character of the English people. This impression was formed mainly because, during the voyage, Lindsay and Gützlaff took the opportunities to distribute a number of Chinese-language pamphlets, which they believed could disseminate favourable images of the British among the natives and help convert them to Christianity. These books, including a brochure entitled *A Brief Account of the English Character*, and various religious tracts as well as some scientific and moral tracts, were described as eagerly sought after whenever they were distributed.[67] Without attempting to ascertain how many of the Chinese were really able to read these pamphlets (the literacy rate was very low in China at this time), advocates of 'free trade' such as 'A correspondent in China' interpreted the phenomenon as a sign that 'there exists among the people of China an unquenchable thirst after knowledge'.[68] To Gützlaff, who was dedicated to spreading the word of God among the Chinese, the demand for the religious tracts not only afforded an inviting field but suggested that the Chinese people wished to read the Gospels. These interpretations led Gützlaff to represent the Chinese as victims who were in need of a moral reformation. 'It is truly distressing', Gützlaff lamented, 'that this people is anxious for the word of eternal life, but unable to obtain it'.[69]

While holding that the Chinese people had no antipathy to commerce, foreigners or external knowledge, the 'free trade' advocates maintained that the Chinese government did not deserve respect. As with leading members of Macartney's embassy, they claimed that the current Qing government did not express the opinions or promote the interests of the Chinese people. An anonymous writer, for example, described the ruling Manchus as barbarians and conquerors 'disliked by the people, and living in constant fear of rebellion which may drive them out of China'.[70] In December 1830, a group of private merchants presented a petition to Parliament. In this document, they stated: 'so many millions of comparatively civilised human beings were subdued by its bitterest enemies, and yielded implicit obedience to a tribe of rude and ignorant barbarians'.[71] Similarly, Lindsay claimed that 'the mere will of a despot ... for the last century ... separate near 400,000,000 of human beings from all communication with their species'.[72] On the basis of these images, the private merchants and their supporters condemned how the present government of China treated foreigners with constant suspicion and made every effort to prevent foreigners from contacting the Chinese people. They believed that, in areas where the country's external trade was conducted, the government promoted mutual antipathy between its subjects and foreign merchants. On the one hand, it gave foreigners 'the worst ideas of the stupid and treacherous natives',[73] while, on the other hand, the government endeavoured to prepossess its people, particularly in Canton, against foreigners by 'representing them ... as a barbarous, ignorant, and depraved race, everyway inferior to themselves, thereby exciting the lower orders to treat them with habitual insolence'.[74] To account for the belief that the contempt of foreigners in Canton was more the result of the government's prejudiced policy than the natural disposition of the people, Lindsay noted that, outside the province of Guangdong, 'we had met with nothing but expressions of friendship and good will'.[75] He found that, in general, 'foreigners in China were better liked the less they were known'.[76] Such first-hand evidence, again, strengthened Crawfurd's idea that the current situation in China was in essence a 'government of the few' against 'the interests of the many'.[77] According to this view, the Qing government, instead of being a respectable institution as the EIC claimed, was but a detestable obstacle which stood between foreigners and the vast majority of the Chinese people, both of whom were desirous of free communications.

In addition, the 'free trade' advocates attempted to present the laws of China as equally unworthy of respect. For instance, with regard to the Chinese laws of limiting the intercourse between foreigners and the Chinese, Gützlaff wrote that 'it was not our wish to oppose the laws of the empire, but we could not believe that there were any laws *compelling* to such misanthropy'.[78] In a similar tone, Gützlaff created an impression that the 'unnatural' laws of China were in conflict with the divine law of the God. He contended that 'All mankind are created and upheld by the same God ... therefore have a natural right to claim fellowship. The refusal of it is a transgression of the divine law of benevolence, which is equally binding upon all the nations of the earth.'[79] On this ground, Gützlaff believed the Chinese people were under the 'the thraldom of Satan'[80] and in need of being rescued. These images complemented the intentions of other observers to attribute all signs of underdevelopment in China, such as poverty in different regions, to the harmful effects of the Chinese laws. Charles Marjoribanks, who served as the head of the Select Committee at Canton and later as an MP from 1832 to 1833, believed that the laws brought 'ruin and impoverishment'[81] to the Chinese nation. 'A correspondent in China' wrote in *The Asiatic Journal* that because of the negative influence of the Chinese laws, the people in China had been reduced to 'nothing more than semi-barbarians'.[82]

Gützlaff also considered the laws to regulate China's internal affairs as problematical. He argued that many laws of China read excellently but could not be put into practice, because they were either too old to be adapted to current circumstances or 'so numerous also and strict, that it is impossible to be a subject and not a transgressor'.[83] For these reasons, the Chinese people did not strictly observe most of their laws. Instead, 'all the restrictive laws of the Celestial Empire receive their validity from interpretation of the mandarins instructed with them, and ... this depends upon the force at their command to enforce them'.[84] The experience of the voyage, again, provided evidence to reinforce this view. Gützlaff reported that, during the voyage, although the mandarins he encountered ordered the foreign visitors to obey the imperial edicts, they actually retained to themselves the power of either overlooking some parts or neglecting the whole of them. For example:

> In the imperial edict, ... all barbarian ships are forbidden to approach the coast of Fuh-keen [Fujian] and Che-keang [Zhejiang] provinces; they are not allowed to anchor for a moment, but ought to be driven away. We anchored for several days, and nobody even endeavoured to drive us away. The barbarians are not allowed to go on shore. We went into the city, and in every direction, and his Excellency never took effectual measures to prevent it. No boat was allowed to approach in order to trade, but no punishment mentioned; and people who dared to look at us were punished very severely. Nobody could therefore make us believe that his Excellency was strictly executing the imperial orders.[85]

Marjoribanks, also speaking from his experience dealing with the Chinese authorities, maintained that, because the Chinese officials had such power to interpret, enforce and ignore the laws, bribery pervaded the government of China. He commented, in that very corrupt system, 'there is no officer ... whose hands are clean, or who is not at all times ready to infringe the law which it is his nominal duty to uphold'.[86]

After demonstrating that it was unnecessary to respect a government which did not represent the interests of its people and whose laws were not observed even by its own officials, campaigners for 'free trade' in China had more reasons to disagree with the EIC's Court of Directors on the need to follow a conciliatory policy towards Chinese authorities. Since no government had a right to exclude its subjects from a peaceful intercourse with foreigners, it was legitimate to challenge the Qing government for the benefit of both the British and the Chinese people. Notably, unlike some of the EIC's supporters such as Fisher who asserted that the Chinese had a natural disposition to appeal to reason, Lindsay asserted that 'much more may be gained by an appeal to their fears'.[87] The anonymous author of *The Foreign Trade of China* agreed with this view. He claimed that, as in the cases of the Macartney and the Amherst embassies, 'those objects which foreigners have sought by means of reason and persuasion, and especially by a show of respect, have scarcely ever been attained', while recent experience had shown that 'a tone of defiance, more particularly when backed by any display of physical force, has nearly always proved successful'.[88] The voyage of 1832, once again, proved useful in showing that the Chinese authorities indeed respected firmness more than conciliation. Gützlaff noted, for example, 'even the least thing was refused when we humbly asked for it',[89] but 'as soon as the mandarins perceived that we were firm and reasonable in our demands, they became polite, and yielded'.[90] Such first-hand finding made it easier for the private merchants and their campaigners to argue that a submissive approach could not improve Britain's relations with China, while a firmer attitude would help.

Although the 'free trade' advocates generally desired a more aggressive line of action, they proposed different approaches. Some of them such as Marjoribanks maintained that 'to command the slightest attention or respect in China, you must appear with an appropriate force'.[91] Believing that the Qing government was weak and timid, Lindsay also suggested a violent approach: 'if four or six Indiamen and one of His Majesty's frigates had entered the port of Fuh Chow-foo [Fuzhou], captured the war-junks, proceeded to Mingan, and thence sent the option to the government of friendship or hostility, trade or war, that the freedom of British intercourse would have been established in perpetuity, without any expenditure either of blood or money'.[92] Others, however, disagreed that military force should be used against the Chinese. Gützlaff concurred with Lindsay that a more steadfast stance was necessary, but he 'highly disapprove[d] of violent measures to obtain an object, which might be gained by firmness and resolution'.[93] In a similar tone, C.W. King of the American firm Olyphant and Co. claimed that, 'We would not trample down the custom of China with cavalry, nor cut up her prejudices with the sabre, nor carry *our* point and *her* cities by storm'.[94] Instead, a policy of 'mild interference of those commercial nations of Europe and America ... by the united expression of their desires'[95] might be a better tactic. Despite the disagreement on whether a violent measure was advisable, the demand for a more determined attitude towards the Chinese government became more vociferous in the early 1830s than before. The foundations for a change in British–Chinese relations had been established to a considerable extent.

In August 1833, the British government decided to abolish the EIC's monopoly of China trade. Trade with China was finally opened to the British private merchants. As for why the government took the decision, Webster's and Kumagai's analyses have presented a range of factors, neither of which favoured the EIC. Economically, since the opening of the India trade to the private merchants in 1813, the EIC's trade with India had declined rapidly. The Company's financial status deteriorated over the 1820s. Britain also faced increasing competition from American companies in the Chinese market. The threat fuelled the anti-monopoly campaigners' argument that, unless trade with China was thrown open, the British merchants would be unable to compete with their American counterparts. Politically, the early 1830s was a time of turmoil. The question of parliamentary reform was the British government's main concern. Many of the landed elite feared that a revolution was going to occur in Britain. Such political climate might have made it easier for politicians to listen to the voices outside the government calling for reform and to compromise if necessary. These underlying trends went hand-in-hand with the formidable campaign created by the opponents of the Company's privileges. According to Webster, 'a decisive factor ... had been the development since 1813 of new political and commercial links between those private trading organisations ..., the London East India agency houses, and the emergent industrial interests of provincial Britain. These had enabled the free trade movement of 1829–33 to present a united campaign which encompassed both provincial and metropolitan commercial financial interests in favour of reform.'[96] Kumagai's research has concentrated on the role that the provincial interests, especially the East India Associations of Glasgow and Liverpool, played in the abolition. Kumagai has shown that how these pressure groups initiated and orchestrated the campaign. They not only rallied wide support in their own localities, bombarded Parliament and government with petitions, but used their connections with MPs, senior politicians, London-based merchants and those with knowledge of Asia to strengthen the impact of the movement. The end of the EIC's China monopoly could not have been possible without the strenuous and tactical efforts made by these provincial interests to influence the opinions of policy-makers as well as the public.[97]

It should be noted, however, that, although the anti-monopoly campaigners won the debate with the EIC, this did not necessarily mean that the images of China presented by them were incontestable. At least, from the following perspectives, their contentions deserve consideration. First, although it seems that some of the critical opinions about China were derived from first-hand discoveries of the voyage, it is difficult to determine whether they were genuine 'discoveries' independent from any predispositions. Similar opinions, in fact, already existed prior to 1832. Since the late 1820s, the Chinese government had been heavily criticised by foreign traders in Canton. As shown earlier in this chapter, in 1830, a group of British merchants in China even petitioned Parliament for the British state's direct intervention in Chinese affairs partly on the basis of the claim that China had an extremely corrupt government that was liked by neither its people nor the foreign traders. Since they did not receive any positive response, the petitioners as well as other 'free trade' advocates were keen to gather more convincing arguments, or 'evidence', about the characters of the Chinese government and people, in order to lobby the British government to take action. In this context, the two central figures of the voyage, Lindsay and Gützlaff, had been inclined to agree with such views of China before they started their journey.

Second, although evidence obtained on the voyage had helped the 'free trade' advocates to claim that the Chinese were naturally friendly to foreigners and that they were keen to know about Christianity, these images could well be representations based on the personal prejudices of the travellers. Gützlaff, for instance, made every effort to record how much his religious tracts were welcomed in China and how hospitable the Chinese became when they lived beyond the reach of the government. He took it for granted that these signs represented the Chinese people's genuine dispositions, but never really questioned whether they had other motives, especially their hope of gaining something from the foreign visitors. Lindsay suggested in his report that it might be the free medical services that Gützlaff provided for the natives that gave rise to the 'the extraordinary degree of respect and friendship shown to us by all classes of Chinese',[98] but no such connection was drawn by Gützlaff himself. Moreover, although Gützlaff did record some occurrences which might have challenged his conclusions, the Prussian missionary made no attempt to explain these phenomena. For example, he once noted that 'We had had a long conversation with the owner of a house, who had posted himself right in the way to prevent our entering his dwelling. I now thought it high time to make them a present of some books. When they found that I really intended to *give* these to them, they changed their tone, became friendly and hospitable.'[99] Such an encounter may well indicate that the claimed friendliness or hospitality of the Chinese did not necessarily represent their real feelings. When Gützlaff came to present the 'genuine' character of the Chinese nation, however, he simply ignored these occurrences.

Third, despite the fact that the 'free trade' campaigners were aware that there was some duplicity innate in the Chinese character, they tended to fix this trait on government officials rather than the common people. To justify his view that the Qing authorities did not represent their subjects, Lindsay maintained that, although there was a friendly disposition on the part of the people, the Chinese mandarins had a 'lying spirit'.[100] Even when the officials treated him in the same favourable manner as some ordinary Chinese people did, Lindsay never forgot to point out that 'there was more of policy than sincerity' in the officials' '*professions* of friendship'.[101] This charge of duplicity, however, was never employed by Lindsay in his portrayal of the hospitality of the common people. Furthermore, when the 'free trade' supporters were satisfied with the comments or actions of some Chinese officials, they never questioned their motives. For example, according to the orders of the emperor, mandarins at various places were anxious to drive foreigners out of their districts. Under such circumstances and perhaps to avert an open conflict, some officials conceded that international trade was beneficial. '[A]s the laws of the Celestial Empire prohibited trade with foreigners', they expressed their wish for the foreign visitors to leave their districts without delay, even though 'for themselves, they would be highly desirous that the trade was opened'.[102] In these cases, the mandarins' favourable remarks on foreign trade, no matter whether they were sincere, were taken out of context and were treated as further evidence of China's general eagerness for external trade – even government officials were not opposed to it. Neither Lindsay nor Gützlaff bothered to try to understand why these mandarins acted in this way, or to relate it to the 'duplicitous' character of Chinese officials.

Fourth, in a similar way, the 'free trade' campaigners attempted to hide some important contexts when they were endeavouring to convince the British public that the Chinese government was extremely suspicious of foreigners. In particular, a few months before the voyage, a serious quarrel broke out between the EIC's factory at Canton and the local authorities. As a result, a rumour spread among the Chinese that the EIC had demanded assistance from India. Instead of referring to this background situation, Gützlaff, Lindsay and others insisted that the Chinese mandarins were 'always suspicious that we [the British] design to attack them',[103] as if this fear were totally unreasonable. During the voyage of 1832, the travellers disguised their connection with the EIC. Since, unlike most non-EIC British merchants, they carried no opium for sale, it gave the Chinese officials ample reason to suspect the real intention of these visitors. These aspects of the voyage might not overthrow the claim that China possessed a suspicious government, but, at least they can suggest that the anxiety and suspicions exhibited by the Chinese authorities were not entirely unwarranted.

Last, in the accounts of the 'free trade' advocates, it was widely contended that the Chinese were a commercially minded nation. These claims were actually speculation based on limited evidence rather than substantial proofs. It is well known that at this time the foreigners had extremely limited contacts with the Chinese people apart from those living in coastal trading communities. Since these Chinese made up only a small proportion of the total population of China, it was unfair to assess the 'national' character of such a vast nation on the basis of meeting some coastal communities. Furthermore, influential opinion formers such as Crawfurd sometimes drew their conclusions on the characteristics of the Chinese mercantile class from information about those who lived outside Chinese territory, especially the Chinese diaspora in South-east Asia. Discoveries about these people who lived thousands of miles away from China, however, were often seen as being representative of the character of all Chinese trading communities, even of the whole nation. For instance, in the writings of Crawfurd and others, the following conjectures were quoted:

> Mr John Deans, ... who resided twenty years in the Eastern archipelago ... [claimed:] 'The Chinese of the Archipelago, who, I *believe*, do not differ from the Chinese in their native country, are very sensible of the importance of commerce, and are, as I have already observed, the keenest speculators perhaps in the country'.[104]

> Robert Rickards, Esq. [claimed:] 'I *believe* that the Chinese are a perfectly commercial people. Wherever the Chinese have been established in Singapore, in Java, in Borneo, and in the other eastern islands where they are settled in great numbers, they are found to be the principal traders, and the most industrious people in the country. I therefore take the Chinese, generally speaking, to be a perfectly commercial people, and exceedingly anxious to extend their commercial dealings, in spite of any restrictive regulations that may be imposed upon them by the Chinese government'.[105]

From such comments it can be seen that these 'beliefs' were purely personal opinions regarding the character of the Chinese. Some of these commentators had never visited China, but, simply because they had some experience of Asia and their opinions supported the private merchants' arguments, their personal interpretations were propagated as proven facts in the anti-monopoly campaign. This vital difference between opinions and facts might have had an important impact in misleading the British government and concerned public to form ideas about the character of the Chinese people. It might also be another reason for the victory of the 'free traders' in the contested debate of the early 1830s.

In conclusion, this chapter shows that the partial opening of Britain's India trade to private merchants led many more Britons to China and enabled them to provide first-hand observations on the country just as diplomatic visitors and EIC employees had been able to do in previous decades. With the aim of completely freeing the China trade, the private merchants and their campaigners advanced various images of China that were in stark contrast to the EIC's assertions. As a result, not only were the Company's representations of Chinese affairs seriously challenged but Britain's overall impression of China deteriorated in the early years of the 1830s. In particular, the Qing government as well as its laws was increasingly presented as unworthy of respect. Although, at this time, opinions were still divided on whether a display of military force was appropriate, the necessity for taking a firmer stance against the Chinese authorities was strengthened. As the types of encounter between Britain and China continued to develop after the abolition of the EIC's China monopoly in 1834, British attitudes towards China would change accordingly.

Notes

1 The 'country trade' began in the late eighteenth century, but significantly expanded after the East India Company Act of 1813.
2 Michael Greenberg, *British Trade and the Opening of China 1800–42* (Cambridge: Cambridge University Press, 1951), p. 16.
3 The Court of Directors was the EIC's executive body, consisting of twenty-four men elected from and by the proprietors (or the stockholders). The directors met regularly to decide on the Company's policies. The Court of Proprietors gathered at least four times a year to elect directors, to discuss their decisions and to oversee their activities.
4 Greenberg, *British Trade and the Opening of China 1800–42*, p. 40.
5 Hosea Ballou Morse, *The Chronicles of the East India Company trading to China 1635–1834* (5 vols, Oxford: Clarendon Press, 1926; reprinted, London: Routledge, 2000), IV; Greenberg, *British Trade and the Opening of China*; C.H. Philips, *The East India Company 1784–1834* (Manchester: Manchester University Press, 1961); Anthony Webster, *The Twilight of the East India Company: The Evolution of Anglo-Asian Commerce and Politics, 1790–1860* (Woodbridge: Boydell, 2009); and Yukihisa Kumagai, *Breaking into the Monopoly: Provincial Merchants and Manufacturers' Campaigns for Access to the Asian Market, 1790–1833* (Leiden: Brill, 2012).
6 Hugh Hamilton Lindsay (1802–81) started working for the East India Company at Canton in 1821. Initially a salaried writer, he became a supercargo in 1829. Lindsay left the Company in 1833. He founded his own company Lindsay & Co. when he returned to Canton in 1836. For more of Lindsay's activities and views, see Robert Bickers, 'The Challenger: Hugh Hamilton Lindsay and the Rise of British Asia, 1832–1865', *Transactions of the Royal Historical Society*, Sixth series, 22 (2012), 141–69.
7 Webster, *The Twilight of the East India Company*, p. 100.
8 Philips, *The East India Company*, p. 291.
9 George T. Staunton, 'Considerations on the China Trade', *The Asiatic Journal*, 28 (Dec. 1829), 684–5.
10 Henry Ellis, *A Series of Letters on the East India Question, Addressed to the Members of the Two Houses of Parliament* (London: John Murray, 1830), p. 60.
11 Ibid., pp. 37–8.
12 R. Montgomery Martin, *The Past and Present State of the Tea Trade of England, and of the Continents of Europe and America* (London: Parbury, Allen, 1832), p. 131.
13 Staunton, 'Considerations on the China Trade', *The Asiatic Journal*, 28 (Dec. 1829), 690–1.
14 Anon., 'The American Commerce with China', *The Asiatic Journal*, 27 (Jan. 1829), 2.
15 Staunton, 'Considerations on the China Trade', *The Asiatic Journal*, 28 (Dec. 1829), 686.
16 'Report of the Select Committee of the House of Commons on the Affairs of the East India Company: China Trade (1830)', in Martin, *The Past and Present State*, p. 132.
17 Staunton, 'Considerations on the China Trade', *The Asiatic Journal*, 28 (Dec. 1829), 686.
18 Ellis, *A Series of Letters*, p. 43.
19 Martin, *The Past and Present State*, p. 4.

THE EIC VERSUS FREE TRADERS

20 This quotation is from 'a celebrated modern and liberal writer, who resided eight years in China, and travelled a great deal in the country', in Martin, *The Past and Present State*, p. 10. Italics in the original.
21 Ellis, *A Series of Letters*, pp. 43–4.
22 *Ibid.*, p. 41.
23 Martin, *The Past and Present State*, p. 127.
24 Ellis, *A Series of Letters*, pp. 56–7.
25 Martin, *The Past and Present State*, p. 6.
26 Thomas Fisher, 'Statistical Notices of China', *The Gentleman's Magazine*, 103 (April 1833), 296.
27 Ellis, *A Series of Letters*, p. 28.
28 Staunton, 'Considerations on the China Trade', *The Asiatic Journal*, 28 (Dec. 1829), 678.
29 *Ibid.*
30 Fisher, 'Statistical Notices of China', *The Gentleman's Magazine*, 103 (May 1833), 392.
31 Martin, *The Past and Present State*, p. 128.
32 Letter from the Court of Directors to the Select Committee, 13 Jan. 1832, in Martin, *The Past and Present State*, p. 214.
33 Martin, *The Past and Present State*, p. 5.
34 *Ibid.*, p. 9. Italics in the original.
35 Fisher, 'Statistical Notices of China', *The Gentleman's Magazine*, 103 (May 1833), 392.
36 *Ibid.*, 389.
37 *Ibid.*
38 Letter from the Court of Directors to the Select Committee, 13 Jan. 1832, in Martin, *The Past and Present State*, p. 214.
39 Anon., *The Foreign Trade of China Divested of Monopoly, Restriction, and Hazard by Means of Insular Commercial Stations* (London: Effingham Wilson, 1832), pp. 8–9.
40 Staunton, 'Considerations on the China Trade', *The Asiatic Journal*, 28 (Dec. 1829), 684.
41 *Ibid.*, 682.
42 Anon., 'The East-India Question', *The Asiatic Journal*, 1 (1830), 116.
43 Webster, *The Twilight of the East India Company*, pp. 98–9.
44 [John Crawfurd], 'Voyage of Ship Amherst', *The Westminster Review*, 20 (1834), 45.
45 [John Crawfurd], 'East India Company – China Question', *The Edinburgh Review*, 104 (1831), 292.
46 [Crawfurd], 'Voyage of Ship Amherst', *The Westminster Review*, 20 (1834), 45.
47 Technically, there were two types of 'unauthorised trade'. One referred to the illegal traffic that was carried on at the mouth of the Canton river. The other was conducted by the Chinese themselves between several Chinese ports and Siam, the Philippine islands, Borneo, Singapore, Java, etc. To the British private merchants, this term mainly meant the former mode of trade.
48 [John Crawfurd], *Observations on the Influence of the East India Company's Monopoly on the Price and Supply of Tea; and on the Commerce with India, China, etc.* (London: Longman, Rees, Orme, Brown, and Green, 1831), p. 26. Italics in the original.
49 [Crawfurd], 'Voyage of Ship Amherst', *The Westminster Review*, 20 (1834), 45.
50 Anon., *The Foreign Trade of China*, p. 41.
51 [Crawfurd], 'East India Company – China Question', *The Edinburgh Review*, 104 (1831), 306.
52 [Crawfurd], *Observations on the Influence*, p. 20. More about Bates and his impact can be found in Webster, *The Twilight of the East India Company*, pp. 97–8.
53 [Crawfurd], 'East India Company – China Question', *The Edinburgh Review*, 104 (1831), 294.

54 As stated earlier, after 1829, some of the EIC's employees in China tended to agree more with the private merchants than the Court of Directors in London. Lindsay was as one of them. He strongly believed the voyage was in the interest of British commerce in China.
55 For more information about Gützlaff and his experience in China, see Jessie Gregory Lutz, *Opening China: Karl F.A. Gützlaff and Sino-Western Relations, 1827–1852* (Grand Rapids, MI: William B. Eerdmans, 2008).
56 [Crawfurd], *Observations on the Influence*, p. 14. Italics in the original.
57 [Crawfurd], 'Voyage of Ship Amherst', *The Westminster Review*, 20 (1834), 37–8.
58 Karl Gützlaff, *Journal of Three Voyages along the Coast of China, in 1831, 1832, & 1833* (London: Frederick Westley and A.H. Davis, 1834), p. 136. As the title suggests, Gützlaff actually made three voyages up the China coast. Before the voyage of 1832, he made an expedition in a Chinese junk from Bangkok to Tianjin. In 1833, Gützlaff sailed in a trading ship from Canton up to Jinzhou, a city in the homeland of the Qing's Manchu rulers. Most comments Gützlaff made on China, however, were drawn from the second voyage.
59 Ibid., p. 172.
60 Gützlaff's Report, in *Report of Proceedings on a Voyage to the Northern Ports of China, in the Ship Lord Amherst: Extracted from Papers, Printed by Order of the House of Commons, Relating to the Trade with China* (London: B. Fellowes, 1833), p. 278.
61 [John Crawfurd], 'Chinese Empire and Trade', *The Westminster Review*, 21 (1834), 254.
62 A correspondent in China, 'Intercourse with China', *The Asiatic Journal*, 13 (1834), 104.
63 Gützlaff, *Journal of Three Voyages*, p. 211.
64 Ibid., p. 172.
65 Ibid., p. 301.
66 [Crawfurd], *Observations on the Influence*, p. 26.
67 Details about the distributed pamphlets can be found in Lindsay's Report, in *Report of Proceedings*, p. 44.
68 A correspondent in China, 'Intercourse with China', *The Asiatic Journal*, 13 (1834), 104.
69 Gützlaff, *Journal of Three Voyages*, p. 155.
70 Anon., *The Foreign Trade of China*, p. 15.
71 *Petition to the House of Commons from British Subjects Residing in China* (also known as 'Canton Petition'), 24 Dec. 1830, in Alain Le Pichon (ed.), *China Trade and Empire: Jardine, Matheson & Co. and the Origins of British Rule in Hong Kong 1827–1843* (Oxford: Oxford University Press, 2006), p. 555. This document was originally published in *The Canton Register*, 18 Dec. 1830, 3 (25).
72 Lindsay's Report, in *Report of Proceedings*, p. 211.
73 Gützlaff, *Journal of Three Voyages*, p. 231.
74 Canton Petition, 24 Dec. 1830, in *China Trade and Empire*, pp. 556–7.
75 Lindsay's Report, in *Report of Proceedings*, p. 10.
76 Ibid., p. 33.
77 [Crawfurd], 'Chinese Empire and Trade', *The Westminster Review*, 21 (1834), 256.
78 Gützlaff, *Journal of Three Voyages*, p. 253. Italics in the original.
79 Ibid., pp. 1–2.
80 Ibid., p. 124.
81 Charles Marjoribanks, *Letter to the Right Hon. Charles Grant, President of the Board of Control, on the Present State of British Intercourse with China* (London: J. Hatchard and Son, 1833), p. 27.
82 A correspondent in China, 'Intercourse with China', *The Asiatic Journal*, 13 (1834), 105.
83 Gützlaff, *Journal of Three Voyages*, p. 15.
84 Gützlaff's Report, in *Report of Proceedings*, pp. 273–4.
85 Ibid., p. 273.

86 Marjoribanks, *Letter to the Right Hon. Charles Grant*, p. 14.
87 Lindsay's Report, in *Report of Proceedings*, p. 57.
88 Anon., *The Foreign Trade of China*, pp. 14–15.
89 Gützlaff's Report, in *Report of Proceedings*, p. 289.
90 Gützlaff, *Journal of Three Voyages*, pp. 284–5.
91 Marjoribanks, *Letter to the Right Hon. Charles Grant*, p. 53.
92 Lindsay's Report, in *Report of Proceedings*, p. 86.
93 Gützlaff, *Journal of Three* Voyages, p. 310.
94 [C.W. King], 'Intercourse with China', *Chinese Repository*, 1:4 (Aug. 1832), 145. Italics in the original.
95 *Ibid.*, 145–6.
96 Webster, *The Twilight of the East India Company*, p. 102.
97 Kumagai, *Breaking into the Monopoly*, pp. 179–89.
98 Lindsay's Report, in *Report of Proceedings*, p. 87.
99 Gützlaff, *Journal of Three Voyages*, p. 418. Italics in the original.
100 Lindsay's Report, in *Report of Proceedings*, p. 78.
101 *Ibid.*, p. 111. Italics added.
102 Gützlaff's Report, in *Report of Proceedings*, pp. 282–3. This was sometimes accompanied with a promise that they would turn a blind eye to the happenings beyond their region, see Lindsay's Report, in *Report of Proceedings*, p. 211; and Marjoribanks, *Letter to the Right Hon. Charles Grant*, p. 23.
103 Gützlaff, *Journal of Three Voyages*, p. 268. Similar views can also be found in Lindsay's Report, in *Report of Proceedings*, pp. 10, 93; and Marjoribanks, *Letter to the Right Hon. Charles Grant*, pp. 23–4.
104 [Crawfurd], *Observations on the Influence*, pp. 300–1. Italics added.
105 Anon., *The Foreign Trade of China*, p. 36. Italics added. Similar examples can be found in the same book that different individuals interpreted the general commercial spirit of the Chinese from their experience in Batavia, Cochin China, Java, Penang and Singapore. See *ibid.*, pp. 24–38.

CHAPTER FOUR

'Show of force'

In August 1833, the British government finally decided to abolish the East India Company's monopoly over the country's China trade. It provided that, after 21 April 1834, trade with China would be open to all British subjects. This decision resulted in a series of changes to British–Chinese relations. Most important, instead of using the Company's Select Committee at Canton, the British government had to take on the task of representing British merchants in China and dealing directly with the Chinese authorities. To this end, a new trade commission was quickly established. William John, ninth Lord Napier, the former shipmate and personal friend of King William IV, was appointed as Britain's first 'chief superintendent of trade' in China. Since Napier had no prior experience of China, John Francis Davis and George Robinson, both EIC representatives in Canton, were named as the second and third superintendents, to assist Napier's mission to 'protect the interests of British subjects in China in the peaceful prosecution of all lawful enterprises'.[1]

Unlike Lord Amherst, whose decision had been heavily influenced by his deputy George Thomas Staunton, Napier totally dominated his mission. In July 1834, Napier arrived at the harbour of Whampoa in a British warship without permission from the Qing government. This unauthorised entry into Chinese territory was followed by an approximately two-month stay at Canton, for which an additional permit should have been required. During this period, Napier, assuming himself to be the representative of the British Crown, refused to accept Hong merchants as the proper channel of communications between himself and viceroy Lu Kun, the highest authority at Canton. To suggest equality, Napier insisted on writing directly to Lu Kun. In his correspondence with the latter, he also resolved to abandon the normal heading of 'pin' (petition), which implies subservience. These acts further challenged China's century-long Canton system and roused much anger in the Chinese government. As a consequence, the local authorities stopped all trade with Britain and demanded Napier's immediate departure from Canton. Napier, in response, adopted some strong measures. He not only circulated a proclamation accusing Lu Kun of 'ignorance and incompetence' but also ordered two British frigates to force a passage to Canton. The situation escalated into a crisis. After a standoff of a few days, on 21 September, Napier's weakened health compelled him to withdraw. He died shortly afterwards in Macao, partly as a result of the very slow journey there in a Chinese boat, the only means by which he was allowed to leave Canton.

The Napier incident, also known as the 'Napier Fizzle', can be viewed in some ways as Britain's first attempt to adopt an aggressive line of action against China. According to prevailing interpretations, most of which are based on findings drawn from the Jardine Matheson papers, Napier's conduct signalled the beginning of a 'forward policy', which was designed to compel the Chinese government to grant the British increased commercial facilities.[2] By examining the private papers of British officials and unpublished Foreign Office records, Glenn Melancon has pointed out that 'the British government had no policy of aggression toward China' in 1834.[3] His argument, however, has not proved strong enough to remove the commonly held perception which regards the Napier affair as a prelude to the Opium War, or at least as an event which made that war more possible or 'justifiable to the British public'.[4] There are a number of reasons for this. First, historians who have written on this subject have concentrated either on the 'Napier Fizzle' itself or on the immediate causes of the Opium War, while little attention has been paid to the period in between, i.e. the mid-1830s. Without detailed investigation into this period, any research focusing on the Napier incident as a free-standing event is not in a position to challenge the traditional narrative about the long-term causes of the First Anglo-Chinese War. Second, although Melancon has shown that no member of the British government was interested in waging a war against China in 1834, he and some other historians, such as Harry G. Gelber, have primarily examined one side of the story, namely the opinions of decision-makers in Britain.[5] Napier's own opinions, public reactions to the incident and discussion within the British-dominated foreign community in China concerning Britain's future course of action have been much less studied. Third, despite the fact that, in the mid-1830s, British residents in China as well as the involved mercantile and legal communities in Britain were not yet a politically significant group,[6] their attitudes have been presented too much as one single voice which 'clearly had no respect for China's rulers or their laws'[7] and was solidly united in promoting a policy of coercing China. Without investigating the complex views held by these opinion formers, a range of questions cannot be answered. For example, apart from those who had direct power to decide on Britain's policies towards China, was a strong-hand course of conduct generally justified and promoted immediately after the 'Napier Fizzle'? Is it true that all British commentators beyond government circles considered a war with China desirable from the mid-1830s onwards? Were any other policies advocated and, if so, what was their impact? To answer these questions, this chapter explores not only Napier's views on China but also popular publications in the mid-1830s, particularly some key English-language newspapers published in Canton. Only after this evidence has been examined can we ascertain whether the British at large were in favour of war in the immediate aftermath of the Napier incident, and whether the contention that open hostilities between China and Britain became almost inevitable from 1834 onwards is reliable.

On the 'Napier Fizzle'

Since Napier died shortly after he returned to Macao from Canton, he had no opportunity to reflect on why his mission was unsuccessful. Nevertheless, Napier's assessment of Chinese affairs, as well as his attitudes towards Britain's conduct in China, can be found in his correspondence with the British government during his superintendency. From this source, we can discover that, although Napier declared that he had 'no delight in war',[8] he did believe that a small-scale demonstration of Britain's arms would earn Britain respect in China. Napier, unquestionably, developed some of his key attitudes from opinions formed as a result of the earlier British embassies to China, especially those published by members of the Amherst mission. For example, Napier came to the same conclusion as several members of that mission that the vast majority of Chinese people were commercially minded and hence in favour of British trade with China. He wrote that 'the Chinese people are most anxious for our trade – from the Great Wall to the southern extremity of the empire', with 'the Tartar Government alone being anti-commercial'.[9] On the basis of this interpretation of the Chinese character as well as having the same negative view of the Qing government as leading members of the Amherst mission, Napier became convinced that a firm British stand against the Chinese government was crucial to the success of his mission. Before his arrival in China, Napier had asserted that 'every act of violence on our part has been productive of instant redress and other beneficial results', while 'every concession made ... has been followed by ensued oppression and spoliation'.[10] In this light, a few months later, Napier wrote to Foreign Secretary Viscount Palmerston to justify his forceful practices in Canton:

> What advantage, or what point did we ever gain by negotiating or humbling ourselves before these people, or rather before their Government? The records show nothing but subsequent humiliation and disgrace. What advantage or what point, again, have we ever lost, that was just and reasonable, by acting with promptitude and vigour?[11]

These lines are obviously similar to the hardline attitude that had evolved after the Amherst embassy, but what is also clear is that Napier did not simply inherit all his views of China by reading the accounts published after the Amherst mission. In particular, Napier disagreed with members of the Amherst embassy on their utterly negative image of the Chinese emperor. Instead of holding the emperor responsible for the difficulties which the British faced in trading with China, Napier entertained some favourable images of the Daoguang emperor. In his opinion, it was the misconduct of the local authorities, rather than that of the monarch, that caused Britain's grievances in Canton. To obtain justice for British merchants, therefore, it was essential to bypass the Canton government. He maintained that it was the 'unprecedented tyranny and injustice ... by the said viceroy' and the 'absurd and tyrannical assumption of power on the part of the governor and lieutenant-governor'[12] that prevented a stable Sino-British trade being established. To remedy this situation, the only way was to protest directly 'with firmness and spirit'[13] to the emperor in Beijing. In this spirit, Napier wrote in his open warning to the Canton government:

> let the Governor or Lieutenant Governor know this, that I will lose no time in sending this true statement to His Imperial Majesty the Emperor at Pekin; and that I will also report to his justice and indignation the false and treacherous conduct of Loo, Governor, and of the present Kwang Chow Foo ... His Imperial Majesty will not permit such folly, wickedness, and cruelty as they have been guilty of, since my arrival here, to go unpunished; therefore tremble Governor Loo, intensely tremble![14]

From this statement, it can be shown that, although Napier had never had an opportunity to meet the Daoguang emperor, he did indeed pin his hopes of establishing good relations with China on the character of His Imperial Majesty, whose positive image overall and impartiality in particular he simply took for granted.

Napier's confidence in the validity of protesting to the emperor was also founded on his belief that the Qing ruler and his army had lost their warlike character. Believing that a serious military clash between China and Britain was virtually impossible, Napier maintained that 'a commanding attitude alone, with the power of following the threat with execution, is all that is required to extort a Treaty which shall secure mutual advantages to China and to Europe'.[15] Even if the Daoguang emperor would not compromise at once, Napier believed that 'three or four frigates and brigs, with a few steady British troops ... would settle the thing in a space of time inconceivably short'.[16] By suggesting this line of action, Napier promised that the Chinese 'would never dare to show a front'[17] and that, for Britain, and perhaps for China as well, this approach would cause 'not the loss of a single man'.[18] Although the British government did not take these words seriously, Napier did officially bring such a hardline policy to its attention for the first time.

Immediately after the 'Napier Fizzle', a heated discussion followed among those who had interest in, or experience of, Chinese affairs on the present state of and future prospects for British–Chinese relations. Within a short period of time, various pamphlets and articles were produced by and circulated in the British community at Canton (with contribution from some foreign writers). This public discussion, as well as the images of China that it presented, has previously been under-studied. In particular, the reasons for the failure of Napier's mission, one of the central topics in this literature, have never been introduced to and analysed for modern readers. A popular opinion at the time was that the 'treacherous and cowardly conduct of the Chinese authorities'[19] caused Napier's failure. Hugh Hamilton Lindsay was convinced that, given the character of the Chinese government, what Napier had suffered in Canton was in fact unavoidable, because 'the Chinese were predetermined to insult him ... no moderation on his part would have procured for him a fitting reception'.[20] As with Lindsay, others considered the incident as a serious insult to the British Crown and nation, rather than simply as the superintendent's personal misfortune. For example, G.J. Gordon, in his *Address to the People of Great Britain*, claimed that 'Our sovereign himself has, in the person of his representative at Canton, the late Lord Napier, been insulted by the Chinese authorities'.[21] An anonymous writer in the *Chinese Repository* asserted that 'the course which the Chinese pursued with regard to Lord Napier ... was most barbarous and unjust ... Wrongs and insults have been heaped on the representative of a great and powerful nation, seeking an amicable, an honorable, and a profitable intercourse ... their government has outraged the laws of common right and humanity'.[22]

From the very beginning, discussion of Napier's unsuccessful diplomacy was closely related to a wider context in which the Chinese government was censured from a variety of perspectives. A common view at this time was to see the Napier mission as Britain's gracious attempt to meet the commercial and social needs of both the Chinese and the British people, while the Qing government had violated the law of nations as well as natural law, especially with regard to economic freedom and freedom of movement. On the principle that 'All men ought to find on earth the things they stand in need of ... The introduction of dominion and property could not deprive men of so essential a right',[23] one of the authors in the *Canton Register* lamented:

> Considering all the nations of the earth as one family, we see no reason why one of them, because it has remained for ages, occupying so large a portion of the common soil, in a state of moral and political idiocy, shall not only deny to the surrounding members all the advantages that may be derived from an interchange of its various productions, but also insult them when they come to them with the most friendly and the most beneficent intentions.[24]

Moreover, some of the personal inconveniences to which the British residents in Canton were subject produced strong complaints. In particular, the prohibition on foreign women entering Chinese territory compelled British (and other Western) merchants to leave their wives during the trading season. This policy really annoyed the foreign community in Canton. James Matheson, co-founder of Jardine, Matheson & Co. and one of the leading opium traders, denounced it as such 'an insult perfectly gratuitous' that 'the laws of nature are outraged' in China.[25] Other writers argued that the arbitrary Qing government had also greatly restricted the rights of its Chinese subjects. In an article entitled 'Universal Peace; obstacles to it in the character and government of nations', an anonymous writer maintained that

> the government destroys the personal liberty of its subjects; none of whom may pass beyond the frontiers of the empire, or hold any intercourse with foreigners. Those who presume to disobey these restrictions are declared outlaws, worthy of death. In this way all the avenues to the introduction of every species of useful knowledge are sealed up ... Moreover, the government affords but very imperfect security for the property of the people. In a word, it acknowledges no rights in its subjects. Such is the unnatural, the unreasonable, and the unrighteous condition in which the monarch of this empire holds his subjects; he robs them of liberty of conscience; annihilates their personal rights; and guaranties [sic] to them no security.[26]

From such accusations, the view that 'the Chinese government is in the highest degree demoralized'[27] became increasingly prevalent. It consequently contributed to the impression that it was the Chinese government that had ruined Napier's friendly mission.

Despite such strong criticism of the Chinese government, not all commentators believed that it was China's fault. Some writers suggested that Napier's misfortune resulted from his own failings. In the *Canton Register*, an anonymous author asserted that Napier's conduct was 'offensive to the Chinese government'. He wrote, 'It is to be regretted that a person so inexperienced and ignorant of Chinese usage should have been sent to China at the critical moment of opening the British trade with that empire'.[28] Staunton, the old China hand who had been involved in Chinese affairs since the Macartney embassy, advanced a similar view. In a more detailed observation, he maintained that 'the case of Lord Napier is not a tenable position in argument against the Chinese'.[29] Napier had infringed Chinese laws in two ways. First, he was 'an individual whose first act within the Chinese territories was a violation of its laws':[30]

> Lord Napier could not be ignorant of the fact, as he had persons of the greatest local experience and information joined with him in his commission, that no foreigners of any description have ever been permitted by the Chinese Government to establish themselves at Canton except in strictly a commercial character; and that, moreover, no person, even if habitually resident at Canton in such commercial character, was permitted to visit that city from Macao, without previously obtaining a certain license or passport ... I fearlessly ask, then, what right or pretext had Lord Napier to signalize his first appearance in China by a violation of the known and acknowledged regulations of the country?[31]

Second, Napier's decision to order two British frigates to proceed to Canton was 'another illegal act':[32]

> All this was done without any actual need of either their assistance or their protection. Lord Napier was perfectly safe – his person was not threatened – he had only to go away, and return from whence he came. The object, therefore, neither was nor could have been any other than that of aiding him in his resistance to the orders of the Government.[33]

As well as expressing these opinions, Staunton refuted some of the viewpoints which were commonly advanced in support of Napier's conduct. Against the claim that Napier represented the British sovereign in China, Staunton stressed:

> He was in no sense whatever the King's Representative. The fact is, however, that as far as the Chinese were concerned, he had no public character at all. No public functionary sent to another state can claim, as we have seen, the rights and privileges of his appointment till he is recognised ... official station or public privilege he had literally none.[34]

In opposition to Napier's assertion that he was 'invited' by the Chinese government but then not treated accordingly,[35] Staunton pointed out that Napier and others who held this view actually misunderstood and even distorted the Chinese authorities' original intention, because:

> the Chinese did *not* contemplate the coming out of an officer from the King, claiming new rights and privileges; but expected and required that, notwithstanding the abolition of the East India Company's trade and privileges, matters should be carried on at Canton, as far as they, the Chinese authorities, were concerned, precisely *'as heretofore'*.[36]

These opinions strengthened Staunton's argument that Napier was by no means innocent in relation to what had occurred at Canton. It is worth noting, however, that similar points of view were rarely found in other works. This was probably because, apart from Staunton, very few British observers at this time were able to appreciate China-related affairs with substantial experience of China and a good knowledge of the Chinese language. Staunton's ability to adopt such an approach was perhaps one of the reasons why his views on the Napier incident differed greatly from what became the more common opinion.

Aside from censuring Napier, some commentators blamed the British government for sending such a high-ranking figure as Napier when the Chinese expected only a commercial representative,[37] and for giving 'foolish' instructions to the superintendents.[38] Staunton pointed out that, although he had made clear to Parliament in 1833 that the prior agreement of the Chinese government was indispensable to the appointment of any British functionary at Canton, his advice had not been taken. Instead, Napier 'seems to have been simply instructed to proceed direct to Canton, and to assume at once his official character there, without the least anticipation of difficulty or discussion, just in the same way as a successor would have been appointed to any vacant Consulship in Europe'.[39] Nonetheless, Staunton maintained that 'a far greater share of the blame appears to lie with his Lordship's instructions, than with himself'.[40] On the government's decision to appoint the second and third superintendents from the EIC representatives at Canton, others maintained that this sent a wrong signal to the Chinese authorities. A writer named 'Viator' believed that the appointment of these EIC officials gave the Chinese the impression that 'the company is still paramount though in abeyance, and that the whole of the late proceedings here were a trick to terrify them into better terms'.[41] James Goddard added that the consequence was that the Chinese authorities were induced to think that 'if they could only eject Lord Napier, they would then be able to preserve the *status quo* of things, and conduct matters as heretofore'.[42]

In brief, in the years after Napier's death, various opinions were presented to explain his diplomatic failure. Although the claims that the Chinese government was at fault were popular, quite a few observers, particularly Staunton, challenged this view. They pointed out that Napier himself, the British government and the EIC were all responsible for Napier's misfortunes. These arguments, however, do not suggest that these commentators had more favourable views of China. On the contrary, some negative images which had long been held by British merchants at Canton were further confirmed by the Napier incident. Even Staunton clearly noted

> the vices of the Chinese national character, and also the vices of their political and commercial system. I shall certainly not undertake to defend either. It has been my lot, during a considerable portion of my life, to have had ample opportunities of witnessing these evils ... These evils ... I have always readily acknowledged and deplored.[43]

'Show of force'

Apart from the debate on the causes of the 'Napier Fizzle', Napier's failed effort to create fear in the Chinese government also excited a heated discussion within the British community in Canton. Was it wrong to adopt this aggressive approach? Or did it fail because it was still not resolute enough? Among various proposals on what approach ought to be employed in Britain's future contacts with China, the most popular one was 'show of force'.

'Show of force' was, in essence, a general idea advanced in miscellaneous pamphlets and articles that were widely distributed in Canton in the mid-1830s. Despite its prevalence, it was neither a policy devised by any British authority nor a rigidly defined strategy promoted by certain interest groups. Little is known about who first employed this term, but it is clear that, in the two years after the Napier incident, a number of writers began demanding the adoption of a more forceful attitude towards China in the local English-language press such as the *Canton Register* and the *Chinese Repository*.[44] Although there was a division of opinion among supporters of this theory about precisely what 'show of force' meant, they generally agreed that, as in Matheson's words, 'The time has arrived when a decisive step must be taken'.[45] In light of the experience of Napier, they argued that the British government had to adopt a harsher stance in its relations with China, otherwise the difficulties in Britain's China trade would never be satisfactorily resolved. These advocates, such as an anonymous writer for the *Chinese Repository*, proposed that a determined plenipotentiary, granted full powers and 'attended by a sufficient maritime force', should proceed to the immediate vicinity of the imperial residence at Beijing, 'for the purpose of demanding redress for injuries sustained, and negotiating a commercial treaty on a liberal basis'.[46] Only by these means, Matheson maintained, would the Chinese authorities be intimidated and the two nations' commercial intercourse be 'easily, speedily, and peaceably placed upon an honourable and secure footing'.[47] This 'show of force' approach had much in common with Napier's coercive policy, particularly in terms of taking a firm stand against the Chinese government. It was, however, based on a profound discussion over about two years and consequently the justifications for it were much more developed.

To begin with, in order to legitimise the suggested line of action, supporters of 'show of force' tended to reinforce the argument that, in so far as China had set itself against the universal laws of nations and the general interests of humankind, the British had just cause to protest. For example, in the *Canton Register*, an author maintained that:

> We must consider the Chinese either as a civilised nation, and one responsible for their own acts, or as barbarians; if as the former, we have an undoubted right to demand with the strong hand, ample satisfaction, not only for their present conduct, but for a long debt of past indignities; if as the latter, according to the usages of nations we see no valid objection to treating them just in the manner that our superior military and naval power can enable us to do, even to the occupation of a portion of their territory.[48]

With regard to the propriety of employing the discourse of universal laws in the case of China, the 'show of force' advocates pointed out that it did not make sense to talk of China being at liberty to disregard the law of nations because of China's having never recognised it. Since the law of nations is but 'the just and rational application of the law of nature to the affairs and conduct of nations', China, as a large branch of the great family of humankind, should not be exempt from 'the obligations of that law which God himself has prescribed for the conduct of his creatures'.[49] In addition, given that 'nations are under obligations to each other', China, whose laws 'are more or less hostile to a free and amicable intercourse with foreigners',[50] had violated the universal law. For these reasons, taking a strong line towards China was absolutely legitimate. From Britain's standpoint, 'it is the sacred duty of every government on earth to protect its subjects and maintain its own honor in foreign countries'.[51] From a wider point of view, it was in 'the *interest of all civilized nations*'[52] that China should be 'compelled to abandon a position so hostile to the general interests of the human race'.[53] In other words, with respect to 'show of force', 'Recent injuries demand this. Humanity demands it. And justice will approve of it.'[54]

Along with the claim that it was legitimate to interfere in Chinese affairs, advocates of 'show of force' attempted to demonstrate that such a coercive approach, supported by a British naval force, was the best course of action to take. First, experience had shown that 'the more forbearance and indulgence are shown to them [the Chinese government], the more proud and overbearing they become'.[55] The conciliatory policy hence must be abandoned. To explain such a view, Matheson maintained, 'Experience ought by this time to have shewn us that it is a foolish and useless policy to attempt to gain the confidence of the Chinese by exhibiting, as was constantly enjoined by the East India Company, a servile deference to their innumerable and absurd peculiarities and customs'.[56] Similarly, in 1834, a number of British merchants signed a memorial to King William IV calling for a more forceful stance against China. In this document, they claimed:

> we cannot but trace the disabilities and restrictions under which our commerce now labours, to a long acquiescence in the assumption of supremacy over the monarchs and people of other countries, claimed by the Emperor of China ... we are forced to conclude that no essentially beneficial result can be expected to arise out of negotiations, in which such pretensions are not decidedly repelled.[57]

Accordingly, if Britain was determined to achieve its commercial goals, it was essential to abandon the submissive policy which had previously been adopted and to employ totally different measures.

Second, advocates of 'show of force' strengthened the notion that in dealing with the 'haughty, semi-civilized, despotic' government of China, 'nothing will bring them to submission, until they have had demonstrative proofs of the force of British argument and reasoning, at the foot of the Imperial throne at Peking'.[58] This meant that a display of Britain's strength was crucial, because, according to 'a Wellwisher', only 'when force is opposed to force, their courage fails, and they prefer concession to a doubtful struggle, in which ... they can never be victorious'.[59] In support of such a view, an anonymous writer compared the Chinese government to a village cur:

> Timidity and insolence are two prominent characteristics of the Chinese government, whose conduct (to compare great things with small) is like that of a village cur. The little animal barks furiously, pursues and tries to bite the stranger who is unprovided with a stick, particularly if he runs; but when he turns round, the cur draws back; if he lifts his stick, the cur flies; if he actually strikes, the cur becomes more cautious in future not to be the aggressor, and even endeavors to conciliate the offended party by fawning and wagging his tail and licking the hand that gave the blow. This is a true picture of the conduct of the Chinese government, as every one knows who is familiar with its history.[60]

With the introduction of such an image, the argument that nothing could be expected from sending humble petitions to the Qing government certainly seemed more reasonable. As the same author asserted, 'if we wish to have a treaty with China, it must be dictated at the point of the bayonet, and enforced by arguments from the cannon's mouth'.[61]

Third, the 'show of force' advocates were confident that such strong measures could be safely adopted. Because of the supposedly timid character of the Chinese, they believed that the Qing court would make every sacrifice to avoid a dangerous confrontation with the British. To reinforce this viewpoint, Matheson maintained that the Chinese had an innate characteristic, which was 'more apt to waste the idle artillery of words in official interdiction, than to resort to serious and really threatening measures'.[62] Another commentator added that, since the emperor was definitely aware of the weakness of his empire and 'the want of loyalty in the people',[63] he would certainly not venture to resort to any hostile measures, but would seek peace. In this respect, an article in the *Chinese Repository* elaborated on this topic:

> Taoukwang [Daoguang], the present emperor of China, is a man of the most pacific disposition, who instead of annihilating daring rebels, begs their leaders to submit, and wages bloodless war against them by means of gold and silver bullets ... if the matter was once brought home to his own bosom, which has never yet been done, and if he began to see the affair in a serious light and has no alternative but acquiescence in our proposals, we are persuaded that he would quietly yield to seeming necessity.[64]

According to this view, concerns that a serious clash would ensue if Britain started a forceful policy were largely discounted.

It can be observed from the above that the advocates of 'show of force' substantially justified the opinion that a firm line of action, supported by British maritime forces, was the wisest way to deal with Chinese affairs. It was not only founded on legitimate grounds, but was also the most effective and safest line of action to force China to comply with Britain's demands. Nevertheless, while generally supporting 'show of force', these writers were divided in their attitudes towards the actual use of arms, or on whether to advocate open war against China. An examination on existing sources can reveal that, notwithstanding the strength of 'show of force', in the mid-1830s there were in fact very few commentators who openly embraced the idea of a war. At least on paper, even Matheson, who is usually considered as the key driving force behind a forceful policy, was anxious to deny at this point that he had 'any wish or suggestion which was likely to involve the two countries in a war'.[65] The Chinese historian Wu Yixiong has produced an in-depth survey of the pro-war sentiment among foreigners in Canton before the Opium War and suggested that the *Canton Register* was the most strident advocate of the hard-line policy.[66] This may be true in the period immediately before the conflict, but, published since 1827, the *Register* produced numerous articles which contained a wide range of viewpoints. In fact, in various issues of 1835 and 1836, its editor explicitly disclaimed that the newspaper had ever had any editorial policy of advocating a war against China.[67] This indicates that, in the mid-1830s, the use of arms was actually not a strategy supported by a majority at Canton.

Although straightforward appeals for open hostilities were rarely expressed in publications, it should be noted that there was widespread discussion opposing the idea of war with China.[68] This suggests that calls for violence were perhaps informally communicated on a greater scale than they appear in the published sources. The fact that there were many more public appeals against rather than in favour of a war, however, indicates that, regardless of the extent to which open hostilities against China were really wanted, the political climate at the time prevented this view from being openly stated through the press. Again, it proves that, in the mid-1830s, there was a certain degree of consensus among the British communities in Canton that it was not wise to raise the issue.

Even though the number of radical calls for war was rather limited, there were some articles expressing a clear desire to resort to force. In September 1835, a commentator wrote, 'no delicacy should be used towards the celestials; and if it be expedient to use power to compel them to our and their own goods, we ought not for a moment to hesitate to use it ... But the Chinese are too wise ever to give us the pretence'.[69] Among the available sources, this passage is probably the best evidence that at this time there were indeed some militant observers who were seeking an excuse to use force against China. As for such a 'pretence', some suggested that Britain could regard China's stoppage of trade – the usual check applied by the Qing government on foreign merchants – as a virtual declaration of war. If the Chinese ever ventured to repeat that policy, it could provide Britain with a great opportunity to avoid the moral responsibility of waging a war. For example, an author named 'an enemy to half-measures' claimed that 'any threat on the part of the Chinese officers to resort to their favourite and hitherto too successful policy – a stoppage of trade ... should be instantly retaliated: for it is a declaration of war, a cartel of defiance, a manifestation of passive hostility'.[70] In such an event, others believed that it would look as if China 'is determined to precipitate an open rupture', and it would 'surely deserve little sympathy'.[71] For this reason, an author for the *Canton Register* was confident enough to write that, 'If her forts have been dismantled, her troops killed and, her laws and territory violated, what induced these acts? her own ignorance, falsehood, treachery and cowardice. Let China avenge her own wrongs; let her redress the grievances of foreigners and she will remove the cause of too probable future wrongs.'[72]

In contrast to such militant views, the vast majority of the 'show of force' advocates, although in support of a more determined attitude from the British government, were clearly not in favour of open hostilities against China. On the grounds of justice and expediency, they disapproved of any step which might lead to bloodshed in China. For instance, an article in the *Canton Register* claimed that 'the act of pillaging and destroying the towns and villages of the Chinese people, merely because they refuse to enter into any treaty of commerce, alliance, or friendship with us' would be 'atrocious' conduct.[73] In the *Chinese Repository*, another author stated that 'We abhor bloodshed and that policy which would build up its own prosperity on the ruins of others. We advocate no course which is repugnant to justice or the laws of nations.'[74] Those who rejected the resort to force for practical reasons were worried that military action might result in unexpected consequences which could ruin Britain's commerce in China. One of them pointed out that 'the Chinese may imitate the example of the Japanese, and exclude all foreigners forever, or cut down the tea shrub and put an effectual stop to foreign commerce'.[75] In that case, the entire Sino-British trade would be endangered. Others, such as the following commentator in the *Canton Press*, reminded the public that:

> this Government ... had, still the extraordinary power and influence to order its subjects to retire ... from the coast into the interior of the country to avoid intercourse ... and to enforce obedience to that order. Suppose that a British force were to land at Tiensing and similar orders were given and obeyed, might not the Expedition be thereby considerably embarrassed? Or if this is not the case, supposing the Emperor sufficiently uncompromising, to render hostilities indispensable, is a force of 600 soldiers sufficient to march up to Peking ... can it for one moment be reasonably supposed that if the Emperor be really willing ... to oppose his forces to this aggression, that he would not succeed in overcoming so very trifling an armament? ... The mildest treatment of the Chinese would be to confiscate our property as a setoff for damage sustained in the north, and expel us for ever from the country. We could in justice not find fault with this.[76]

In the mid-1830s, these considerations led many to maintain that it would be improper to wage war against China. As a result, the majority of the 'show of force' advocates were further persuaded that open hostilities against China were inappropriate under the present circumstances.

For most 'show of force' supporters, their concerns over the danger of resorting to military action did not prevent them from insisting on the necessity of impressing the Chinese government with a sense of Britain's power. Although some of them identified their views in different ways such as a 'middle course' or a 'half-way measure' (these terms perhaps have confused some modern readers), these observers tended to agree that Britain should adopt neither open violence nor unconditional submission in its relations with China.[77] They were convinced that a firm resolve, accompanied by a demonstration of Britain's ability to resort to extreme measures, would be the most effective measure, because 'we can demand everything from the fears of the Chinese Government, but nothing from their good will'.[78] For this reason, it was vital to dispatch a plenipotentiary who was 'firm of purpose and strong of nerve, armed with discretionary powers',[79] to remonstrate with the emperor, both to command respect from the Chinese and to allow 'no encroachment on our rights or insult to our national honor to pass with impunity'.[80] Commentators such as 'A Wellwisher' and Matheson considered this course of conduct as the surest way to success. For one thing, 'Such firmness carries greater force of conviction to the Chinese than the best diplomatic arguments ... the less that proof by words is resorted to, and the more it is shown by incontestable facts, that the plenipotentiary is an immovable man, the greater will be his success'.[81] For another, given the present state of China and the character of the nation, a 'show' of Britain's naval power would definitely not result in open violence, but would hasten the conclusion of an amicable arrangement with the country: 'A glimpse of one or two of our men-of-war stationed off the north-eastern coast of China, would send a thrill of consternation through the whole empire, and do more to incline the Chinese to listen to the dictates of reason and justice than centuries of "temporizing" and submission to insult and oppression.'[82] Matheson hence concluded that 'the surest preventive of war is an unequivocal manifestation of our being neither unable nor unprepared, on its becoming necessary, to resort to it'.[83]

In sum, although 'show of force' was the most prominent strategy advocated in Canton in the mid-1830s, there was no agreement about how it should be implemented. Among the advocates of this approach were those who simply wanted the Chinese to recognise the strength of the forces at Britain's disposal, whereas others were much readier to support the actual use of force. A detailed examination of the available sources can show that the vast majority of observers in Canton at this time held the former point of view. On the one hand, they insisted that it was crucial to adopt a resolute line of action, supported by a display of Britain's maritime power; but, on the other hand, it was unjust and impractical to resort to a serious use of violence or to open war. It can therefore be inferred that, for most of the 'show of force' advocates, the significance of this new strategy rested not on any physical harm being inflicted on the Chinese empire but on the psychological impact that it would have on the Qing authorities. These commentators were most concerned that advocating this new course of action would signal a change in Britain's official attitude towards China, that is from unresisting submission to firm determination. It was for this change, rather than for direct armed intervention, that the majority of British residents in Canton had been waiting and lobbying.

'Minor' voices

In addition to the widespread discussion of 'show of force', other 'minor' voices were advanced in this period on Britain's future relations with China. As with the 'show of force' advocates, those who held these 'minor' views can be found across different social groups, including the British merchants and missionaries in Canton. These observers concurred with the majority of the 'show of force' supporters in opposing open hostilities, but they also attempted to find better alternatives to aggressive military actions:

First, instead of advocating a show of strength in the vicinity of Beijing, some proposed economic blockade as a means to exert pressure on the Chinese government. A correspondent for the *Canton Register* suggested that, if the local authorities in Canton ventured to stop the trade again, the British should respond strongly to ensure that 'their [the Chinese] own trade will be stopped as long as ours continued to be so'.[84] Karl Gützlaff, the Protestant missionary, agreed that this was 'the least bloody and the most efficacious' plan, because 'The trade along the coast is enormous and feeds myriads; as soon as it ceases ... the effects would be dreadful, so much so, that the local government, as well as the Court, would pray for the resuming of the trade, with more humanity than we ever intend to do'.[85] The correspondent for the *Canton Register* went on to argue that this course of action was feasible. Given the numerous navigable rivers leading to some of China's major cities, and that the forts along the coast were 'in the most defenceless state', he drew up a plan to cut off communications between key ports along the coast and the rest of the country by only thirteen British warships.[86] In this way, he hoped and believed that, through a non-violent but resolute economic blockade, the British could make the Qing court realise that Britain was able to threaten the economic vitality of its maritime provinces and even to endanger its control over the whole country. As a consequence, the Chinese government would soon change its attitude and policies towards Britain in a way favourable to the latter.

Second, in his public letter to Palmerston, Lindsay advanced another proposal alongside his references to a coercive line of action. He suggested the withdrawal of all political establishments from China, and the appointment of 'a person of no pretensions' as agent for the customs, whose duty was simply 'registering ships' papers, and countersigning manifests'.[87] Lindsay explained that:

> This mode of procedure will be highly embarrassing to the Chinese authorities, who are most anxious to see some recognised chief at Canton for the purpose, as they term it, of 'managing and controlling all affairs of the English nation;' and on the very first difficulty or dispute which occurs, they will most anxiously inquire, why no such authority exists. Our reply then is obvious: 'It is your own fault; for, when we sent one to you, you treated him with insult; and it is incompatible with the dignity of England that a representative of her sovereign should be subject to such indignity; no chief will, therefore, be sent until you promise him "proper reception and treatment"'.[88]

Goddard agreed that it was wiser to develop a purely commercial intercourse than to preserve expensive political establishments. In his opinion, to leave the trade to the 'patient, thrifty, dexterous assiduity of private and untrammelled enterprise' would be helpful to British merchants in Canton. As 'guardians of their own anomalous privileges', they should be allowed to 'protect themselves in the best way they could against the encroachments of the Chinese'.[89] Staunton, in his *Remarks on the British Relations with China*, also expressed his support for Lindsay's second proposal. He described it as 'a plan, easy and simple, perfectly peaceable as well as legitimate'.[90] Instead of seeking to instil fear in the Chinese, this proposal, 'by a merely negative course of proceeding', placed them 'in such a highly embarrassing predicament ... that they must very shortly become most anxious to do that of their own accord, which it is not quite certain that all our embargoes and blockades would extort from them'.[91] In addition, Staunton suggested that, in concert with the political withdrawal, Britain should try to set up a trading post beyond the limits of Chinese jurisdiction: 'there is an infinite number of intermediate islands ... which might be taken possession of, not only without a contest, but without the violation of any right in practical exercise'.[92] Given the commercially oriented character of the Chinese, Staunton predicted that the Chinese 'would not hesitate to trade with foreigners there, if they could be assured of receiving protection'.[93] In this way, such a trading station could put British–Chinese relations on to a thoroughly commercial basis. As a result, Britain's profitable trade with China would be conducted in the most pacific and lawful manner.

Third, others who believed in the peaceful benefits of commerce contended that nothing was more trustworthy than the 'irresistible and expansive energy of the free trade'.[94] Some of these observers maintained that, since China had enough resources to isolate itself from the rest of the world, too precipitate an attempt to coerce its government to change its commercial policy would only retard the progress of mutually beneficial trade.[95] Moreover, 'the Chinese government and people are not yet sufficiently advanced in civilisation to be capable of forming a reasonable commercial treaty'.[96] For this reason, an immediate demand for a treaty might place unnecessary burdens on the British government. The best course of action at this stage, therefore, should simply be to trust 'the gradual operation of time',[97] so that, with the progress of trade, the obstacles and prejudices in China would ultimately be overcome. An article in the *Canton Press* elaborated on what would happen as a result of such a policy:

> whilst on continuing a course of quiet and unassuming trade, which brings us in continual and ... extensive intercourse with the mass of the people, these will soon become aware of many of the disabilities under which we labour, and from which they equally suffer. Such a state of things must lead to evasion of the imposed regulations. The people find it their interest to treat us well to secure their own welfare, and public opinion among Chinese even is strong enough to make itself heard by its rulers ... The rapacity of the Local Government is too great to allow so rich a prize to escape without attempting to draw large profits from it individually. The consequence will be, that the too heavily taxed commodity will not only continue to be smuggled into the ports of the eastern coast, but will be sent there in greater quantities than ever ... and the Government at Peking failed in obtaining the object it had in view, viz, that of preventing foreign ships from visiting other ports than Canton will have at no very remote date to concede to us the freedom of these ports, in order to enjoy the revenue of which under the present system it is deprived.[98]

According to this view, although 'The process will be slow, [and] the result doubtful',[99] the advantages that might arise would be enormous once the Chinese authorities realised the reciprocal benefits of international trade. For this reason, as well as for its perfectly peaceful nature, an author named R.I. (possibly Sir Robert Inglis) considered this course of action as 'the true policy of foreign states in their communications with China, and the only policy which the Chinese government in its present state of knowledge is likely, or possibly, able to pursue towards foreigners'.[100]

Last, some commentators, perhaps mostly Protestant missionaries, did not agree with the belief in the progressive impact of commerce. They maintained that the spread of Christianity and of useful knowledge was the best means to develop Britain's future relations with China. These observers contended that a purely commercial course of action was more applicable to the uncivilised races of the islands than to the comparatively refined Continental nations. In the case of China, the most effective line of action would be not to wait passively for the long-term results of economic improvement but to actively '*attempt the amelioration of the condition of China*',[101] through 'the diffusion of knowledge and the dissemination of religious truth'.[102] In the opinions of these writers, China had long been suffering an intellectual and moral darkness, which had suppressed the genius of the Chinese people and inhibited 'almost entirely that interchange of thought and those kind offices of humanity, which the Almighty has vouchsafed to his creatures as their birth right'.[103] For this reason, the Chinese 'cannot make known their wishes or sufferings to each other, or join in any determination to acquire new privileges or redress old wrongs'.[104] Furthermore, the previously advanced Chinese civilisation had fallen far behind the cultivated nations of the West. Nevertheless, 'The Chinese are by no means such a forlorn race, so incapable of improvement'.[105] What they needed was nothing but the moral power of Christianity and the knowledge of Western sciences and arts. Hence, it was the divine duty of the spiritually advanced nations to enlighten the minds and secure the salvation of the Chinese. Once darkness was dispelled, the foundations of friendly relations between China and Western countries would be laid and, consequently, they would remove the evils which restricted foreign trade. As one commentator stated: 'Truth is our object ... we do wish and hope and desire to bear a humble part in labours to concentrate the energies of all in just and generous efforts to improve the condition of China. This is DUTY.'[106] 'Knowledge is strength', another one added, 'if we can show our mental superiority, and excite congenial feelings in the breast of those to whom we communicate our sciences, we shall marshal the minds of the people, and have public opinion in our favour'.[107]

In conclusion, apart from the support for 'show of force', a variety of opinions were expressed in the press at Canton about the best line of action to be employed against China. Although individually none of these 'minor' voices was able to outweigh the former in terms of scale and influence, their significance seems greater when they are

'SHOW OF FORCE'

viewed as a whole. Since those who suggested alternative approaches concurred with the majority of the 'show of force' advocates in opposing open hostilities, the voices against a violent policy were in fact in a clear majority, even though a war with China did become more imaginable after the Napier incident. For this reason, the prevailing historical interpretation that 1834 marked the beginning of Britain's pro-war attitude towards China deserves serious reconsideration. Since no one at the time could have known that a war would break out in just a few years, we cannot view it retrospectively and maintain that the Opium War had become inevitable from this time onwards. The mid-1830s, therefore, should be considered more as a period of confused thinking with regard to Britain's China policy, rather than a clear stage in the preparation for a military conflict.

Notes

1. Extract from the Royal Sign Manual Instructions to the Superintendents of Trade in China, 31 Dec. 1833, in Great Britain, Parliament, *Correspondence Relating to China, Presented to Both Houses of Parliament, by Command of Her Majesty* (London: T.R. Harrison, 1840), p. 3.
2. For example, Michael Greenberg, *British Trade and the Opening of China 1800–42* (Cambridge: Cambridge University Press, 1951), p. 191; Maurice Collis, *Foreign Mud: Being an Account of the Opium Imbroglio at Canton in the 1830s and the Anglo-Chinese War that Followed* (London: Faber, 1964), pp. 108–25; and Brian Inglis, *The Opium War* (London: Hodder and Stoughton, 1976), p. 89.
3. Glenn Melancon, 'Peaceful Intentions: The First British Trade Commission in China, 1833–5', *Historical Research*, 73 (2000), 33–47, at p. 47. Melancon has elaborated this argument in his book *Britain's China Policy and the Opium Crisis: Balancing Drugs, Violence and National Honour, 1833–40* (Aldershot: Ashgate, 2003).
4. Ulrike Hillemann, *Asian Empire and British Knowledge: China and the Networks of British Imperial Expansion* (Basingstoke: Palgrave Macmillan, 2009), p. 92. Julia Lovell has suggested that Napier 'succeeded ... in moving Anglo-Chinese relations closer towards the possibility of armed conflict', see Julia Lovell, *The Opium War: Drugs, Dreams and the Making of China* (London: Picador, 2011), p. 8.
5. Chapter 2 of Gelber's book deals specifically with the general outlook of the British government in London. See Harry G. Gelber, *Opium, Soldiers and Evangelicals: Britain's 1840–42 War with China, and Its Aftermath* (New York: Palgrave Macmillan, 2004), pp. 19–39.
6. Greenberg maintained that perhaps 'the most important consequence of 1834' was that the weight of the home manufacturing interests in Britain was thrown behind a 'forward policy' in China (see Greenberg, *British Trade and the Opening of China*, p. 195). Nevertheless, no matter whether they are viewed individually or as a whole, in the mid-1830s the British community in China and concerned interest groups in Britain did not yet possess a strong voice in shaping government policies. The British government did not take the China question seriously until reports about the opium crisis reached London in August 1839.
7. Melancon, 'Peaceful Intentions', p. 47. Similar opinion can be found in W.T. Hanes III and F. Sanello, *The Opium Wars: The Addiction of One Empire and the Corruption of Another* (Naperville, IL: Sourcebooks, 2002), p. 32. Song-Chuan Chen has recently identified a 'warlike party' and a 'pacific party'. His book emphasises more the

PRELUDE TO THE OPIUM WAR

views of the former. See Song-Chuan Chen, *Merchants of War and Peace: British Knowledge of China in the Making of the Opium War* (Hong Kong: Hong Kong University Press, 2017).

8 Napier to Palmerston, 14 Aug. 1834, in *Correspondence Relating to China*, p. 14.
9 Napier to Grey, 21 Aug. 1834, in *ibid.*, p. 26.
10 Napier, 10 Mar. 1834, 'From the MS. Memoir Vol. 2', Remarks and Extracts Relative to Diplomatic Relations with China, Napier and Ettrick Papers, in Melancon, *Britain's China Policy and the Opium Crisis*, p. 37. Napier, however, was not specific about these past experiences.
11 Napier to Palmerston, 14 Aug. 1834, in *Correspondence Relating to China*, p. 14.
12 Napier to the Hong merchants and Chinese authorities, 8 Sept. 1834, in *ibid.*, p. 36.
13 Napier to Palmerston, 14 Aug. 1834, in *ibid.*, p. 15.
14 Napier to the Hong merchants and Chinese authorities, 8 Sept. 1834, in *ibid.*, p. 36.
15 Napier to Palmerston, 14 Aug. 1834, in *ibid.*, p. 14.
16 Same letter, in *ibid.*, pp. 13–14.
17 Napier to Grey, 21 Aug. 1834, in *ibid.*, p. 28.
18 Napier to Palmerston, 14 Aug. 1834, in *ibid.*, p. 13.
19 Hugh Hamilton Lindsay, *Letter to the Right Honourable Viscount Palmerston on British Relations with China* (London: Saunders and Otley, 1836), p. 6.
20 *Ibid.*, p. 3.
21 G.J. Gordon, *Address to the People of Great Britain, Explanatory of Our Commercial Relations with the Empire of China* (London: Smith, Elder, 1836), p. 12.
22 Anon., 'British Authorities in China', *Chinese Repository*, III, no. 10 (Feb. 1835), 472.
23 A quote of Vattel's, cited in James Matheson, *The Present Position and Prospects of the British Trade with China; Together with an Outline of Some Leading Occurrences in Its Past History* (London: Smith, Elder, 1836), p. 34.
24 *Canton Register*, VIII, no. 39 (29 Sept. 1835), 156. The *Canton Register* was China's first English-language newspaper. It was founded in November 1827 by the Scottish merchants James Matheson and his nephew Alexander, together with Philadelphian William Wightman Wood, who was the first editor.
25 Matheson, *The Present Position*, p. 49.
26 Anon., 'Universal Peace; Obstacles to It in the Character and Government of Nations', *Chinese Repository*, III, no. 11 (March 1835), 527. The *Chinese Repository* was founded in May 1832 by Elijah Coleman Bridgman, the first American Protestant missionary appointed to China.
27 Anon., 'Brito-Chinese Politics', *Canton Press*, I, no. 49 (13 Aug. 1836), 388.
28 Anon., 'The Chinese Trade', *Canton Register*, VIII, no. 28 (14 July 1835), 113.
29 George Thomas Staunton, *Remarks on the British Relations with China, and the Proposed Plans for Improving Them* (London: Edmund Lloyd, 1836), p. 26.
30 *Ibid.*, pp. 18–19.
31 *Ibid.*, pp. 17–18.
32 *Ibid.*, p. 23.
33 *Ibid.*, pp. 23–4.
34 *Ibid.*, pp. 26–7.
35 On 16 January 1831, the viceroy Li Hongbin, after being informed about the possible dissolution of the East India Company, issued an edict requiring the chief of the British factory to pass on the message that 'it was incumbent on the British Government to appoint a Chief to come to Canton, for the general management of commercial dealings, and to prevent affairs from going to confusion'. Some British commentators used it as evidence that the Chinese government invited the British superintendent of trade to come to Canton. For Napier's original wording, see Napier, 'Present State of Relations between China and Great Britain – Interesting to the Chinese Merchants – A True and Official Document', Canton, 26 Aug. 1834, in *Correspondence Relating to China*, p. 33.

'SHOW OF FORCE'

36 Staunton, *Remarks on the British Relations with China*, p. 43. Italics in the original.
37 James Goddard, *Remarks on the Late Lord Napier's Mission to Canton; in Reference to the Present State of Our Relations with China* (London: printed for private circulation, 1836), p. 12.
38 *Canton Press*, I, no. 36 (14 May 1836), 283.
39 Staunton, *Remarks on the British Relations with China*, p. 19.
40 *Ibid*.
41 Viator, 'To the Editor of the Canton Register', *Canton Register*, VIII, no. 11 (17 March 1835), 44.
42 Goddard, *Remarks on the Late Lord Napier's Mission*, p. 5.
43 Staunton, *Remarks on the British Relations with China*, p. 40.
44 Some of these writers can be identified as British. Some are anonymous.
45 Matheson, *The Present Position*, p. 79.
46 Anon., 'British Authorities in China', *Chinese Repository*, III, no. 8 (Dec. 1834), 363; Lindsay, *Letter to the Right Honourable Viscount Palmerston*, p. 12.
47 Matheson, *The Present Position*, p. 70.
48 *Canton Register*, VIII, no. 39 (29 Sept. 1835), 156.
49 Matheson, *The Present Position*, pp. 49–50.
50 Anon., 'Negotiation with China', *Chinese Repository*, III, no. 9 (Jan. 1835), 422.
51 Anon., 'War with China', *Canton Register*, VIII, no. 8 (25 Feb. 1835), 31.
52 An enemy to half-measures, 'What Steps Should the Expected Strength from England Take?', *Canton Register*, VIII, no. 14 (7 Apr. 1835), 54. Italics in the original.
53 Gordon, *Address to the People of Great Britain*, p. 16.
54 Anon., 'Negotiation with China', *Chinese Repository*, III, no. 9 (Jan. 1835), 421.
55 Anon., 'British Authorities in China', *Chinese Repository*, III, no. 8 (Dec. 1834), 362.
56 Matheson, *The Present Position*, p. 63.
57 'To the King's most Excellent Majesty in Council: the Petition of the undermentioned British Subjects at Canton' (also known as the 'Canton Petition'), 9 Dec. 1834, in A. Le Pichon (ed.), *China Trade and Empire: Jardine, Matheson & Co. and the Origins of British Rule in Hong Kong 1827–1843* (Oxford: Oxford University Press, 2006), p. 563.
58 *Canton Press*, I, no. 18 (9 Jan. 1836), 138.
59 A Wellwisher, 'Intercourse with China', *Chinese Repository*, III, no. 9 (Jan. 1835), 401.
60 Anon., 'Treaty with the Chinese, a Great Desideratum', *Chinese Repository*, IV, no. 10 (Feb. 1836), 448. The author of this article may be Charles W. King, an American merchant.
61 *Ibid.*, 446.
62 Matheson, *The Present Position*, p. 59.
63 *Canton Register*, VII, no. 16 (22 April 1834), 62.
64 Anon., 'Treaty with the Chinese', *Chinese Repository*, IV, no. 10 (Feb. 1836), 446.
65 Matheson, *The Present Position*, p. 59.
66 Wu Yixiong, 'Yapian Zhanzheng qian Zaihua Xiren yu Duihua Zhanzheng Yulun de Xingcheng (The Formation of a General Sentiment among Westerners in China for Waging War against China before the Opium War)', *Jindai Shi Yanjiu* (Modern Chinese History Studies), 2 (2009), 23–43.
67 For example, 'Supplement to the Calcutta Courier, Feby. 7', *Canton Register*, VIII, no. 21 (26 May 1835), 83; *Canton Register*, IX, no. 33 (16 Aug. 1836), 134.
68 See, for example, Anon., 'Free Trade to China', *Canton Register*, VII, no. 26 (1 July 1834), 101–3; Anon., 'Treaty with the Chinese', *Chinese Repository*, IV, no. 10 (Feb. 1836), 441–9; Anon., 'Brito-Chinese Polities', *Canton Press*, I, no. 49 (13 Aug. 1836), 387–9.
69 *Canton Register*, VIII, no. 39 (29 Sept. 1835), 156.
70 An enemy to half-measures, 'What Steps Should the Expected Strength from England Take?', *Canton Register*, VIII, no. 14 (7 Apr. 1835), 54.

PRELUDE TO THE OPIUM WAR

71 Anon., 'War with China', *Canton Register*, VIII, no. 8 (25 Feb. 1835), 31.
72 *Canton Register*, IX, no. 33 (16 Aug. 1836), 134.
73 Anon., 'Free Trade to China', *Canton Register*, VII, no. 26 (1 July 1834), 102.
74 Anon., 'Treaty with the Chinese', *Chinese Repository*, IV, no. 10 (Feb. 1836), 447.
75 *Ibid.*, 446.
76 Anon., 'Brito-Chinese Politics', *Canton Press*, I, no. 49 (13 Aug. 1836), 388.
77 See, for example, A Wellwisher, 'Intercourse with China', *Chinese Repository*, III, no. 9 (Jan. 1835), 393–405; Anon., 'Treaty with the Chinese', *Chinese Repository*, IV, no. 10 (Feb. 1836), 441–9. The former contains four letters by different writers.
78 The National Archives of the UK: Public Record Office, FO 17/9/148, Gützlaff, 'Present state of our relations with China', separate enclosure, Robinson to Palmerston, 26 March 1835.
79 A Wellwisher, 'Intercourse with China', *Chinese Repository*, III, no. 9 (Jan. 1835), 403.
80 Anon., 'Treaty with the Chinese', *Chinese Repository*, IV, no. 10 (Feb. 1836), 447.
81 A Wellwisher, 'Intercourse with China', *Chinese Repository*, III, no. 9 (Jan. 1835), 404.
82 Matheson, *The Present Position*, pp. 62–3.
83 *Ibid.*, p. 78.
84 A correspondent, 'Character of the Chinese', *Canton Register*, VII, no. 50 (16 Dec. 1834), 200.
85 TNA: PRO, FO 17/9/152, FO 17/9/150, Gützlaff, 'Present state of our relations with China'.
86 A correspondent, 'Character of the Chinese', *Canton Register*, VII, no. 50 (16 Dec. 1834), 200–1.
87 Lindsay, *Letter to the Right Honourable Viscount Palmerston*, p. 5.
88 *Ibid.*
89 Goddard, *Remarks on the Late Lord Napier's Mission*, pp. 16–17.
90 Staunton, *Remarks on the British Relations with China*, p. 31.
91 *Ibid.*
92 *Ibid.*, p. 42. This opinion coincided with Napier's view in August 1834. In his correspondence with Earl Grey, to 'take possession of the island of Hong Kong' was mentioned for the very first time to the British government. See Napier to Grey, Canton, 21 Aug. 1834, in *Correspondence Relating to China*, p. 27.
93 Staunton, *Remarks on the British Relations with China*, p. 42.
94 A correspondent, 'Commercial Treaty with China', *Canton Register*, VIII, no. 4 (27 Jan. 1835), 14.
95 R.I., 'Notices of Modern China', *Chinese Repository*, V, no. 5 (Sept. 1836), 211–12.
96 A correspondent, 'Commercial Treaty with China', *Canton Register*, VIII, no. 4 (27 Jan. 1835), 14.
97 *Ibid.*
98 Anon., 'Brito-Chinese Politics', *Canton Press*, I, no. 49 (13 Aug. 1836), 388.
99 Goddard, *Remarks on the Late Lord Napier's Mission*, p. 18.
100 R.I., 'Notices of Modern China', *Chinese Repository*, V, no. 5 (Sept. 1836), 207.
101 Anon., 'Free Intercourse between China and Christendom', *Chinese Repository*, V, no. 6 (Oct. 1836), 242. Italics in the original.
102 An American Merchant, 'Remarks on British Relations and Intercourse with China', *Chinese Repository*, III, no. 9 (Jan. 1835), 412.
103 Anon., 'British Authorities in China', *Chinese Repository*, III, no. 8 (Dec. 1834), 361.
104 Anon., 'Free Intercourse between China and Christendom', *Chinese Repository*, V, no. 6 (Oct. 1836), 257.
105 *Canton Register*, VII, no. 16 (22 April 1834), 62.
106 Anon., 'Free Intercourse between China and Christendom', *Chinese Repository*, V, no. 6 (Oct. 1836), 242.
107 *Canton Register*, VII, no. 16 (22 April 1834), 62.

CHAPTER FIVE

Justifying the Opium War

Lord Napier and most British observers in the mid-1830s could not have foreseen that a large-scale military conflict would break out between Britain and China within just a few years. As discussed in the Introduction, much has been written about this milestone in the history of Sino-Western encounters – the First Anglo-Chinese War, or the Opium War – but some important questions have escaped our close attention. When exactly did the war begin? Some maintain that it was in 1839; others believe that it began in 1840. What was the immediate trigger for this conflict? Was it Lin Zexu's campaign to stamp out the opium trade, or Charles Elliot's 'heroic' intervention in the opium crisis, or the murder of Lin Weixi, a Chinese villager who was allegedly killed by a British seaman? A war in defence of a contraband trade, of course, sounds morally unjustifiable, but then why should MP George Palmer claim, in the parliamentary debate held in April 1840, that 'no member was willing to declare himself directly opposed to a war with China'?[1] If this was the case, what is even more puzzling is that the Whig government won the debate by only a narrow majority (271 votes to 262) – how can we explain this close result? Moreover, the timing of the debate seems doubtful. If the war started in 1839 or early the following year, why were British MPs still debating the question of how Britain should deal with the China dispute in April 1840? These questions are not merely technical issues, but help us to understand how such an important event as the Opium War has been remembered, neglected, contested and 're-invented' in different settings. Answers to these questions, therefore, need to be addressed to advance our understanding of the origins of the Opium War.

PRELUDE TO THE OPIUM WAR

1839 or 1840?

The starting point of the Opium War is disputable because neither the British nor the Chinese government officially declared war on the other. Scholars in the People's Republic of China overwhelmingly believe that the war started in 1840 when the British expeditionary force arrived in China and went into action. The dating used by those outside PRC academia varies – some of them clearly state that the war began in 1839 when the first shots were fired in the aftermath of the Lin Weixi incident; others simply pick either 1839 or 1840 without looking further into it. To determine a precise time for the beginning of the warfare, however, is not a trivial matter, because, one could argue, recognising 1839 as the starting point of the conflict can indicate a greater degree of sympathy with the contemporary official British narrative justifying the war. The main storyline offered in such a narrative normally runs as follows: for most of the eighteenth century, opium, recognised as a form of medicine, was admitted into China on the payment of an import duty. The Jiaqing emperor banned the trade in 1796, but this prohibition proved to be ineffectual because of the connivance of corrupt local authorities and the perseverance of foreign opium traders, most of whom were British. The supply of opium kept increasing at a dramatic rate. By the late 1830s, the quantity imported into China annually reached 40,200 chests, approximately forty times more than the amount when opium was first declared contraband (each chest contained 140 lb/63.5 kg). As a result, opium smoking spread rapidly in China and it caused a series of problems for the Qing. Not only was the physical and moral welfare of the Chinese people threatened, but a vast amount of silver was flowing out of the country to pay for the opium imports. In this context, after some deliberation on whether to legalise the trade, the Daoguang emperor finally decided to adopt stringent measures. He appointed Lin Zexu, an honest, energetic and determined man, as imperial commissioner with extraordinary powers to eliminate the opium trade.

As soon as Lin Zexu reached Canton, in March 1839, he issued an edict requiring all opium to be surrendered. In order to enforce obedience to this demand, Lin Zexu suspended all international trade in Canton and detained the entire foreign community within their factories. He also demanded that all foreigners sign a 'no-opium-trade' bond, the breaking of which was subject to capital punishment. Learning of these events, Charles Elliot, the chief superintendent of British trade with China, who was then at Macao, lost no time in going to Canton. No sooner had he arrived at the British factory than he found himself under restraint as well. On 27 March, in this 'imprisoned and harassed condition',[2]

Elliot yielded to circumstances. Believing that 'the safety of a great mass of human life hung upon my [his] decision',[3] Elliot ordered all British subjects to give up their opium to Chinese authorities, with a promise of compensation from the British government. In consequence, 20,283 chests of opium were handed over to the Qing.[4] The confinement of foreigners in Canton ended and the British retreated to Macao. Soon afterwards, however, not only did the British merchants resume the sale of opium, which exasperated Lin Zexu, but a riot took place in Kowloon (Jiulong) in July. Six drunken British sailors vandalised a temple and were involved in killing Lin Weixi, a Chinese native. Lin Zexu demanded the surrender of these British suspects, but Elliot refused to hand over anyone for trial under Chinese justice, for fear that the Chinese might use torture to secure confessions. Angered by the violation of China's sovereignty, Lin Zexu stopped trade again, cut off supplies for Macao and moved two thousand troops to an adjacent town. Meanwhile, rumours began to spread that the Chinese had poisoned some wells. Under these circumstances, all British subjects, including women and children, were compelled to abandon their dwellings and to seek refuge on board the merchant fleet off Hong Kong. Determined to drive the British out of Chinese territory, Lin Zexu prohibited the sale of food to the British. He also commanded the natives to fire upon and seize the British whenever they went on shore. In this situation, on 4 September 1839, a skirmish took place at Kowloon. To some historians, 'the first shots' in the Opium War were 'exchanged' in this event, later known as the battle of Kowloon,[5] although technically it was the British who started shooting.

This storyline underlines three aspects in explaining the origins of the Opium War, and none of these empathises greatly with the Chinese. To begin with, historians often stress that, before the Daoguang emperor took the decision to wipe out the opium trade, he faced an internal debate within his court over the legalisation of the trade. James Polachek has commented extensively on this debate and he used it to coin the title of his famous book *The Inner Opium War*.[6] According to his narrative, which has now become a common way to contextualise the Opium War, a legalisation faction, mostly mandarins from the Guangdong government, argued that banning opium would achieve nothing, while legalising the trade could end the corruption in Canton and bring in a steady revenue through import tariffs. An anti-opium lobby led by Huang Juezi opposed this proposal. This group maintained that opium smoking was enfeebling the nation and urged the Daoguang emperor to pursue the prohibitions with greater rigour than before. After serious consideration, the emperor opted for a vigorous crackdown on opium. He chose Lin Zexu, one of Huang Juezi's staunch supporters, to carry out this policy. On the basis on this storyline, Polachek not only identified a group of literati officials of the 'Spring Purification party'[7] as the prime movers of the Qing's foreign-trade policies, but claimed that the Chinese were responsible for the outbreak of the Opium War. It was 'the Ch'ing [Qing] government, and *not* the British', he maintained, which 'took the really active role in forcing a diplomatic and military showdown ... under the influence primarily of *internal* political pressures, and not foreign economic or military threat'.[8] It is unclear what inspired Polachek to develop this line of reasoning, but similar ideas did exist in the propaganda of nineteenth-century British opium merchants in Canton and their campaigners back home.[9] Although they had neither the opportunity nor the ability to access the materials that Polachek used as primary historical sources, such interpretations of Chinese court politics well suited their agenda to abdicate responsibility for causing the war. They also helped them to understate the harmfulness of opium, because emphasising the emperor's hesitation on the prohibition carried the connotation that the Qing's anti-opium campaign was to a great extent prompted by commercial concerns – to stop the outward flow of silver – rather than by moral concerns as claimed by the Qing government. More of this will be discussed later in this chapter.

Mao Haijian's in-depth research on Chinese sources has shown that these interpretations of prewar Qing politics are untenable. Most importantly, Polachek and others have overlooked a key aspect of Chinese political culture. Unlike in the party politics of today's West, in imperial China the personal opinions of officials were never as significant as one might think. Trying to anticipate and cater to the perceived outlook of the emperor had long been a feature of many members of the Chinese bureaucracy (although this might also apply to other premodern bureaucracies). Particularly, in the Daoguang reign, the court was staffed by many 'irresponsible, fraudulent and incompetent functionaries',[10] who 'did not express their own convictions', but 'sought to please the emperor by figuring out his intensions and putting them into practice'.[11] In such a political climate that only promoted 'yes-men', to conform to the emperor's expectations was of paramount importance. Therefore, whether an official decided to be for or against anti-opium measures, he did so to a great extent because he was trying to interpret the monarch's will and to align himself with policies emanating from the throne. Moreover, the Daoguang emperor actually received only two memorials advocating the lifting of the opium ban – one in 1834 by Lu Kun, the governor of Guangdong and Guangxi, the other in 1836 by Xu Naiji, a junior minister in the Court of Imperial Sacrifice who had worked in Guangdong – both memorials attempted to sound out whether the emperor had sympathy for legalisation and both were rejected. Since the emperor later forced Xu Naiji into retirement, no official dared to risk his position by putting forward a similar proposal. For these reasons, Mao reached the conclusion that the call for legalising the opium trade was just a minority opinion and that there was no such 'legalisation faction'.[12] The Japanese scholar Inoue Hiromasa's study on the Qing opium policy can also confirm this view. He added that since the talk about legalisation had ended in 1836, the so-called internal debate between the legalisation and the anti-opium lobbies did not actually exist. According to Inoue's close reading of Qing edicts and memorials, there were indeed officials who disagreed with Huang Juezi, but that was on his proposal in 1838 (two years later than Xu Naiji's memorial) to execute opium addicts. Disagreeing with this extreme measure did not make these officials supporters of a policy of legalisation. In fact, the vast majority of the twenty-nine officials who responded to the Daoguang emperor on Huang Juezi's call for death penalty made clear to the monarch that the government should act strongly against the trade.[13] Hence, again, it proves that the Daoguang emperor's indecisive attitude towards the opium ban has been exaggerated in some of the existing scholarship.

Another aspect that has previously been highlighted to explain the outbreak of the Opium War is that Lin Zexu's strong measures in the 1839 crisis were inconsistent with Western standards of justice, morality and humanity and that they gave Britain reasons to justify a war in the name of vindicating its national honour and protecting British citizens overseas.[14] What has been less commented upon, however, is what Lydia Liu called 'the colonial discourse of injury'[15] and China's attempts to avoid more serious (and in their eyes unnecessary) offences. According to Liu, at the heart of European colonial history, 'When the freedom to trade, to travel and to proselytize comes to rest on the rights and principles granted by *ius gentium*, the opposition by a native population cannot but be interpreted sui generis as an injury to the life and property of the Europeans and therefore cause for just war'.[16] This discourse of injury, moreover, went hand-in-hand with the popular image of 'oriental brutality' in the nineteenth-century West. It was in these contexts that the contemporary British pro-war narrative tended to concentrate on Lin Zexu's cruelty in enforcing the Chinese laws and how his conduct violated international law. Lin Zexu, indeed, blockaded the foreign factories to force the surrender of opium. He threatened those who engaged in the opium trade with the death penalty. He also tried his best to drive the British community out of China, after the British merchants resumed the opium smuggling and in response to Elliot's refusal to hand over those suspected of involvement in the Lin Weixi incident. But, what has been remembered, or at least better remembered, is Elliot's accusation of Lin Zexu's actions as insults 'against British life, liberty, and property, and ... the dignity of the British crown'.[17] The following facts and details largely escaped the popular memories about the Opium War. As Li Chen has recently pointed out, the Chinese in fact exhibited a high degree of forbearance both before and during the opium crisis. The American trader Charles King's eyewitness account can show that, before Lin Zexu took action to detain the foreign community in Canton, he tried all means to urge the opium merchants to leave China voluntarily, together with their stock of opium. The Chinese 'warnings, threats, entreaties', however, failed to 'convince the smugglers of the reality of the danger'.[18] Lin Zexu also declared on different occasions that the Qing government had shown extraordinary favour to foreign merchants in confiscating only the opium stock on board their ships in Chinese waters while forgiving their misbehaviour in conducting this trade. The foreign merchants were to be allowed to continue their legal trade so long as they signed a pledge not to trade in opium again. This bond did, indeed, prescribe capital punishment for continuing the opium trade, but there was a long period of grace – originally one year and then extended to eighteen months – before it would take effect. Although the local authorities did execute some Chinese opium smugglers in front of the foreign factories, an act that can be considered cruel, such cruelty was never practised towards the British.[19]

As for the blockade of the foreign factories that Elliot described as 'imprisonment', various primary and secondary sources have suggested that there was no real danger to the safety of the foreigners. Li Chen has gathered a variety of such evidence, which allows him to maintain that 'people confined to the thirteen foreign factories during the blockade might have suffered humiliation, anxiety, boredom, or "obesity" from too little exercise but were not exposed to other serious physical harm or real danger to their lives. Save for mental distress and losing some domestic comforts and the liberty to leave Guangzhou, their condition was materially different from "imprisonment".'[20] Mao Haijian has discovered the dates on which Lin Zexu allowed the resumption of supplies (29 March 1839 – five days after the blockade and the first day after Elliot's promise to hand over opium), permitted the servants to return to the factories (12 April – when he received the first load of opium) and lifted the blockade (2 May – when the timely surrender of the rest of the opium could be anticipated).[21] All of these developments can suggest that Lin Zexu's actions were not as brutal as previously portrayed. He was concerned with the discomfort of the foreign community and was happy to relieve it as long as these foreigners did not obstruct his anti-opium campaign, the very reason the Daoguang emperor sent him to Canton.

In addition to exaggerating Lin Zexu's aggressive measures, and perhaps even more important, is the downplaying of the key role that Elliot played in shaping the opium crisis. This can be shown in at least two ways. First, when Lin Zexu blockaded the foreign factories, Elliot was not in Canton, but in Macao. Despite being the chief superintendent of trade, Elliot never had good control over the conduct of the British merchants in China. It is not known what motivated him to go to Canton and get deeply involved in the crisis there, but Elliot's voluntary entry into the confinement zone did significantly change the nature of Lin Zexu's conduct. From the British perspective, the Chinese certainly had a right to act strongly against foreign smugglers and to seize their opium. Confining only this community in their own residences until they surrendered the contraband goods might not have been considered unacceptable or unjust. It definitely was not the most extreme measure that could have been imagined. Having Britain's superintendent of trade with them, however, was a different story. It allowed the British advocates of war to point out that the Chinese had unjustly imprisoned an innocent representative of the British monarch, *together with* the community whose welfare he was to superintend. This logic, according to Li Chen, 'turned Elliot ... into the *primary* subject and victim of Chinese injustice, while the original targets of Chinese law enforcement, the opium smugglers, now became secondary'.[22] Glenn Melancon's argument that Britain went to war to defend its national honour would not have been possible without this important development.

Second, Elliot's promise that the British government would pay compensation for the surrendered opium was made without any authorisation from London. Hearing Elliot's guarantee, the British opium traders handed over not only their opium stock within Chinese waters that had originally been demanded by Lin Zexu, but also their cargoes in the outer waters. Elliot's explanation is that he had no other choice under such unusual circumstances, but this decision was a key explanation as to why Britain went to war with China. On the one hand, it prevented the Chinese from confiscating the opium stock directly from the British merchants. This made Lin Zexu's conduct sound even more unlawful from the British standpoint, because the Commissioner had seized the opium not by legitimate actions but as a ransom for a representative of the British Queen and hundreds of British subjects. On the other hand, since technically speaking the opium was surrendered to Elliot (in the name of his government) rather than to Lin Zexu, the British government was forced to react. Li Chen has analysed the difficult position that Elliot put the government in by his decision, as well as the limited options that London faced at the time.[23] The British government had no funds to pay such a huge sum (about £2 million to £3 million sterling) and Parliament was unlikely to approve a budget for this purpose. In this situation, to make China pay for it became the Whig government's naturally preferred option. For all the above reasons, we cannot explain the cause of the Opium War without stressing Elliot's role. Elliot's actions, to be fair, are widely mentioned in the narratives of the existing literature, but it can still be argued that the significance of his conducts could be emphasised more, especially compared to that of Lin Zexu's moves. Certainly, it is difficult to know whether Elliot meant to provoke a war when he decided to go to Canton in March 1839, but his subsequent actions did push the policy-makers in London to confront the Chinese without further delay, and provided them with a justifiable *casus belli*. Therefore, if Lin Zexu was responsible for causing the Sino-British hostilities, he could not have accomplished it without Elliot's intervention. In other words, Lin Zexu's policies did not *directly* lead to the conflict. Elliot's actions, or at least the interaction between the two, did.

The final aspect that deserves clarification about the outbreak of the Opium War is what should be considered as the 'immediate trigger' of the war. The answer to this question is closely linked with the query raised in the beginning of this chapter – when exactly did the Opium War begin, in 1839 or 1840? Those who believe that the conflict began in 1839 generally regard the Lin Weixi incident as the trigger. Such historical accounts of the First Anglo-Chinese War tend to highlight both the opium crisis in Canton and the Lin Weixi incident, before noting that the two sides exchanged the first shots in the battle of Kowloon, and that the British government had to intervene under such circumstances. This certainly forms a coherent narrative, but what has been overlooked is the timing of the information-exchange and decision-making processes. Unlike today when an email can reach any part of the world almost instantly, in the first half of the nineteenth century it took about four to five months for officials in London to get intelligence either from or to Canton. Mao Haijian's book includes the exact dates on which the British government received reports from Canton,[24] so that it is possible to work out what decision was made upon what information. The first batch of Elliot's letters, written between 30 March and 3 April 1839, reached the Foreign Office in London on 29 August. Palmerston received the second batch, written from 6 April to 29 May, on 21 September. According to Li Chen, a secret dispatch from Elliot to Palmerston, dated 3 April 1839, is a key document in shaping the British government's decision to fight a war against China.[25]

JUSTIFYING THE OPIUM WAR

This dispatch, written amid the blockade, was virtually Elliot's war proposal. It included not only his justification for the war but a detailed military plan with demands for treaty negotiations – including compensation for the surrendered opium, cession of an island to Britain and the opening of new ports to British merchants. Song-Chuan Chen has recently maintained that William Jardine, one of Britain's leading opium traders, played a pivotal role in influencing the government's decision. Palmerston interviewed Jardine on 27 September. On this occasion, bringing with him maps and charts of China, Jardine supplied the Foreign Secretary with his war strategy and military intelligence, as well as a range of new knowledge about the country that Song-Chuan Chen believed to be 'paramount to the war decision'.[26] No matter whose impact on the government was greater, it was with such information that, on 1 October, the decision to send a military expedition to China was taken in a closed-door cabinet meeting held in Windsor Castle. On 18 October, Palmerston wrote to Elliot, secretly notifying him that the expeditionary force would reach China the following March, before the third batch of Elliot's reports, written between 8 and 18 June, reached the Foreign Office (on 2 November). Elliot received this message in February 1840.

Here it is important to note that when ministers in the Whig government made up their mind to use armed force against China, the news about the Lin Weixi incident, which had occurred in July 1839, had not reached London. Neither was Elliot aware of the government's order and assistance to fight against the Chinese, when the battle of Kowloon occurred. For these reasons, although retrospectively one could argue that the period of conflict started to unfold in September 1839 because this was the point when the actual hostilities began, neither side at this time believed that the exchange of fire in Kowloon marked the beginning of a Sino-British war. From the sources he gathered, Mao Haijian has discovered that Lin Zexu assumed that he was battling with British warships that came to China without permission from the British throne/government, but in private alliance with merchants who were also out of their government's control. Lin Zexu's famous letter to Queen Victoria, written on 18 January 1840, showed that he did not think that China was at war with Britain at this time. On Elliot's side, the superintendent still had not received the British government's response to his actions during the crisis in Canton. He saw the battle of Kowloon as nothing more than the armed protection of British merchants.[27] On this basis, Mao Haijian concluded, 'although the curtains had already risen on the war, neither side began to play their part in earnest straight away. Because of this, it is more appropriate to consider the war as having begun in late-June 1840 [when the entire British expeditionary forces arrived in Chinese waters].'[28] This conclusion seems reasonable, because, if the Whig government had made a different decision, if no expeditionary force was going to be sent to China, no one would have argued that the conflict in September 1839 alone constituted the beginning of the First Anglo-Chinese War. The Lin Weixi incident, indeed, triggered the battle of Kowloon, but the battle should not be considered as the beginning of the Opium War, given the fact that both sides did not see the skirmish in the same way as some people have interpreted it in hindsight.

What makes the overall picture even more complicated is that, after the Whig ministers had made the formal decision to start the conflict, they tried to keep it a secret. News leaked out only gradually and rumours had it that a war was already under way. In March 1840, it finally came to the attention of Parliament. The Tory MP James Graham raised a motion against the government for mishandling the dispute with China. This led to the famous parliamentary debate from 7 to 9 April, on which occasion the Whigs defeated the critical motion by nine votes. So, to be clear, this was not a debate on whether Britain should wage a war against China, but a vote of no confidence in the Whig government's management of the crisis. Although the full British fleet did not arrive off Canton until June 1840,[29] at the time of the parliamentary debate there was reason to believe that the war had already started. Therefore, it is not a surprise that the term 'war' had been used by British MPs and the British public at this point – another fact that might mislead one to assume that the war had started before April 1840. For those who are not familiar with nineteenth-century British politics, what the government did in sending a fleet to China was not illegal or unconstitutional. The British Parliament did not make war or peace until modern times and the government, as the executive, did not need the approval of Parliament to start a war. Parliament, however, passed laws and voted taxes as the legislature. Although declaring and conducting war was an executive action, war always required high taxes so Parliament could subsequently make it easy or difficult for the government to continue any war. This explains why the debate did not happen before the expeditionary force was sent and why it occurred in April 1840 – the Tories, as the opposition, were unhappy about the Whig ministry's decision. They introduced the motion to censure the government for causing the conflict and hence made the issue a political dispute. By this time, news about the Lin Weixi incident and the battle of Kowloon had reached London. It probably had some impact on the outcome of the vote, but the vote did not mark or influence the actual beginning of the Opium War.[30]

JUSTIFYING THE OPIUM WAR

In retrospect, the insertion of the Lin Weixi incident and the ensuing battle into the narrative on the drift to the Opium War has helped to reinforce the image that Lin Zexu crossed the line of acceptable conduct in too many ways. This image served further to make the British appear as victims in the nineteenth-century 'colonial discourse of injury' and made it easier to justify British military retaliation in its particular historical contexts. It is however worth noting that this image was formed on the basis of a partial telling of the story. In particular, the forbearance on the Chinese side and the significance of Elliot's intervention should have received more attention, and emphasis, in the historiography of mounting Sino-British hostilities before the war. Moreover, an investigation into the information-exchange and decision-making processes has shown that, even if the Lin Weixi incident had not happened, China could not have avoided the task of confronting the British force sent to its coast. Britain's decision to go to war with China was made in October 1839, triggered very importantly but not exclusively by Elliot's reports on the opium crisis in Canton. The actual war began in June 1840, when the British troops arrived and the Daoguang emperor finally realised what was happening and issued his commands to destroy the invading British force.

The opium controversy

The Introduction of this book presents various views that previous historians put forward to explain the outbreak and significance of the Opium War. This scholarship has offered wide-ranging interpretations for the origins of the event, but a common limitation is that most of these studies sought to identify a principal cause of the war – either trade, or culture, or opium, or honour and so on – but paid less attention to some highly relevant but also substantially different questions: how exactly was the opium trade imagined and the opium question disputed within Britain, and how were open hostilities against China justified upon these grounds? If the war was caused by Britain's wish to expand trade, or to protect an illegal traffic in China – neither sounds easily justifiable – then how did the decision-makers in nineteenth-century Britain become convinced that this war ought to be fought? Based on a range of pamphlets, newspaper articles published by Britons in China, official and government correspondence and records of parliamentary debates, the rest of this chapter addresses these questions. By focusing on the diverse views presented on the opium question, rather than trying to determine a fundamental cause of the conflict, this research attempts to reconstruct how exactly the opium trade and related Chinese affairs were presented and discussed prior to the war. It seeks to show that, in this extremely complicated controversy, although the debates on the opium trade, the proceedings of the opium crisis and the British government's intervention in Chinese affairs were heavily interwoven, they can be analysed separately. In this way, we can see more clearly that the dispute over the opium trade should not be considered as the most immediate cause of hostilities. To be fair, nor was the First Anglo-Chinese war produced by Britain's 'defiance of ethics' or 'irresponsible imperialism',[31] as was claimed by Tan and others.

Well before Lin Zexu's anti-opium campaign, a controversy over the nature of opium and the opium trade had taken place among concerned Britons, both in Canton and in Britain. In 1835, the first anti-opium pamphlet, *No Opium! Or, Commerce and Christianity, Working Together for Good in China*, was published anonymously for Robert Philip in London.[32] Around the same time, the *Chinese Repository* in Canton began to present various views on the opium question, as well as translations of Chinese sources on this issue. It was not until 1839, however, that opium came to the forefront of public consciousness. A.S. Thelwall's pamphlet *The Iniquities of the Opium Trade* drew the public's attention to the deplorable effects of opium-smoking and the problem this trade posed to the extension of Christianity in China. Subsequently, an Anti-Opium Society was formed. A number of pamphlets and articles followed and a debate on opium began almost simultaneously in Canton and Britain.

The first subject of dispute was the nature of opium. The principal impression introduced by the anti-opium campaigners was that opium was 'a certain poison',[33] whose injurious effects threatened the health, morals and lives of the Chinese people. The more this drug was consumed, the greater became the need for it. Although there was a claim at the time that opium was a medicine of great value when properly used, anti-opium activists insisted that the drug sold by the British traders was actually 'deficient in the sedative principle for which opium is chiefly valued'.[34] Opium produced in British India was simply 'unfit for medicine, [and] applicable only to purposes of vicious indulgence'.[35] Moreover, as Stephen Lushington pointed out in the House of Commons, 'not a thousandth part of the quantity of opium exported from India, and introduced into China, was used for medical purposes'.[36] Hence, in the opinion of anti-opium campaigners, the destructive effects of the drug were beyond all doubt. They believed that, unlike the consumption of alcohol, moderation in opium-smoking was almost impossible, because, once a person was induced to smoke it, 'the habit fasten[s] itself on him so rapidly, and so forcibly, that he ... becomes in a short time inveterately addicted to it'.[37] According to an article in the *Chinese Repository*, 'There is no slavery on earth to name with the bondage into which opium casts its victim. There is scarcely one known instance of escape from its toils.'[38] To stress that opium was unwelcome to the Chinese, those who resided in China referred to their local experience. For instance, an anonymous author maintained that, 'So far as we know – and we have read and heard the sentiments of thousands of the Chinese – no one ever regards the use of the drug in any other light than as a physical and moral evil. ... "It is a noxious thing," they say, ... This is truth.'[39] For this reason, the anti-opium campaigners were further convinced that opium was, as Thelwall wrote, 'a deleterious drug which ruins those who indulge in it, in mind, body, and estate – which depraves and enervates them, physically, intellectually, and morally, and finally brings them to an untimely grave'.[40]

On the basis of beliefs about opium's harmful nature, the anti-opium campaigners condemned the opium trade from different perspectives. First, since the trade was illegal in China, it was 'highly injurious to the legitimate commerce' and endangered 'a most important branch of our revenue'.[41] According to some of these observers, the contraband nature of the opium trade justified the Chinese government's policy of exclusion, as well as its suspicious attitude towards the British. In consequence, not only had Britain's export of woollens and cottons declined but the Qing court had reason not to extend Britain's regular trade to other Chinese ports. Second, the opium traffic was 'dishonourable to the British name',[42] because, so long as the British were involved in such a disreputable trade, 'it renders us [the British] contemptible in the eyes of the Chinese, or rather it seals and confirms them in that disdain with which their pride has always prompted them to regard us'.[43] According to this view, since the British flag had been constantly implicated in the opium trade, Great Britain held a bad reputation in China. This made it difficult to achieve good relations with the Chinese. Third, the opium trade was a major obstacle to the introduction of Christianity into China. Philip, the author who first raised the opium issue in Britain, attributed the failure of the Chinese mission to the fact that 'our Chinese missionaries have all along been counteracted by the influence of the Opium Trade'.[44] To explain this view, William Storrs Fry claimed that 'every individual who is once enslaved by the use of Opium, is *morally and physically* incapacitated from giving any attention to the voice of Christian instruction'.[45] Another author called 'S.S.S.' pointed out that the Chinese were 'not able to distinguish the hands which were stretched out to rescue them with the Bible from those which offered them the opium pipe'.[46] This led the Chinese to form their views of Christians from the conduct of opium merchants. Because of this nefarious traffic, Thelwall lamented, 'how should they be able to imagine that any real good or true kindness can come from a nation and people whom they look upon as smugglers and dealers in poison, for their ruin and destruction?'[47] To reinforce his point, Thelwall wrote with indignation:

> I ask of every considerate and reflecting man, Can it be doubted but that the name and profession of Christianity is grossly dishonoured by the fact (well known throughout Eastern Asia), that those who profess and call themselves Christians are systematically and perseveringly engaged in this iniquitous and poisonous traffic? that our national character is degraded, and covered with infamy too well deserved, among the nations of the East? ... that the greatest market in the world is comparatively closed – and that justly – against the productions of our national industry? that we are deservedly excluded from all honourable and comfortable intercourse – commercial or diplomatic – with the most populous Empire upon earth? that the cause of the glorious Gospel of Christ itself is compromised, and the progress of Christian missions among half the population of the globe is effectually impeded? and that among three hundred, or rather five hundred, millions of our fellow-men, we are justly branded as wholesale corrupters and murderers of an unoffending people?[48]

Since they regarded the opium trade as derogatory to the British name and harmful to the British interests, the anti-opium campaigners created rather unfavourable images of those merchants who conducted this trade. They denounced the opium traders as lawless smugglers who were 'greedy and pestilent corrupters and poisoners of the Chinese nation',[49] and 'the most deceitful, dishonest, grasping, criminal party'.[50] Since these merchants did not smoke opium themselves, nothing but the lust for financial gain induced these men to violate the principles of justice, truth and humanity. The anti-opium activists also drew comparison between the iniquities of the opium traders and those who had conducted the slave trade. As an anonymous author wrote in his *British Opium Trade with China*: 'they are equally hateful, and equally productive of human misery'.[51]

The strength of the anti-opium campaign did not prevent contrasting images of opium, the trade and its participants being put forward. The defenders of the opium trade declared that the destructive effects of opium were grossly exaggerated. Some argued that, instead of being a pernicious poison, opium was undeniably 'one of the most beneficial medicines at present in use'.[52] As 'a perfect substitute for quinine',[53] it was not only 'one of the most powerful remedies for numerous diseases which science had discovered and art applied'[54] but a 'balm' which heaven 'bestowed upon us ... to our suffering bodies and our troubled minds'.[55] D. Stewart even described the discovery of this substance as having brought 'the greatest good to the cause of humanity'.[56] Other supporters of opium did not go so far, but they still believed that, as Henry Ward claimed in the House of Commons, 'if used in moderation, opium was not injurious to morals or health'.[57] Hence, it was not the use, but the abuse, of opium that caused the problems. As 'a resident in China' maintained, 'the smoking of opium, if not less, was not more deleterious than the use of ardent spirits at home; both depending upon the quantity taken'.[58] In other words, any damage was caused by the self-indulgence of the Chinese smokers, rather than by the nature of opium. Moreover, in contrast to the fearful danger of opium causing general depravity in China, supporters of the opium trade maintained that 'the mass of the people seem healthy, industrious, and cheerful, where the greatest quantity of the drug is consumed'.[59] 'One long resident in China' even claimed that opium to the Chinese was 'as great a national luxury as tea with us [the British]'.[60] As in the anti-opium campaign, local experience was also utilised to support the opium trade defenders' views. H. Hamilton Lindsay described the Chinese natives along the coast as 'flocking on board the opium ships, bringing bags of dollars to purchase it'.[61] 'A resident in China' noted that 'Their great solace ... is the opium-pipe. There is nothing they would substitute for it. ... They have told me, "Opium is to us what tea is to you. You cannot do without tea, and we must have opium. Deprive us of opium, and you drive us to despair."'[62] In this way, supporters of the opium trade represented what its critics considered an unwanted poison as a largely innocuous substance greatly desired by the Chinese.

The opium trade defenders also defined the nature of the trade in ways that conflicted with the assertions of the anti-opium campaigners. To start with, they stressed that the foreign merchants had 'never themselves introduced the opium into the country';[63] instead, it was the natives that came to collect the stock beyond the jurisdiction of the China. This was because, after the Chinese government warned the British in 1820 not to bring opium to Canton, all vessels with opium retreated to the so-called outer waters. Since then, although the British merchants still 'sold' opium in Canton, their Chinese clients only received an order for delivery. To obtain their cargoes, these natives had to take their own risk in collecting them from the ships anchored near Lintin island. This fact allowed the opium merchants to argue that they did not violate the Chinese laws. It was their Chinese clients who bribed the customs officers and introduced opium into China, while the British did nothing beyond the 'undoubted right of every British subject to trade in opium on the high seas'.[64]

Furthermore, in lieu of the nefarious images that their critics constructed of the opium trade, defenders of the trade attempted to represent the traffic as a *de facto* regular trade. Lindsay, for instance, maintained that 'such a trade cannot fairly be considered smuggling in the ordinary acceptation of the term',[65] because 'this falsely called smuggling trade had for a series of many years been conducted with greater regularity, facility, and mutual confidence, than any trade of similar magnitude in any part of the world'.[66] When comparing the opium trade with legitimate trade, another commentator insisted that 'both were equally regular trades, although differently conducted, each paying the duties, and fees instead of duties, to the government officers, with the same punctuality'.[67] Instead of blaming the opium merchants, supporters of the trade chose to highlight 'the open and undisguised connivance of the local authorities'[68] as the very reason why such a trade had subsisted over the decades. They repeatedly emphasised that, because of the venality of the Chinese officers and the widespread corruption within their system, 'opium enjoyed the clandestine patronage of the court'.[69] Accordingly, the local officials in Canton, rather than anybody else, were 'the most blame-worthy parties'.[70] The responsibility was once again shifted from the British to the Chinese.

In addition, the opium trade defenders challenged the legitimacy of the Chinese law, blurring the boundary between justice and unlawfulness in the case of the opium trade. They contended that, since there were no official diplomatic relations between China and Britain, the opium merchants had to subject themselves to the local authorities in Canton, unable to discover whether the 'imperial edicts' presented to them actually emanated from the emperor in Beijing. An anonymous writer, for example, noted that the laws of China were often implemented differently in practice, to such an extent that 'the Chinese say of their own law, it was made for the officers, not for the people; it is a net no one can escape if the mandarin throws it; for a fee, anything is declared legal, and every thing is illegal to extract a fine, especially as regards trade duties are said among themselves to be almost always matter of bargain, not regular established charges'.[71] Under these circumstances, since the legality and practicality of these laws were doubtful, submission to the Chinese law became problematic *per se*. In this respect, local experience was used again to demonstrate that, in the past decades, local officers had issued 'so many absurd, frivolous, vexatious, inconsistent, and contradictory regulations'[72] that the British merchants had no other option but to disregard them. For these reasons, 'there are no laws in China demanding conscientious obedience – beyond the universal law of truth, justice, and mercy – and that all questions there regarding legality or illegality, are questions of prudence, not of principle'.[73]

By such means, defenders of the opium merchants presented the images of the opium trade in a totally different way. The trade was neither against the desires of the Chinese population, nor was it conducted contrary to morality or justice. The term 'smuggler' was hence 'a stigma' on the character of the opium traders.[74] Since opium was introduced into China because of the demands of the natives and the business was transacted with the tacit and almost open consent of the local authorities, one supporter of the trade declared that an opium dealer could best be described as 'the *importer* of opium into Whampoa' or 'the disposer of his *own property*'.[75] Others even maintained that these merchants commanded much respect, because they 'thought it their duty ... to submit to inconvenience and seeming degradation'[76] in China, in order to enrich 'their country far more than themselves'.[77] They were, in the meantime, the 'most intelligent, and useful, and charitable persons',[78] who not only acquired extensive knowledge of China but 'dispensed the most munificent charities among the poor Chinese'.[79] In any case, 'no resemblance at all could be drawn between the opium merchants and those engaged in the slave trade'.[80] All accusations against the moral character of these people were unfounded.

In sum, the anti-opium campaigners and their opponents presented conflicting images about the nature of opium, the opium traffic and its British participants. Supporters of the trade, at this stage, were largely forced on to the defensive. While the views of the anti-opium campaigners did not entirely prevail, the strength of their opinions was not in the slightest degree inferior to that on the other side. On opium-related issues, the general verdict did not lean towards the opium trade defenders, nor was any of their arguments strong enough to justify a war against China. This state of affairs, however, altered greatly when the opium crisis was taken into consideration.

The crisis debate

As with the controversy over opium and the opium trade, the crisis in 1839 touched off a heated debate both within the British community in China and between concerned parties in Britain. These commentators advanced various opinions as to the fairness or injustice of Lin Zexu's conduct. According to the most radical wing, who were mainly solid supporters of the opium trade, the Chinese side was entirely in the wrong because Lin Zexu's action was 'a gross infraction of the law of nations'.[81] They maintained, first of all, that the Chinese had violated the principle of free trade. Since every article was 'in itself good, and ... may be cultivated, manufactured, bought, sold, and distributed all over the world', opium was 'no exception as an article, nor China as a country'.[82] According to War Secretary Thomas Macaulay, no political system had the right to keep out 'those luxuries which the people enjoyed, or were able to purchase, or to prevent the efflux of precious metals, when it was demanded by the course of trade'.[83] Therefore, even though the Chinese government had declared opium to be an illicit article and had erected legal barriers to its trade with Western countries, foreign merchants were still justified in carrying on the trade in any product that was desired by the Chinese people – 'with or without her consent, contraband or otherwise', as 'a resident in China' claimed.[84] Second, Lin Zexu had committed a serious insult 'not only against British subjects and property, but also against the dignity of the British crown'.[85] For one thing, Lin Zexu's decision to put Elliot under house arrest was a direct affront to the British sovereign, because according to international law Elliot's public character as the Queen's representative at Canton was not merely 'sacred and inviolable, but independent of the jurisdiction of the Chinese government'.[86] For another, the blockade and then expulsion of the British community, as well as the confiscation of their property without a judicial hearing, were also unlawful proceedings. Samuel Warren, for example, alleged that these Britons came to China 'under the full protection of the British flag, and under the sanction of British authority ... in pursuit of the objects of national commerce'.[87] However, according to the description by 'a barrister at law', the foreign community in Canton had been treated 'like a parcel of wild animals, and, without ... an opportunity of pleading the cause'.[88] By seeking to propagate such perceptions, British commentators had reason to be outraged by these offences on the persons and property of their fellow countrymen.

To justify the necessity of taking retaliatory measures, these radical commentators presented China as an arbitrary 'other' that had long held other countries in contempt and had often set at defiance the laws of civilised nations. An anonymous writer asserted, 'the single fundamental cause' of both the present crisis and past disputes was 'the arrogant assumption of supremacy on the part of China over foreigners'.[89] Others pointed out that, as China had no real sense of its relative place in the scale of nations, its rulers believed China to be first among nations in knowledge and power, so that they were accustomed to acting as an absolute authority. Even though China seemed to have the right to regulate its own affairs, according to the principle that the majority should give law to the minority, the Chinese were not entitled to challenge any international law with impunity. To justify this view, another anonymous writer claimed, since they were numerically only one-third of the human race, 'China, as one, cannot be allowed to oppose the rest of the world, who are two, and more particularly when she is asked to do any thing that cannot injure herself, or place her in a worse state than she is at present'.[90] On such grounds, any challenge to China's authority was justified in the service of protecting international law. Among others, Foreign Secretary Palmerston was clearly in favour of this view. In the House of Commons, he condemned Lin Zexu's conduct as 'totally at variance with international law, a course of the most arbitrary kind, and liable to every possible objection'.[91] For this reason, the key decision-maker was convinced that Britain was legitimately 'entitled to demand satisfaction, reparation, and redress' from the Chinese authorities.[92]

In opposition to these views, the anti-opium campaigners raised a number of counter-arguments. They averred that many of the aforesaid remarks were contrary to the truth, while as Sydney S. Bell maintained, 'right and justice are entirely on the side of China'.[93] First, it was incorrect to regard Elliot as the representative of the Queen, because the Chinese government had never recognised any official personage at Canton. Given that Elliot had to communicate with the Guangdong government through Hong merchants, Horatio Montagu believed that he was 'nothing more than chief commercial agent'.[94] William Gladstone shared this view. In Parliament, he claimed that, since Elliot had no political authority to represent Britain, 'it was unjust to contend that the Chinese were responsible as if they had known him in the character of a regularly-accredited diplomatic agent'.[95] Second, although Lin Zexu's decisions to stop all trade and to act against the whole foreign community sounded cruel, it was not entirely unreasonable in the circumstances. This was because, in Canton, it was neither necessary nor possible to fix the guilt on individuals, because 'the entire British community, at Canton, was directly or indirectly implicated in this odious traffic'.[96] In this regard, even Elliot himself had admitted that 'the Chinese Government had a just ground for hard measures towards the lawful trade, upon the plea that there was no distinguishing between the right and the wrong'.[97] As to the Lin Weixi incident, because Elliot refused to hand over those who were involved in the murder, the Qing government certainly had a right to refuse any suspects the right to remain on Chinese territory. Particularly, in light of Britain's long-standing reputation as dangerous trouble-makers, it was perfectly understandable that the Qing court remained suspicious of the British and chose to expel the whole community whenever it deemed necessary. Furthermore, against the charge of China being unwilling to abide by international law, the anti-opium campaigners suggested that every nation was entitled to choose for itself what contributed most to its own wellbeing. Any interference with this right should be considered as an infringement of its liberty. Since the Chinese government never recognised what the West called international law, its principles were inapplicable to China. Therefore, 'the Chinese Government had the "unquestionable right"

... to prohibit the importation of Opium ... to enforce it by penalties',[98] while 'every foreigner was bound to pay absolute, implicit, unconditional, obedience'[99] to these laws.

At variance with the contention that either Britain or China was completely in the wrong, a less biased opinion met with the most favourable response in the debate. Supporters of this attitude saw the insults offered to Britain during the crisis as separate from the immorality of the opium trade. They generated an influential case, which to a great extent justified Britain's decision to wage war against China. In comparison with the assertion that justice was entirely on the Chinese side, these commentators seemed to be more persuaded by Jardine's claim that those who upheld the view 'very foolishly, mix up the insult and violence with the illicit trade'.[100] Alexander Graham, for instance, stressed that *'a legitimate end is no justification of illegitimate means'*.[101] John Hobhouse claimed in the House of Commons that, although China had an undeniable right to stamp out a contraband trade for its own safety and wellbeing, 'the circumstances of severity under which it took place'[102] were a serious insult to British subjects and their property, as well as to the honour of the British nation. In particular, the surrender of opium beyond China's jurisdictional limits was a great offence that deserved punishment.[103] George Thomas Staunton, now Britain's leading China expert and the translator of *Ta Tsing Leu Lee* (*The Penal Code of China*), proclaimed in his speech before Parliament: 'there was absolutely no law authorising the confiscation of goods, under any circumstances, outside the port. The opium lying in the receiving ships at Lintin, was no more liable to confiscation by any existing fiscal law of the Chinese, than if it had been lying in the river Thames'.[104]

Perhaps because Staunton was not a friend of the opium trade and he actually 'yielded to no Member of the House in his anxiety to put it down altogether',[105] his view seemed to be very well received. Since Lin Zexu did not attempt to distinguish the participants in the opium trade from those involved in the legal trade, British observers in China were able to argue that 'the innocent and the guilty have both had to suffer – and in some cases it may be the former have sustained greater losses than the latter'.[106] Opinions such as this allowed the creation of the popular narrative on the opium crisis that has been sketched earlier in this chapter. Without sufficient information about the forbearance on the Chinese side and the key role Elliot played, the following key images emerged. First, during the crisis, all British men in Canton (women were not allowed to enter), whether or not they were opium traders, were indiscriminately taken hostage by Lin Zexu. Even Britain's chief officer in China was not made an exception. Second, for seven weeks or so, they were not only deprived of supplies and servants but threatened with capital punishment.[107] Third, a few months later, when Elliot was unable to identify the murderer of Lin Weixi, not only British men but also women and children, who were certainly innocent, were treated with equal severity. Lin Zexu expelled them from their residences at very short notice, with all means of subsistence cut off. On the basis of these images, there was no doubt that the lives and property of quite a number of law-abiding British subjects were put in jeopardy at the hands of Chinese authorities. For this reason, some observers were convinced that Lin Zexu's measures to mix the innocent with the guilty had crossed the line of acceptable conduct. Even although China was not bound by international law, its recent actions were against any sense of justice, or, as Lushington put it, 'every principle of justice and eternal truth ... which must exist so long as man and man had the power of conversation and intercourse with one another'.[108] On such grounds, Joseph Hume claimed that, 'from the moment British subjects at Canton were placed in prison to the danger of their lives, the Chinese became the aggressors'.[109] Since the British government had an obligation to protect British life, liberty, and property, it was absolutely just and necessary to take vigorous measures against the 'crimes' committed by the Chinese.

To legitimise further the actions of the British government, supporters of this view paid much attention to identifying the nature of the opium trade and that of Lin Zexu's actions as two separate issues. Staunton maintained that 'the question between us and the Chinese, in a national point of view, has nothing to do with the immorality or the impolicy of the trade'.[110] The British government had never intended to protect whoever violated the Chinese law, but meanwhile it could not disregard the insult and injuries that the Chinese had inflicted upon the British nation. As to the opium crisis, Benjamin Hawes believed that despite the fact that China had been on the right side when it began its anti-opium campaign, 'The Chinese Government, by seizing upon the persons of British merchants, putting them in prison, seizing the opium of the parties under threats, put themselves in the wrong'.[111] It was these latter outrages, rather than the opium trade, to which Britain should respond. Macaulay, in his celebrated speech, made it very clear

> that government had a right to keep out opium, to keep in silver, and to enforce their prohibitory laws, by whatever means which they might possess, consistently with the principles of public morality, and of international law; and if, after having given fair notice of their intention, to seize all contraband goods introduced into their dominions; they seized our opium, we had no right to complain; but when the government, finding, that by just and lawful means, they could not carry out their prohibition, resorted to measures unjust and unlawful, confined our

innocent countrymen, and insulted the Sovereign in the person of her representative, then ... the time had arrived when it was fit that we should interfere.[112]

According to such arguments, the Chinese government was once again defined as an arbitrary power in which Britain could not trust. The government's intervention hence became even more important, not just to respond to what had happened but, as Elliot wrote, 'for the effectual prevention of the like dark proceedings'[113] in future. Considering the significance of the China trade, as well as the perception that 'British commerce can never safely be carried on, and certainly can never flourish in a country where our persons and property are alike at the mercy of a capricious and corrupt Government',[114] many opinion formers at this time concurred on the necessity of changing Britain's relations with China. They either strongly urged the government to intervene immediately, or, at the least, accepted that Britain was entitled to demand redress for the injuries to British honour and interests.

Therefore, it can be seen that, after the opium crisis of 1839 was taken into consideration, a remarkable change had occurred in the content and tenor of British debates on Chinese affairs. In contrast with the previous debate, which was based solely on the opium question, the focus had now digressed from the character of the opium trade to the nature of the Chinese government's actions. To debate what the Chinese authorities did to British subjects, rather than what the British merchants did to Chinese subjects, became the main concern. As a result, those who formerly had to defend the legitimacy of the opium trade gained much ground, because their demand for the British government's forcible intervention coincided with the views of a group of observers such as Staunton who had less sympathy for the opium merchants but saw this crisis as distinct from the immorality of the opium trade. They jointly produced an image that the lives and property of British subjects had been subjected to gross insults offered by an arbitrary and presumptuous Chinese government. This view eventually overwhelmed the voices raised on the other side, which now adopted a defensive position and anyhow were unable to convince the public that all of Lin Zexu's actions had been based on just grounds. In consequence, a prompt response from the British government was regarded as legitimate and reasonable. A significant change in perceptions had occurred and vigorous intervention was finally going to happen.

War

As highlighted in the beginning of this chapter, in the parliamentary debate held in April 1840 'no member was willing to declare himself directly opposed to a war with China'.[115] This may be surprising to some readers, especially given the fact that the Whig government won by only nine votes. Then, why was it the case? As explained earlier, the decision to go to war with China was made by the Whig ministry in October 1839. Technically speaking, the Parliament had no right to make or stop the decision. The MPs were also aware that the conflict had been unavoidable because, by the time of the debate, the British expeditionary force should have arrived in China. In other words, the war might have started. What the Parliament could do at this point was to discuss whether the Whig government had made a mistake and to decide what measures Britain should take subsequently – to continue or terminate the hostilities. Although historians have recognised the general importance of Britain's interest and honour to the war decision, less attention has been paid to what specific considerations of the nation's interests and honour led Britain to interfere so violently in the dispute with China. In the late 1830s and 1840, British observers advanced various ways as the best means to carry out the interventionist policy. Discussion on these subjects formed an essential part of the pre-Opium War debates.

One of the most important factors that prompted Britain's determination to take military action against China was the anxiety felt about the need to preserve the empire in India. In this respect, some commentators maintained that the crisis in China was a crucial financial issue. As Graham pointed out in Parliament, since 'one-sixth of the whole united revenue of Great Britain and India depended on our commercial relations with that country',[116] the elimination of Britain's trade with China would be 'one of the greatest calamities which could befall the East India Company and the nation'.[117] Others believed that the China question had become a security matter. Hume, for example, alleged that 'the peace of India greatly depended on our vindicating British supremacy before China'.[118] Among others, the anonymous author of *Some Pros and Cons of the Opium Question* shared this concern. He was apprehensive that, if Britain continued to show forbearance towards China, it would be 'degrading in the eyes of the world generally, but especially destructive of that respect and confidence among our Indian fellow-subjects, which maintains our empire of opinion in the East'.[119] In such a case, Staunton maintained, 'the day is not far distant when the consequences will be visited on our great empire in India, and our political ascendancy there will be fatally undermined'.[120] From this perspective, the China question was now associated with important matters about the preservation of the British Empire.

Meanwhile, in the debate leading up to the Opium War, some previously favourable images of the Chinese emperor and his people were challenged, so that nothing else seemed more reliable to the British than their own actions. Previously, with the exception of the Amherst mission, no matter how hard the British had censured the local authorities of Canton, they had entertained a more or less positive image of the Chinese monarch. The emperor had long been assumed to be a merciful sovereign who was kept in ignorance of the corruption of the Guangdong government. This impression changed dramatically after the opium crisis. For one thing, it had become well known that, keen to eradicate the opium trade, the Daoguang emperor appointed Lin Zexu to an imperial commissionership, an office of extreme importance which had been conferred only four times before in the Qing dynasty. Unlike the local officials of Canton, Lin Zexu could be seen as 'the interpreter of the Imperial wishes and of the principles that actuate the administration'.[121] Moreover, intelligence (or rumour) suggested that the Daoguang emperor might indeed have quite unkind intentions towards the British. 'A resident in China' reported that during the crisis the emperor had forwarded to Lin Zexu a memorial, presented by another mandarin, that proposed to 'call out the best swimmers and divers ... cause them at night to divide into groups, to go diving straight on board the foreign ships, and taking the said foreigners unawares, *massacre every individual among them*'.[122] Such information led the author to deplore that: 'how can any of us continue of our former opinions? ... How greatly should we appreciate the Emperor's tender mercies towards us, past, present, and future, when he has lent his sign manual and signet to give authority to such a document!'[123] Clearly, as a result of the opium crisis, the previously positive image of the Chinese monarch was contested. The British commentators now began to doubt whether the emperor could be, or indeed had ever been, a reliable protector of Britain's interests in China.

Similarly, the character of the ordinary Chinese people was also challenged. In the past, British visitors to China had tended to consider the Chinese as generally friendly and hospitable. As more contact with them occurred, some British observers such as Warren began to claim that they had been deluded by the Chinese people's outward forms, because, on closer inspection, 'nothing is visible but fraud, hypocrisy, and falsehood'.[124] According to this new attitude, 'a disregard for veracity'[125] was a common character of ordinary Chinese people. 'Personal profit and convenience is all they look to', 'a resident in China' wrote, 'so long as we contribute anything to pamper that selfish feeling, they will profess themselves to be our friends. But hollow are their promises, and fragile the ties that bind them to us.'[126] For this reason, even though these British commentators still believed that the Chinese people were passionate about trade, they had to bear in mind that the hospitality displayed by their Chinese 'friends' might not be genuine. Since they now regarded neither the Chinese emperor nor his subjects as trustworthy, the British in Canton and at home had more reasons to argue that 'there is no security for us in future but the strong hand of power, such as we can wield for our own protection'.[127]

Thus, the pressing need for the British government to intervene was justified from a variety of perspectives. Although the Whig government won the debate in April 1840 by only a small majority, the disparity of views over the propriety of 'intervention' was actually not as great as has been commonly presumed. A closer analysis of primary sources reveals that the inclination to take action against China was much stronger than the voting in Parliament appears to indicate. What really divided opinions in and outside Westminster was not the legitimacy for Britain to attack China, but the *extent* to which Britain should fight against the Chinese, or, in other words, whether an immediate large-scale war was Britain's best option at the time. In this respect, concerned British commentators put forward various views on what specific means should be adopted.

Most notably, open violence against China was favoured much more in the late 1830s than ever before. Unlike the advocates of the 'show of force' strategy in the mid-1830s, during and after the opium crisis quite a number of observers insisted that the desire to improve Britain's relations with China 'must be enforced at the cannon's mouth'.[128] Warren, for example, claimed that, since China had insulted Britain's honour and caused injury to its commercial interests, it deserved 'the most signal chastisement in our power'.[129] Others proposed that the British force should, first of all, blow up 'every fort at the mouth of the Canton river',[130] and then to 'demand, in the highest tone, defined treaties, both political and commercial, or the alternative to China of an aggression on her territory, or the occupation of an island, to secure the due protection of our subjects and their property'.[131] To those who held this view, this course of conduct was fully justified, because history had shown that it was useless to conciliate the Chinese authorities. Only a firm military response would check their insolence and compel their submission. Under such circumstances, these commentators believed that, in comparison with a mere 'show' of force, the actual use of arms would create a much stronger sensation that could force the Chinese government to make concessions. Otherwise, 'as long as the forts are allowed to remain in the hands of the Chinese, all negotiation will be useless'.[132]

Aligned with this opinion, these commentators also maintained that the present crisis had provided 'a golden opportunity'[133] to teach the Chinese a lesson. According to this view, unlike in the Napier incident of 1834, the conduct of Lin Zexu had provided ample grounds for legitimising Britain's forcible intervention in Chinese affairs. Since the Qing court had adopted force to compel compliance with its demands, the British, with greater justice, were entitled to adopt a similarly vigorous policy. Probably influenced by similar opinions, Elliot declared that 'a more just, necessary, or favourable conjunction for action never presented itself'.[134] Given an awareness of these arguments, policy-makers in Britain became increasingly able to understand the pro-war sentiments – since justice was on the British side, and force was the most effective means, the present opportunity must not be lost if Britain wished to place its relations with China on a satisfactory footing.

It is also worth noting that, at this time, many of those who were in favour of open hostilities with China were no longer disposed to underestimate the difficulty of overawing the Chinese. As shown in the previous chapters, ever since Macartney's time, British visitors to China had entertained rather optimistic views on the weakness of the Chinese defences. Almost all of them seemed to have been extremely confident that a small-scale demonstration of Britain's naval force, such as 'three or four frigates and brigs',[135] would be enough to create such a strong impact on China that the Qing court would yield to Britain's demand right away. By the time Britain had encountered Lin Zexu's tough measures, this view had altered significantly. Quite a number of commentators began to argue that 'the conviction [that] the Chinese are a nation of cowards, is a very unwarranted and a very unsafe one',[136] and that 'we are equally erroneous in our estimate of their resources and their power'.[137] On this basis, in official documents as well as in popular publications, British observers of China began to propose that, if Britain was to launch an expedition, not only as many warships as possible should be deployed but a sufficient military force would also be helpful.[138] To justify such a view, commentators such as Philip Stanhope contended that, after all, China possessed 'a people unbounded in population, animated by the purest patriotism, and by the most enthusiastic attachment to the laws and institutions under which they had enjoyed prosperity and peace'.[139] It was, therefore, difficult to imagine that the Chinese would succumb to a foreign invasion without offering stiff resistance. For this reason, to produce the most favourable results, it was vital to make sure that the British troops succeeded in all their undertakings, so that the Chinese would be sufficiently impressed with and overawed by Britain's strength. Expounding on this argument, an author in the *Canton Press* wrote that

> In putting any of our military or naval plans in execution, we employ such numbers and such *moyens militaires* as always to make victory

certain, so that on no occasion may we allow the Chinese the slightest pretext for claiming the smallest advantage over us ... if we permit the Chinese to beat us even if the odds be twenty to one, still if they *beat us*, our *prestige* of superiority is gone, and our cause lost even before we have well begun it.[140]

Hence, in the late 1830s, not only did a war against China become more conceivable than before but it seemed more sensible that, in the anticipated conflict, the British expedition should be composed of sufficient strength to ensure ultimate success.

Contrary to the commentators who were vehemently calling for a large-scale war, others pointed out that, although Britain had just grounds to intervene and the success of open warfare was almost certain, military action against China might not be the best option. These observers such as an author of *Chinese Repository* named 'C.R.' argued that a war would threaten the safety of the Chinese people as well as Britain's long-term interests in Asia, hence '*every peaceful resort must be exhausted, before force is employed against China*'.[141] According to this view, even if the most extreme measures had to be adopted eventually, the scale of Britain's initial operations should be as limited as possible. This was because the purpose of Britain's action was to demand reparation for the injuries inflicted on the British honour and interests, rather than to seek aggrandisement in China or promote aggression of any kind. Otherwise, Britain's strength might become over-extended. 'If we once planted our flag and built a fort within the Chinese dominions', Lindsay wrote, 'circumstances would compel us to extend our limits, and our career of British India would be repeated in China'.[142] Since China was much bigger in size and population than India, any attempt to obtain territorial acquisitions might impose an incredible burden for Britain and might weaken its empire in Asia.

Other observers pointed out that because Britain's ultimate goal was to improve its trade with China, the British force should take particular care to preserve amicable relations with ordinary Chinese people. Any hostile measures should hence be designed to involve them as little as possible. To avoid rousing vindictive feelings among the populace in China, it was crucial to restrict bloodshed to 'the mandarins and military who would come to interfere with our works',[143] while, at the same time, to 'protect, cherish, and refrain from injuring the Chinese people'.[144] Even though a war against China might be inevitable, Lushington stressed that it should not be 'a war of blood and of reprisals'.[145] Nor should the means applied to obtain justice exceed what was necessary. In this respect, Robert Peel strongly urged Parliament:

> do not enter into this war without a becoming spirit – a spirit becoming the name and character of England. Do not forget the peculiar character

of the people with whom you have to deal, and so temper your measures that as little evil as possible may remain. ... It is your duty to vindicate the honour of England where vindication is necessary, and to demand reparation wherever reparation is due. But God grant that all this may lead to the restoration of amicable relations with China.[146]

From these lines, we can see that, for those adhering to this opinion, although a war was not absolutely unacceptable, Britain should take into consideration its long-term effects. Any military action against China, if it had to be adopted, should proceed with the utmost prudence.

Compared to the abovementioned observers, those who completely disagreed with the idea of using violence against China were in a small minority. As in the crisis debate, the main arguments advanced by these commentators still rested on the iniquity of the opium trade. Fry, for example, contended that the only just method of intervention was to 'prohibit the growth of the poppy and manufacture of opium in British India'.[147] Montagu added that Britain should co-operate with the Chinese government to 'seize all smugglers from henceforth, and deal with them as with pirates'.[148] With regard to a potential war against China, these commentators continued to condemn it upon the principles of justice and humanity. They maintained that, although the Chinese authorities had used violence, they should not be regarded as the unjust party. What the Chinese had done, according to John Fisher Murray, 'was only a reciprocation of outrage and violence. ... the crime does not originate in secondary, but in primary causes ... these reciprocal injuries are but symptoms of that evil disease our people have carried into the land of others'.[149] On the basis of similar opinions, Philip Stanhope claimed in Parliament that the opium traffic was 'the sole cause of the war'.[150] For this reason, he and others believed that, if Britain adopted a violent line of action against China, it would not only be 'a most unjust and unfair attack upon the Chinese, who had done nothing more than we had compelled them to do',[151] but would 'add another gross insult to humanity, and to the laws of nations'.[152]

Moreover, some of these commentators found it hard to believe that the war could be terminated in a single campaign. Once operations commenced, Graham was afraid that it 'would be no little war'.[153] Believing 'an independent nation will always resent any condition imposed upon it at the point of the Bayonet',[154] Bullock predicted that a war of conquest would become necessary to achieve Britain's ultimate goals. Since Britain was obviously not able to conquer the whole of China, the consequences of starting such a war would be not only disgraceful for Britain but harmful to the nation's trade in China. In the long term, if China was awakened from its present dormant state, 'the combined nations of Europe, would hardly compete with her single

JUSTIFYING THE OPIUM WAR

and united power'.[155] In that case, not only Britain's rule in India but its influence across the British Empire might be in danger.

It can be seen that the main ground on which these arguments were based – the immorality of the opium trade – did not vary greatly from that employed in the earlier debates. By this time, however, other commentators had gathered enough reasons to justify a war against China – to protect Britain's interests and honour in Asia, or to defend the principles of free trade and international law. Although they had not entirely agreed with each other on the scale and specific means of intervention, a general agreement was reached on the justice and viability of taking reasonably strong measures against China. In contrast, the arguments unconditionally against the war were a minority voice. This significant change of attitude, obviously, would not have been possible without the altered circumstances and the changed British perceptions of China, occasioned by Lin Zexu's strong measures in conjunction with Elliot's intervention in and representations of the crisis. It also finally explains why Palmer maintained that in Parliament 'no member was willing to declare himself *directly* opposed to a war with China'.[156] The word 'directly' is the key in this quotation.

In conclusion, in the complex pre-Opium War controversies over China-related and opium-related issues, although the debates on the subjects of opium, crisis and war were interwoven with each other, they can also be viewed separately in their own right. In each of these discussions, the impact and relative strength of different views varied greatly. Initially, the arguments against the opium trade were not weak at all. After the opium crisis, however, the case for the British government's intervention gradually gained the upper hand, while those who insisted that justice was entirely on the Chinese side and hence a war against China was absolutely unacceptable were reduced to a small minority. Although in April 1840 the Whig government won the vote only narrowly, there was in fact more common ground among the concerned observers in support of Britain adopting a policy of vigorous intervention. What swayed opinion in Westminster, to be exact, was not whether Britain ought to attack China but whether it was essential to pursue an immediate large-scale war. Some sort of military conflict with China, at any rate, became an acceptable prospect to most MPs. Moreover, contrary to what many modern readers might have imagined, general support for government intervention in Chinese affairs was not justified for the sake of protecting the lucrative opium trade. In fact, very few Britons attempted to demonstrate the legitimacy of war on the basis of the sheer economic importance of that trade. Instead, the immorality of the opium trade was often viewed separately from the 'injustice' of the actions that the Chinese took against the British.

It was on the latter ground, rather than the former, that the British commentators disputed the different interpretations of justice and legality. Eventually, notwithstanding the notoriety of the opium trade, the necessity and timeliness of using violence against China was justified on the grounds of protecting the British subjects from an allegedly despotic Chinese government and its unreliable people, and defending the long-term and short-term interests as well as honour of Britain and its empire.

Notes

1 *Hansard's Parliamentary Debates*, House of Commons, 8 April 1840, Third series, vol. 53, 836.
2 Elliot to Palmerston, Canton, 30 Mar. 1839, in Great Britain, Parliament, *Correspondence Relating to China, Presented to Both House of Parliament, by Command of Her Majesty* (London: T.R. Harrison, 1840), p. 355.
3 *Ibid.*, p. 357.
4 Of these, 1,540 chests belonged to American merchants.
5 See, for example, Edgar Holt, *The Opium Wars in China* (London: Putnam, 1964), p. 56; Gerald S. Graham, *The China Station: War and Diplomacy 1830–1860* (Oxford: Clarendon Press, 1978), p. 97; Lawrence Sondhaus, *Naval Warfare, 1815–1914* (London; New York: Routledge, 2001), p. 35; Julia Lovell, *The Opium War: Drugs, Dreams and the Making of China* (London: Picador, 2011), p. 369.
6 James M. Polachek, *The Inner Opium War* (Cambridge, MA: Harvard University Press, 1992).
7 Polachek claims that Lin Zexu was an ally with this group. Polachek repeatedly mentions this 'Spring Purification party', but he does not give its Chinese translation (apart from the annual gathering it hosted in Beijing from 1829 onwards – *Zhanchun Ji*). He also states that it was a successor group to Xuannan Poetry Club (*Xuannan Shishe*). Also known as *Xiaohan Shishe* (Dispersing-the-Cold Poetry Club), Xuannan Poetry Club was believed to be a harbinger of China's reform or even anti-imperialist movement by Chinese intellectuals in the 1950s. From the 1960s, however, Chinese historians had begun to challenge this interpretation. They pointed out that the club was merely a traditional literary society which had nothing to do with the 'progressive' movements later seen in China. Lin Zexu was a member for a short period, but there is no evidence that the club had a significant impact on his political views. See Yang Tianshi, 'Guanyu Xuannan Shishe (On Xuannan Shishe)' (written in 1961), in *Xunqiu Lishi de Midi: Jindai Zhongguo de Zhengzhi yu Renwu* (In Pursuit of Answers to History: Politics and Personages in Modern China) (Beijing: Renmin University of China Press, 2010), pp. 1–6; Yang Guozhen, 'Xuannan Shishe yu Lin Zexu (Xuannan Shishe and Lin Zexu)', *Xiamen Daxue Xuebao* (Journal of Xiamen University), 2 (1964), 107–17; Wang Junyi, 'Guanyu Xuannan Shishe (On Xuannan Shishe)', *Wenwu* (Cultural Relics), 2 (1979), 72–3; and Wang Chunlin, 'Shishu Yapian Zhanzheng Qianxi de Xuannan Shishe de Xingzhi (On the Nature of Xuannan Shishe)', *Lishi Jiaoxue* (History Teaching), 12 (1999), 49–51.
8 Polachek, *The Inner Opium War*, p. 102. Italics in the original.
9 Song-Chuan Chen's recent study on the British 'warlike party' shows that it is far from fair to blame these Qing literati for prompting the war. See Chen, *Merchants of War and Peace*.
10 Julia Lovell, 'Introduction to the English edition', in Mao Haijian, *The Qing Empire and the Opium War: The Collapse of the Heavenly Dynasty*, trans. Joseph Lawson, Craig Smith and Peter Lavelle (Cambridge: Cambridge University Press, 2016), p. xvi.

11 Mao, *The Qing Empire and the Opium War*, p. 12.
12 *Ibid.*, pp. 11–12.
13 Inoue Hiromasa, *Qingdai Yapian Zhengceshi Yanjiu* (Studies in the History of Qing Policy towards Opium), trans. Qian Hang (Lhasa: Tibet Renmin Chubanshe, 2011), pp. 182–209.
14 Glenn Melancon, 'Honour in Opium? The British Declaration of War on China, 1839–1840', *International History Review*, 21 (1999), 855–74; Glenn Melancon, *Britain's China Policy and the Opium Crisis: Balancing Drugs, Violence and National Honour, 1833–1840* (Aldershot: Ashgate, 2003).
15 Lydia H. Liu, *The Clash of Empires: The Invention of China in Modern World Making* (Cambridge, MA; London: Harvard University Press, 2004), pp. 59–69.
16 *Ibid.*, p. 67. Italics in the original.
17 Foreign Office [hereafter FO], 17/31/13. Elliot to Palmerston, 2 April 1839.
18 'The Opium Trade and War', *Eclectic Review*, 7 (May 1840), 712–13, in Li Chen, *Chinese Laws in Imperial Eyes: Sovereignty, Justice, and Transcultural Politics* (New York: Columbia University Press, 2016), p. 227.
19 Chen, *Chinese Laws in Imperial Eyes*, pp. 227–8.
20 *Ibid.*, p. 229.
21 Mao, *The Qing Empire and the Opium War*, p. 92.
22 Chen, *Chinese Laws in Imperial Eyes*, pp. 228–9. Italics in the original.
23 *Ibid.*, pp. 220–1.
24 Mao, *The Qing Empire and the Opium War*, p. 100.
25 Chen, *Chinese Laws in Imperial Eyes*, pp. 232–5.
26 Chen, *Merchants of War and Peace*, p. 121.
27 Mao, *The Qing Empire and the Opium War*, pp. 118–19.
28 *Ibid.*, p. 132. There is an error in the translation here. Mao wrote 'late-June' in his original text. The translator mistakenly put 'mid-June' in the English version of the book. For the Chinese version, see Mao Haijian, *Tianchao de Bengkui: Yapian Zhanzheng Zai Yanjiu* (The Collapse of the Celestial Empire: The Opium War Reconsidered) (Beijing: Sanlian Shudian, 1995), p. 132.
29 On 21 June 1840, James Bremer, the commander of the East Indies and China Station, arrived with warships from India. On 28 June, George Elliot, the commander-in-chief of the expeditionary force and joint plenipotentiary (also, Charles Elliot's cousin), arrived with warships from South Africa. Mao Haijian has provided the detailed composition of the British expeditionary force, including a table on 'British warships outside Humen by the end of June 1840', with the number of cannons they carried. See Mao, *The Qing Empire and the Opium War*, pp. 126–7.
30 It is worth noting that although the Tories failed to win enough votes at this point, when they came into office in 1841 they did not abandon the war. Sir Robert Peel's government continued to fight against China until the Treaty of Nanjing was signed in August 1842.
31 Tan Chung, *China and the Brave New World: A Study of the Origins of the Opium War 1840–42* (Durham, NC: Carolina Academic Press, 1978), p. 230.
32 [Robert Philip], *No Opium! Or, Commerce and Christianity, Working Together for Good in China: A Letter to James Cropper, Esq., of Liverpool* (London: Thomas Ward, 1835).
33 Horatio Montagu, *A Voice for China: which must be heard* (London: Nisbet, 1840), p. 9.
34 Anon., *British Opium Trade with China* (Birmingham?: B. Hudson, 1840?), p. 14.
35 *Ibid.*
36 *Hansard's Parliamentary Debates*, House of Commons, 9 April 1840, Third series, vol. 53, 855–6.
37 Anon., 'Abuse of Opium: Opinions on the Subject Given by One Long Resident in China', *Chinese Repository*, VIII, no. 10 (Feb. 1840), 517.
38 Anon., 'Remarks on the Opium Trade with China', *Chinese Repository*, V, no. 7 (Nov. 1836), 300.

39 Anon., 'Remarks on the Present Crisis in the Opium Traffic, with Inquiries Respecting Its Causes, and the Best Course to Be Pursued by Those Now Connected with It', *Chinese Repository*, VIII, no. 1 (May 1839), 4.
40 A. S. Thelwall, *The Iniquities of the Opium Trade with China; Being a Development of the Main Causes Which Exclude the Merchants of Great Britain from the Advantages of an Unrestricted Commercial Intercourse with that Vast Empire* (London: Wm H. Allen, 1839), pp. 129–30.
41 William Storrs Fry, *Facts and Evidence Relating to the Opium Trade with China* (London: Pelham Richardson, 1840), p. 6.
42 William Groser, *What Can Be Done to Suppress the Opium Trade* (London: J. Haddon, 1840), p. 4.
43 Anon., 'Means of Doing Good in China, or Remark upon a Few of Those Expedients of a Benevolent Kind that Are Still within Our Reach', *Chinese Repository*, VII, no. 4 (Aug. 1838), 196.
44 Robert Philip, *Peace with China! Or The Crisis of Christianity in Central Asia: A Letter to the Right Honourable T.B. Macaulay, Secretary at War* (London: John Snow, 1840), p. 4.
45 Fry, *Facts and Evidence*, p. 6. Italics in the original.
46 S.S.S., 'To the Editor of the Canton Press', *Canton Press*, III, no. 51 (25 Aug. 1838).
47 Thelwall, *The Iniquities of the Opium Trade*, p. 131.
48 *Ibid.*, pp. 173–4.
49 Anon., *British Opium Trade with China*, p. 24.
50 Montagu, *A Voice for China*, p. 9.
51 Anon., *British Opium Trade with China*, p. 22.
52 Anon., 'Mr. King's Letter to the British Chief Superintendent, dated Macao, 19th May, 1839', *Canton Register*, XIII, no. 7 (18 Feb. 1840).
53 Anon., 'Substitutes for Sulphate or Quinine', *Canton Register*, XI, no. 39 (25 Sept. 1838).
54 *Hansard's Parliamentary Debates*, House of Lords, 12 May 1840, Third series, vol. 54, 32.
55 A resident in China, *The Rupture with China and Its Causes; Including the Opium Question, and Other Important Details: in a Letter to Lord Viscount Palmerston* (London: Sherwood, Gilbert, and Piper, 1840), p. 8. The author is believed to be H. Hamilton Lindsay.
56 D. Stewart, 'Dr. Stewart's Report', *Canton Register*, XIII, no. 21 (26 May 1840).
57 *Hansard's Parliamentary Debates*, House of Commons, 8 April 1840, Third series, vol. 53, 824.
58 A resident in China, *The Rupture with China*, p. 4.
59 Anon., *Some Pros and Cons of the Opium Question; With a Few Suggestions Regarding British Claims on China* (London: Smith, Elder, 1840), pp. 12–13.
60 One long resident in China, 'The Opium Trade, to John Harsley Palmer, Esq', *Canton Press*, V, no. 16 (18 Jan. 1840).
61 H. Hamilton Lindsay, *Is the War with China a Just One?* (London: James Ridgway, 1840), p. 30.
62 A resident in China, *The Rupture with China*, p. 33.
63 Anon., 'Foreign Relations with China', *Canton Press*, IV, no. 47 (24 Aug. 1839).
64 Anon., 'Mr. King's Letter to the British Chief Superintendent, dated Macao, 19th May, 1839', *Canton Register*, XIII, no. 7 (18 Feb. 1840).
65 Lindsay, *Is the War with China a Just One?* p. 9.
66 *Ibid.*, p. 8.
67 Anon., *Review of the Management of Our Affairs in China, since the Opening of the Trade in 1834* (London: Smith, Elder, 1840), p. 54.
68 Anon., 'To the Right Honorable Lord Viscount Palmerston, Secretary of State for Foreign Affairs', *Canton Press*, IV, no. 38 (25 May 1839).
69 Anon., 'Foreign Relations with China, III', *Canton Press*, IV, no. 43 (21 July 1839).
70 *Canton Register*, XIII, no. 11 (17 March 1840).
71 Anon., *Some Pros and Cons*, p. 19.

72 *Ibid.*, p. 23.
73 *Ibid.*, p. 24.
74 Lindsay, *Is the War with China a Just One?* p. 8.
75 *Canton Register*, XII, no. 11 (12 March 1839). Italics in the original.
76 Anon., *Some Pros and Cons*, pp. 21–2.
77 Samuel Warren, *The Opium Question* (London: James Ridgway, 1840), p. 78.
78 Anon., *Some Pros and Cons*, p. 21.
79 Warren, *The Opium Question*, p. 78.
80 Anon., *Review of the Management*, pp. 56–7.
81 Warren, *The Opium Question*, p. 101.
82 Anon., *Some Pros and Cons*, p. 34.
83 *Hansard's Parliamentary Debates*, House of Commons, 7 April 1840, Third series, vol. 53, 717.
84 A resident in China, *The Rupture with China*, p. 44.
85 Alexander Graham, *The Right, Obligation, and Interest of the Government of Great Britain to Require Redress from the Government of China for the Late Forced Surrender of British-owned Opium at Canton* (Glasgow: Robert Stuart, 1840), p. 17.
86 *Ibid.*, p. 16.
87 Warren, *The Opium Question*, p. 114.
88 A Barrister at Law, *The Opium Question*, p. 44.
89 Anon., 'On the Causes of Rupture between England and China', *Chinese Repository*, VIII, no. 12 (April 1840), 622.
90 Anon., *Review of the Management*, p. 90.
91 *Hansard's Parliamentary Debates*, House of Commons, 9 April 1840, Third series, vol. 53, 939.
92 *Ibid.*, 27 July 1840, vol. 55, 1047.
93 Sydney S. Bell, *Answer to 'The Opium Question' by Samuel Warren* (London: Smith, Elder, 1840), p. 7.
94 Montagu, *A Voice for China*, p. 24.
95 *Hansard's Parliamentary Debates*, House of Commons, 27 July 1840, Third series, vol. 55, 1036.
96 Anon., *British Opium Trade with China*, p. 19.
97 Elliot to Palmerston, 30 Jan. 1839, in *Correspondence Relating to China*, p. 343.
98 T.H. Bullock, *The Chinese Vindicated, or Another View of the Opium Question* (London: Wm H. Allen, 1840), p. 101.
99 *Hansard's Parliamentary Debates*, House of Lords, 12 May 1840, Third series, vol. 54, 2.
100 William Jardine in London to James Matheson in China, 25–7 Sept. 1839, in Alain le Pichon (ed.), *China Trade and Empire: Jardine, Matheson & Co. and the Origins of British Rule in Hong Kong 1827–1843* (Oxford: Oxford University Press, 2006), p. 387. James Matheson (1796–1878) was a leading opium trader and co-founder of Jardine, Matheson and Company.
101 Graham, *The Right, Obligation, and Interest*, p. 16. Italics in the original.
102 *Hansard's Parliamentary Debates*, House of Commons, 27 July 1840, Third series, vol. 55, p. 1039.
103 These commentators were obviously unaware that it was Elliot's promise about the British government's compensation that prompted the British merchants to hand over their opium stock voluntarily in the outer waters.
104 *Corrected Report of the Speech of Sir George Staunton, on Sir James Graham's Motion on the China Trade, in the House of Commons, April 7, 1840* (London: Simpkin, Marshall, 1840), p. 13.
105 *Hansard's Parliamentary Debates*, House of Commons, 7 April 1840, Third series, vol. 53, 740.
106 Anon., 'The New Year; Posture of Public Affairs; Prospects and Probable Consequences of War between the Governments of China and Great Britain', *Chinese Repository*, VIII, no. 9 (Jan. 1839), 443.

107 As explained earlier, Mao Haijian's finding has shown that the deprivation of supplies and servants was actually much shorter than seven weeks.
108 *Hansard's Parliamentary Debates*, House of Commons, 9 April 1840, Third series, vol. 53, 864.
109 *Ibid.*, 27 July 1840, vol. 55, 1051–2.
110 *Corrected Report of the Speech of Sir George Staunton*, p. 11.
111 *Hansard's Parliamentary Debates*, House of Lords, 8 April 1840, Third series, vol. 53, 753.
112 *Hansard's Parliamentary Debates*, House of Commons, 7 April 1840, Third series, vol. 53, 717.
113 Elliot to Palmerston, Canton, 13 April 1839, in *Correspondence Relating to China*, p. 389.
114 Anon., 'To the Right Honorable Lord Viscount Palmerston, Secretary of State for Foreign Affairs', *Canton Press*, IV, no. 38 (25 May 1839).
115 *Hansard's Parliamentary Debates*, House of Commons, 8 April 1840, Third series, vol. 53, 836.
116 *Ibid.*, 7 April 1840, 670.
117 *Ibid.*, 674.
118 *Ibid.*, 27 July 1840, vol. 55, 1052.
119 Anon., *Some Pros and Cons*, pp. 39–40.
120 *Corrected Report of the Speech of Sir George Staunton*, pp. 14–15.
121 *Canton Press*, V, no. 8 (23 Nov. 1839).
122 A resident in China, *Remarks on Occurrences in China, since the Opium Seizure in March 1839 to the Latest Date* (London: Sherwood, Gilbert and Piper, 1840), p. 28. Italics in the original. Again, H. Hamilton Lindsay is believed to be the author. No record from the Chinese side, however, could confirm that the Daoguang emperor indeed received and forwarded such a document.
123 *Ibid.*, pp. 27, 29.
124 Warren, *The Opium Question*, p. 76.
125 Anon., *Review of the Management*, p. 39.
126 A resident in China, *Remarks on Occurrences*, p. 32.
127 *Ibid*.
128 Anon., *Chinese Commerce and Disputes, from 1640 to 1840* (London: W. Morrison, 1840), p. 31.
129 Warren, *The Opium Question*, p. 108.
130 Lindsay, *Is the War with China a Just One?* p. 37.
131 One long resident in China, 'The Opium Trade, to John Harsley Palmer, ESQ', *Canton Press*, V, no. 16 (18 Jan. 1840).
132 *Canton Press*, VI, no. 10 (5 Dec. 1840).
133 Anon., 'China', *Canton Press*, IV, no. 45 (10 Aug. 1839).
134 Elliot to Palmerston, 22 April 1839, in *Correspondence Relating to China*, p. 391.
135 Napier to the Hong merchants and Chinese authorities, 8 Sept. 1834, in *ibid.*, p. 13.
136 'Ramrod: To the Editor of the Canton Press', *Canton Press*, V, no. 11 (14 Dec. 1839).
137 Anon., *British Opium Trade with China*, p. 18.
138 See, for example, Elliot to Auckland, Governor-General of India, 16 April 1839, in *Correspondence Relating to China*, p. 431; Graham, *The Right, Obligation, and Interest of the Government*, p. 16; and A resident in China, *The Rupture with China and Its Causes*, p. 56, etc.
139 *Hansard's Parliamentary Debates*, House of Lords, 12 May 1840, Third series, vol. 54, 25.
140 'Ramrod: To the Editor of the Canton Press', *Canton Press*, V, no. 2 (12 Oct. 1839). Italics in the original.
141 C.R., 'Progress of the Difficulties between the English and Chinese', *Chinese Repository*, VIII, no. 9 (Jan. 1839), 476. Italics in the original.
142 Lindsay, *Is the War with China a Just One?* pp. 36–7.
143 'Ramrod: To the Editor of the Canton Press', *Canton Press*, V, no. 11 (14 Dec. 1839).

144 'Ramrod: To the Editor of the Canton Press', *Canton Press*, V, no. 2 (12 Oct. 1839). Italics in the original.
145 *Hansard's Parliamentary Debates*, House of Commons, 9 April 1840, Third series, vol. 53, 866.
146 *Ibid.*, 924.
147 Fry, *Facts and Evidence*, p. 61.
148 Montagu, *A Voice for China*, p. 55.
149 John Fisher Murray, *The Chinese and the Ministry. An Inquiry into the Origin and Progress of Our Present Difficulties with China, and into the Expediency, Justice, and Necessity of the War* (London: T. Cadell, 1840), p. 51.
150 *Hansard's Parliamentary Debates*, House of Lords, 12 May 1840, Third series, vol. 54, 26.
151 *Hansard's Parliamentary Debates*, House of Commons, 8 April 1840, Third series, vol. 53, 836.
152 Montagu, *A Voice for China*, p. 55.
153 *Hansard's Parliamentary Debates*, House of Commons, 7 April 1840, Third series, vol. 53, 702.
154 Bullock, *The Chinese Vindicated*, p. 113.
155 *Ibid.*, p. 111.
156 *Hansard's Parliamentary Debates*, House of Commons, 8 April 1840, Third series, vol. 53, 836. Italics added.

Conclusion

The Opium War lasted longer than the British had expected. This was partly because resistance from the Chinese was more resolute than anticipated, partly because Britain did not launch a full-scale attack according to Charles Elliot's 'fight-and-talk' strategy. In August 1841, as Sir Henry Pottinger replaced Elliot as the plenipotentiary, Britain's determination to win the war by force became evident. Within a year, the British troops stormed up China's south coast, blockaded the Grand Canal, and occupied the large island of Zhoushan at the mouth of the Yangtze River, as well as several ports to the south, including Canton, Amoy, Ningbo and Shanghai. Despite the fact that the Chinese soldiers fought with bravery and even desperation, they were clearly no match for British arms and discipline. When the British expedition pushed on to the walls of Nanjing, the second city of the empire, the Qing court sued for peace. On 29 August 1842, the Treaty of Nanjing was signed aboard the *Cornwallis*, the British fleet's flagship moored in the Yangtze. The First Anglo-Chinese War had come to an end.

The Treaty of Nanjing, with its supplementary agreement signed in October 1843, has often been regarded as 'the most important treaty settlement in China's modern history'.[1] These historic documents allowed Britain to achieve what it had failed for so long to obtain by diplomacy. The restrictive Canton system was abolished and five 'treaty ports' were opened to British trade and residence. The Chinese government had to pay 21 million dollars to Britain as compensation for the war costs and the destroyed opium. In addition, the island of Hong Kong was ceded to Britain as its trading base. To the Chinese, the conclusion of the war and the Treaty of Nanjing signified that the era when China determined the terms of Sino-British relations was over. The country was ushered into a period of 'Western domination and

CONCLUSION

increasing Chinese humiliation',[2] in which the Qing court gradually lost control of the key elements of its commercial, social and foreign policies. As John Gregory has stated, from the middle years of the nineteenth century 'the Chinese world began to be turned upside down'.[3]

This study has traced British–Chinese encounters in the half century before the Opium War. Unlike previous publications on early Sino-British relations, this book has focused closely on British imperial attitudes towards China, with emphasis on how the idea of war against the Chinese empire was created, developed and debated on the basis of these changing views. It has shown that British perceptions of China, by and large, became increasingly negative over this period. These unfavourable views, to a great extent, were important underlying influences which helped justify Britain's decision to embark on a war against China. In retrospect, leaders of the Macartney embassy tended to argue that it was a very few hostile ministers in the Qianlong court who had obstructed the mission's official business in 1793, while the emperor himself was an amicable and open-minded figure who was prepared to protect Britain's trade. During their travels across China, these British observers formed the idea that the patriarchal government of China had rendered Chinese civilisation stagnant, but they still held a certain degree of respect for that regime. Despite the fact that the Macartney mission failed to achieve its commercial and diplomatic objectives, Macartney and Staunton did not find anything inappropriate in the course of conduct that Britain had adopted in its relations with China. Instead of suggesting a radical change of policy, they suggested that patience and perseverance were extremely important to future British–Chinese relations. They were convinced that, 'by time and management',[4] favourable results would eventually follow, while 'no shorter way will do it'.[5] Macartney, in particular, advised against an aggressive line of action on the grounds that it would harm the interests of Britain and its empire in Asia. Although Macartney did mention a possible breakdown in Sino-British relations, he asserted that 'nothing could be urged in favour of an hostile conduct, but an irresistible conviction of failure by forbearance'.[6]

When the Amherst mission visited the Qing court in 1816, these British representatives developed rather different attitudes towards China. They overthrew the benevolent image of the Chinese emperor, which was promoted by Macartney's embassy. Instead, members of the Amherst embassy perceived the Chinese sovereign (now the Jiaqing emperor) as a capricious despot whose personal character was the very reason for the failure of the mission. Moreover, as the embassy provided British travellers with new opportunities to explore the interior of China, the backward state of the Qing empire was increasingly exposed to British eyes. As a result, members of the Amherst mission reached a general consensus on the half-civilised image of China, believing that the Qing government was the primary cause of China's decline or lack of progress. Such 'discoveries' not only lowered these British observers' respect for the current Chinese government but provided new perspectives for Britain to deal with in its relations with China. Since experience had shown that, to obtain an objective in China, it was more effective either to ignore the authority of the government or to offer a firm remonstration, the conciliatory line of action advised by Macartney was seen as problematical. Complimentary embassies to the Qing court were hence no longer considered a good idea. In order to produce favourable results in British–Chinese relations, members of the Amherst embassy such as Davis suggested that a 'determined step' was 'more requisite'.[7] Although the call for coercive measures was still not popular at this time, a change of attitude towards China, as well as a demonstration of Britain's steadfast image, first appeared on the agenda.

Not long after the Amherst embassy, British merchants who traded with China replaced diplomatic visitors as the main providers and interpreters of images of China. In the early 1830s, the controversy over the renewal of the East India Company's China trade monopoly touched off a heated debate on the China question. To justify that the free trade theory was inapplicable to the case of China and that the Company was irreplaceable in dealing with the Chinese, the EIC and its supporters stressed the peculiarity, or cultural otherness, of China. They maintained that China's unique history and economic system had led its people to undervalue international communication. Since Chinese institutions were simply different from (but not necessarily inferior to) the European models, the Chinese government and its laws deserved respect. Given the Chinese people's natural disposition to 'appeal to reason',[8] the EIC's campaigners insisted that persuasion and a peaceful approach would be more effective than an aggressive line of action in improving Britain's trade with China. In contrast, the 'free traders', who wished the Chinese market to be opened to all, presented diametrically different views. They asserted that the universal laws of international commerce could certainly be applied to the China trade, because the Chinese people were friendly, commercially minded and desirous of communication with foreigners. According to these commentators, the principal problem for China was that the Qing government, which did not represent the vast majority of the nation, had set itself against the interests of both the Chinese and foreign people. For this reason, it was fully legitimate to challenge the authority of the Qing government and to hold its restrictive laws in defiance. Since 'it is a Chinese maxim to trample on the voluntary submissive and abject, while they respect firmness and decision',[9] 'free trade' advocates such as Lindsay promoted the notion that 'much more may be gained by an appeal to their fears than to their friendship'.[10] Although in the early years of the 1830s opinions were divided on whether a display of military force was appropriate, with the abolition of the EIC's monopoly in 1834 the necessity for a more determined stance against China was strengthened.

In the mid-1830s, Napier's failed effort to create fear in the Chinese government excited new discussions on Britain's future policy in China. Various British residents in Canton began to allege that it was time to officially abandon the conciliatory policy and to adopt a 'show of force' attitude. They argued that the key to success was to impress the Chinese government with a sense of Britain's power and firmness. To achieve this end, Britain should send a determined plenipotentiary, attended by sufficient maritime force, to the vicinity of Beijing to demand a mutually beneficial commercial treaty. Given the perceived timidity of the Chinese government, some of these observers predicted that, once Britain pursued such an approach, the Qing court would make every concession to avoid a clash with the force at Britain's disposal and thus comply with Britain's demands. It should be noted that, however, although 'show of force' advocates proposed an aggressive stance and a display of Britain's naval force, very few of them supported the actual use of arms. The majority of British residents in China at this time, as with the British government, regarded it unjust and impractical to resort to a significant use of force against China. Due to the fact that the 'show of force' theory aimed only to intimidate the Chinese authorities by the presence of British force and was clearly opposed to a large-scale armed conflict, the mid-1830s cannot be viewed as the beginning of Britain's pro-war attitude towards China, even though it made a war with China more imaginable than ever.

In the late 1830s, the rapidly growing opium trade on the China coast and the ensuing crisis, in which Lin Zexu suppressed the traffic with a strong hand, brought Chinese affairs to the forefront of British attention. Although, by and large, the opium merchants' arguments in favour of their trade were not well supported, they, together with other opinion formers, successfully produced an impression that the British nation was suffering gross insult in China as a result of Lin Zexu's actions. In this context, since history had repeatedly shown that it was useless to conciliate the Chinese authorities, the actual use of arms was much more favoured by the British than it had been a few years earlier. On the basis of this general sentiment, and because of a variety of concerns over the interests and honour of Britain and its empire, the British government (and then Parliament) finally approved the justice, necessity and timeliness of a war against China. A new chapter in British–Chinese relations unfolded.

To conclude, this book investigates British imperial attitudes towards China during their early encounters from 1792 to 1840. By focusing on this medium-term (*moyenne durée*) period, we can discover that Britain's decision to go to war against China was created as a result of both continuing and changing attitudes towards that country. On the one hand, from the Macartney embassy to the opium crisis, informed and influential British observers, many of who had participated in these encounters, produced increasingly hostile feelings towards the Chinese empire. In consequence, a war with China became more and more imaginable to the British. On the other hand, over this period, opinion formers and decision-makers in Britain disagreed with each other on various aspects such as the disposition of the Chinese emperor, the extent to which Britain should adopt coercive measures and whether a small-scale demonstration of Britain's military strength would be enough to compel China to make concessions. Although, at last, it was Lin Zexu's campaign and Elliot's intervention in the opium crisis that triggered Britain's determination to involve itself vigorously in Chinese affairs, open hostilities with China would probably not have appeared justifiable or acceptable without these attitudes that had slowly developed from the Macartney mission to the eve of the Opium War.

Notes

1 Jonathan D. Spence, *The Search for Modern China* (New York and London: Norton, 1999), p. 160.
2 John S. Gregory, *The West and China since 1500* (Basingstoke: Palgrave Macmillan, 2003), p. 73.
3 Ibid., p. 88.
4 George L. Staunton, *An Authentic Account of an Embassy from the King of Great Britain to the Emperor of China* (2 vols, London: W. Bulmer, 1798) II, 334.
5 J.L. Cranmer-Byng (ed.), *An Embassy to China: Being the Journal Kept by Lord Macartney during His Embassy to the Emperor Ch'ien-lung 1793–1794* (London: Longmans, Green and Co., 1962), p. 210.
6 Ibid., p. 213.
7 John Francis Davis, *Sketches of China; Partly during an Inland Journey of Four Months between Peking, Nanking, and Canton* (2 vols, London: Charles Knight, 1841), II, 143.
8 Thomas Fisher, 'Statistical Notices of China', *Gentleman's Magazine*, 103 (May 1833), 389.
9 Karl Gützlaff, *Journal of Three Voyages along the Coast of China, in 1831, 1832, & 1833* (London: Frederick Westley and A.H. Davis, 1834), p. 12.
10 Hugh Hamilton Lindsay's Report, in *Report of Proceedings on a Voyage to the Northern Ports of China, in the Ship Lord Amherst: Extracted from Papers, Printed by Order of the House of Commons, Relating to the Trade with China* (London: B. Fellowes, 1833), p. 57.

BIBLIOGRAPHY

Primary sources

Manuscripts

British Library, London: India Office Library and Records: India Office Amherst correspondence, Lord Amherst's embassy, 1815–17, vols 196–8, G/12/196–8.
British Library, London: India Office Library and Records: India Office Macartney correspondence, Lord Macartney's embassy, 1787–1810, vols 91–3, G/12/91–3.
British Museum, London: Alexander, William, *Journal of Lord Macartney's Embassy to China, 1792–1794*, Add 35, 174 (I. 9).
Durham University, Durham: Political and Public Papers of Charles, 2nd Earl Grey.
National Library of Ireland, Dublin: Winder, Edward, *Account of a Journey in China in 1793 in Lord Macartney's Mission*, MS 8799 (1).
Royal Geographical Society, London: Else, Stephen, *Journal of a Voyage to the East Indies and an Historical Narrative of Lord Macartney's Embassy to the Court of Pekin*, 1793, B.K.S. case 260 H.
The National Archives of the UK: Foreign Office, Political and Other Departments: General Correspondence before 1906, F.O. 17.

Parliamentary debates

Hansard's Parliamentary Debates, 1840, Third Series, vols 53–5 (London: Thomas Curson Hansard).

Periodicals

The Asiatic Journal, 1829–34.
The Canton Press, 1835–40.
The Canton Register, 1834–40.
The Chinese Repository, 1832–40.
The Edinburgh Review, 1830–4.
The Gentleman's Magazine, 1831–4.
The Westminster Review, 1831–4.

Books and pamphlets

A Barrister at Law, *The Opium Question, as between Nation and Nation* (London: James Bain, 1840).
A resident in China, *Remarks on Occurrences in China, since the Opium Seizure in March 1839 to the Latest Date* (London: Sherwood, Gilbert and Piper, 1840).

BIBLIOGRAPHY

A resident in China, *The Rupture with China and Its Causes; Including the Opium Question, and Other Important Details: in a Letter to Lord Viscount Palmerston* (London: Sherwood, Gilbert and Piper, 1840).

Abel, Clarke, *Narrative of a Journey in the Interior of China in the Years 1816–1817* (London: Longman and Hurst, 1818).

Anderson, Aeneas, *A Narrative of the British Embassy to China, in the Years of 1792, 1793 and 1794* (London: J. Debrett, 1795).

Anon., *Brief Observations Respecting the Pending Disputes with the Chinese, and a Proposal for Bringing Them to a Satisfactory Conclusion* (London: James Ridgway, 1840).

Anon., *British Opium Trade with China* (Birmingham?: B. Hudson, 1840?).

Anon., *Chinese Commerce and Disputes, from 1640 to 1840* (London: W. Morrison, 1840).

Anon., *Review of the Management of Our Affairs in China, since the Opening of the Trade in 1834* (London: Smith, Elder, 1840).

Anon., *Some Pros and Cons of the Opium Question; with a Few Suggestions Regarding British Claims on China* (London: Smith, Elder, 1840).

Anon., *The Foreign Trade of China Divested of Monopoly, Restriction, and Hazard by Means of Insular Commercial Stations* (London: Effingham Wilson, 1832).

Anson, George, *A Voyage Round the World in the Years 1740–1744* (London: John and Paul Knapton, 1748).

Barrow, John, *The Life of George Lord Anson* (London: John Murray, 1839).

Barrow, John, *Some Account of the Public Life and a Selection from the Unpublished Writings of the Earl of Macartney* (London: T. Cadell, 1807).

Barrow, John, *Travels in China* (Philadelphia: W.E. M'Laughlin, 1805).

Bell, Sydney S., *Answer to 'The Opium Question' by Samuel Warren* (London: Smith, Elder, 1840).

Boswell, James, *Boswell's Life of Johnson: Together with Boswell's Journal of a Tour to the Hebrides and Johnson's Diary of a Journey into North Wales*, ed. L.F. Powell (6 vols, Oxford: Clarendon Press, 1934–50).

Bullock, T.H., *The Chinese Vindicated, or Another View of the Opium Question: Being in Reply to a Pamphlet, by Samuel Warren, Esq., F.R.S., Barrister at Law in the Middle Temple* (London: Wm H. Allen, 1840).

Chambers, William, *A Dissertation on Oriental Gardening* (Dublin: W. Wilson, 1773).

Chambers, William, *Designs of Chinese Buildings, Furniture, Dresses, Machines and Utensils* (London, 1757; reprinted, Farnborough: Gregg International, 1969).

Chang, Elizabeth Hope (ed.), *British Travel Writing from China, 1798–1901* (5 vols, London: Pickering & Chatto, 2010).

Compendium of Facts Relating to the Opium Trade [London, 1840?], in *The Dublin Literary Journal*, vol. 1 (Dublin: Joshua Abell, 1843).

Corrected Report of the Speech of Sir George Staunton, on Sir James Graham's Motion on the China Trade, in the House of Commons, April 7, 1840 (London: Simpkin, Marshall, 1840).

BIBLIOGRAPHY

Cranmer-Byng, J.L. (ed.), *An Embassy to China: Being the Journal Kept by Lord Macartney during His Embassy to the Emperor Ch'ien-lung, 1793-1794* (London: Longmans, Green and Co., 1962).

[Crawfurd, John], *Chinese Monopoly Examined* (London: James Ridgway, 1830).

[Crawfurd, John], *Observations on the Influence of the East India Company's Monopoly on the Price and Supply of Tea; and on the Commerce with India, China, etc.* (London: Longman, Rees, Orme, Brown and Green, 1831).

Crisis in the Opium Traffic: Being an Account of the Proceedings of the Chinese Government to Suppress that Trade, with the Notices, Edicts, &c., Relating Thereto ([Canton: ?], 1839).

Davis, John Francis, *Sketches of China; Partly during an Inland Journey of Four Months between Peking, Nanking, and Canton* (2 vols, London: Charles Knight, 1841).

Davis, John Francis, *The Chinese: A General Description of the Empire of China and Its Inhabitants* (2 vols, London: Charles Knight, 1836).

Defoe, Daniel, *The Life and Adventures of Robinson Crusoe* (1719; reprinted, Edinburgh: James Ballantyne, 1812).

Downing, C. Toogood, *The Fan-Qui in China in 1836-37* (3 vols, London: Henry Colburn, 1838).

Du Halde, Jean Baptiste, *A Description of the Empire of China and Chinese Tartary, Together with the Kingdoms of Korea, and Tibet* (2 vols, London: Edward Cave, 1738-41).

Du Halde, Jean Baptiste, *The General History of China: Containing a Geographical, Historical, Chronological, Political and Physical Description of the Empire of China, Chinese-Tartary, Corea and Thibet* (London: John Watts, 1736).

East India Company, *Three Reports of the Select Committee, Appointed by the Court of Directors to Take into Consideration the Export Trade from Great Britain to the East Indies, China, Japan, and Persia* (London: J.S. Jordan, 1793).

Ellis, Henry, *A Series of Letters on the East India Question, Addressed to the Members of the Two Houses of Parliament* (London: John Murray, 1830).

Ellis, Henry, *Journal of the Proceedings of the Late Embassy to China* (London: John Murray, 1817).

Fry, William Storrs, *Facts and Evidence Relating to the Opium Trade with China* (London: Pelham Richardson, 1840).

Goddard, James, *Remarks on the Late Lord Napier's Mission to Canton; in Reference to the Present State of Our Relations with China* (London: printed for private circulation, 1836).

Gordon, G.J., *Address to the People of Great Britain, Explanatory of Our Commercial Relations with the Empire of China* (London: Smith, Elder, 1836).

Graham, Alexander, *The Right, Obligation, and Interest of the Government of Great Britain to Require Redress from the Government of China for the Late Forced Surrender of British-owned Opium at Canton* (Glasgow: Robert Stuart, 1840).

[Graham, James], *The War in China, Sir J. Graham's Speech in the House of Commons, Tuesday, April 7, 1840* ([London?]: W.E. Painter, [1840?]).

BIBLIOGRAPHY

Great Britain, Parliament, *Correspondence Relating to China, Presented to Both Houses of Parliament, by Command of Her Majesty* (London: T.R. Harrison, 1840).

Groser, William, *What Can Be Done to Suppress the Opium Trade* (London: J. Haddon, 1840).

Gützlaff, Karl, *A Sketch of Chinese History, Ancient and Modern: Comprising a Retrospect of the Foreign Intercourse and Trade with China* (2 vols, London: Smith, Elder, 1834).

Gützlaff, Karl, *China Opened: or a Display of the Topography, History, Customs, Manners, Arts, Manufactures, Commerce, Literature, Religion, Jurisprudence, etc, of the Chinese Empire* (2 vols, London: Smith, Elder, 1838).

Gützlaff, Karl, *Journal of Three Voyages along the Coast of China, in 1831, 1832, & 1833* (London: Frederick Westley and A.H. Davis, 1834).

Hall, Basil, *Narrative of a Voyage to Java, China and the Great Loo-Choo Island* (London: Edward Moxon, 1840).

Hayne, Henry, *Henry Hayne Diary 1816–1817* (4 vols), *China through Western Eyes: Manuscript Records of Traders, Travellers, Missionaries and Diplomats, 1792–1942* (London: Adam Matthew Microform Publications, 1996).

Holmes, Samuel, *The Journal of Mr Samuel Holmes, Serjeant-Major of the Sixth Light Dragoons, during His Attendance, as one of the Guard on Lord Macartney's Embassy to China and Tartary, 1792–3* (London: W. Bulmer, 1798).

Hunter, William C., *Bits of Old China* (London: Kegan Paul, Trench, 1885).

Jones, William, *The Works of Sir William Jones* (6 vols, London: G.G. and J. Robinson, 1799).

[King, Charles W.], *Opium Crisis, a Letter Addressed to Charles Elliot, Esq., Chief Superintendent of the British Trade with China* (London: Edward Suter, Duncan and Malcolm, and Hatchard and Son, 1839).

Lindsay, H. Hamilton, *Is the War with China a Just One?* (London: James Ridgway, 1840).

Lindsay, H. Hamilton, *Letter to the Right Honourable Viscount Palmerston on British Relations with China* (London: Saunders and Otley, 1836).

Lockman, John (ed.), *Travels of the Jesuits into Various Parts of the World* (2 vols, London: John Noon, 1743).

Macleod, John, *Narrative of a Voyage in His Majesty's Late Ship Alceste to the Yellow Sea, along the Coast of Corea, and through Its Numerous Hitherto Undiscovered Islands, to the Island of Lewchew* (London: John Murray, 1817).

Marjoribanks, Charles, *Letter to the Right Hon. Charles Grant, President of the Board of Control, on the Present State of British Intercourse with China* (London: J. Hatchard and Son, 1833).

Martin, R. Montgomery, *The Past and Present State of the Tea Trade of England, and of the Continents of Europe and America* (London: Parbury, Allen, 1832).

Matheson, James, *The Present Position and Prospects of the British Trade with China; Together with an Outline of Some Leading Occurrences in Its Past History* (London: Smith, Elder, 1836).

BIBLIOGRAPHY

Medhurst, Walter Henry, *China: Its State and Prospects, with Special Reference to the Spread of the Gospel* (London: John Snow, 1838).
Montagu, Horatio, *A Voice for China: Which Must Be Heard* (London: Nisbet, 1840).
Monteith, Robert, *Reasons [for Investigation into Charges against Lord Palmerston]* (Glasgow?: William Collins, 1840?).
Morrison, Eliza (ed.), *Memoirs of the Life and Labours of Robert Morrison, D.D.* (2 vols, London: Longman, 1839), I.
Morrison, Robert, *A Memoir of the Principal Occurrences during an Embassy from the British Government to the Court of China in the Year 1816* (London: Hatchard & Son, 1820).
Morrison, Robert, *A View of China, for Philological Purposes: Containing a Sketch of Chinese Chronology, Geography, Government, Religion and Customs* (London: Black, Parbury, and Allen, 1817).
Murray, John Fisher, *The Chinese and the Ministry. An Inquiry into the Origin and Progress of Our Present Difficulties with China, and into the Expediency, Justice, and Necessity of the War* (London: T. Cadell, 1840).
Palace Museum (ed.), *Qingdai Waijiao Shiliao (Jiaqing Chao)* (Qing Dynasty Diplomatic Documents (the Jiaqing period)) (6 vols, Taipei: Chengwen Press, 1968).
[Palmer, Roundell, Earl of Selbourne?], *Statement of Claims of the British Subjects Interested in Opium Surrendered to Captain Elliot at Canton for the Public Service* (London: Pelham Richardson, 1840).
[Philip, Robert], *No Opium! Or, Commerce and Christianity, Working Together for Good in China: A Letter to James Cropper, Esq., of Liverpool* (London: Thomas Ward, 1835).
Philip, Robert, *Peace with China! or The Crisis of Christianity in Central Asia: A Letter to the Right Honourable T.B. Macaulay, Secretary at War* (London: John Snow, 1840).
Proudfoot, William Jardine, *Biographical Memoir of James Dinwiddie: Embracing Some Account of His Travel in China and Residence in India* (Liverpool: E. Howell, 1868).
Report of Proceedings on a Voyage to the Northern Ports of China, in the Ship Lord Amherst: Extracted from Papers, Printed by Order of the House of Commons, Relating to the Trade with China (London: B. Fellowes, 1833).
Robbins, Helen H., *Our First Ambassador to China, an Account of the Life of George, Earl of Macartney* (London: John Murray, 1908).
Shuck, J. Lewis, *Portfolio Chinensis: Or a Collection of Authentic Chinese State Papers Illustrative of the History of the Present Position of Affairs in China. With a Translation, Notes and Introduction* (Macao: New Washington Press, 1840).
Smith, Adam, *An Inquiry into the Nature and Causes of the Wealth of Nations*, ed. R.H. Campbell and A.S. Skinner (2 vols, Oxford: Oxford University Press, 1976).
Staunton, George L., *An Authentic Account of an Embassy from the King of Great Britain to the Emperor of China* (2 vols, London: W. Bulmer, 1798).

Staunton, George Thomas, *Memoirs of the Chief Incidents of the Public Life of Sir George T. Staunton* (London: L. Booth, 1856).
Staunton, George Thomas, *Miscellaneous Notices Relating to China, and Our Commercial Intercourse with that Country* (London: John Murray, 1822).
Staunton, George Thomas, *Notes of Proceedings and Occurrences during the British Embassy to Pekin in 1816* (London: Habant, 1824; reprinted, with an introduction by Patrick Tuck, London: Routledge, 2000).
Staunton, George Thomas, *Remarks on the British Relations with China, and the Proposed Plans for Improving Them* (London: Edmund Lloyd, 1836).
Staunton, George Thomas, *Ta Tsing Leu Lee; Being the Fundamental Laws, and a Selection from the Supplementary Statutes of the Penal Code of China* (London: T. Cadell and W. Davies, 1810).
[Taylor, Henry?], *A Digest of the Despatches on China (Including Those Received on the 27th of March): With a Connecting Narrative and Comments* (London: James Ridgway, 1840).
Temple, William, *The Works of Sir William Temple* (4 vols, London: J. Brotherton, 1770; reprinted, New York: Greenwood, 1968).
Thelwall, A.S., *The Iniquities of the Opium Trade with China; Being a Development of the Main Causes Which Exclude the Merchants of Great Britain from the Advantages of an Unrestricted Commercial Intercourse with that Vast Empire* (London: Wm H. Allen, 1839).
Thompson, George, *Report of a Public Meeting and Lecture at Darlington on China and the Opium Question* (Durham: J.H. Veitch, 1840?).
Van Braam, André Everard, *An Authentic Account of the Embassy of the Dutch East-India Company, to the Court of the Emperor of China, in the Years 1794 and 1795* (London: R. Phillips, 1798).
Warren, Samuel, *The Opium Question* (London: James Ridgway, 1840).
Webb, John, *An Historical Essay Endeavoring a Probability that the Language of the Empire of China is the Primitive Language* (London: Nath. Brook, 1669).
Williams, S. Wells, *The Middle Kingdom: A Survey of the Geography, Government, Education, Social Life, Arts, Religion, etc. of the Chinese Empire and Its Inhabitants* (New York and London: Wiley & Putnam, 1848).
Winterbotham, W., *A Historical, Geographical and Philosophical View of the Chinese Empire, with an Appendix: 'Narrative of the Embassy to China'* (London: Ridgeway and Buttom, 1795).
Young, William Curling, *The English in China* (London: Smith, Elder, 1840).

Secondary sources

Books

Adas, Michael, *Machines as the Measure of Men: Science, Technology, and Ideologies of Western Dominance* (Ithaca, NY: Cornell University Press, 1989).
Appleton, William W., *A Cycle of Cathay: The Chinese Vogue in England during the Seventeenth and Eighteenth Centuries* (New York: Octagon Books, 1979).
Bai, Shouyi and Gong, Shuduo, eds, *Zhongguo Tongshi* (General History of China) (12 vols, Shanghai: Shanghai Renmin Chubanshe, 2013).

BIBLIOGRAPHY

Ballaster, Rosalind, *Fabulous Orient: Fictions of the East in England 1662–1785* (Oxford: Oxford University Press, 2005).

Barringer, Tim and Flynn, Tom (eds), *Colonialism and the Object: Empire, Material Culture and the Museum* (London; New York: Routledge, 1998).

Bartlett, Beatrice S., *Monarchs and Ministers: The Grand Council in Mid-Ch'ing China, 1723–1820* (Berkeley, CA: University of California Press, 1991).

Beevers, David (ed.), *Chinese Whispers: Chinoiserie in Britain 1650–1930* (Brighton: The Royal Pavilion and Museums, 2008).

Bello, David Anthony, *Opium and the Limits of Empire: Drug Prohibition in the Chinese Interior, 1729–1850* (Cambridge, MA: Harvard University Asia Center, 2005).

Bickers, Robert A. (ed.), *Ritual and Diplomacy: The Macartney Mission to China, 1792–1794* (London: Wellsweep, 1993).

Bickers, Robert, *The Scramble for China: Foreign Devils in the Qing Empire, 1832–1914* (London: Penguin, 2011).

Blake, Robert, *Jardine Matheson: Traders of the Far East* (London: Weidenfeld and Nicolson, 1999).

Braudel, Fernand, *On History*, trans. Sarah Matthews (London: Weidenfeld and Nicolson, 1980).

Brockley, Matthew Liam, *Journey to the East: The Jesuit Mission to China, 1579–1724* (Cambridge, MA: Belknap Press of Harvard University Press, 2007).

Brook, Timothy and Blue, Gregory (eds), *China and Historical Capitalism: Genealogies of Sinological Knowledge* (Cambridge: Cambridge University Press, 1999).

Bulley, Anne, *Free Mariner: John Adolphus Pope in the East Indies 1786–1821* (London: British Association for Cemeteries in South Asia, 1992).

Chang, Elizabeth Hope, *Britain's Chinese Eye: Literature, Empire and Aesthetics in Nineteenth-Century Britain* (Stanford, CA: Stanford University Press, 2010).

Chang, Hsin-pao, *Commissioner Lin and the Opium War* (Cambridge, MA: Harvard University Press, 1964).

Chen, Li, *Chinese Laws in Imperial Eyes: Sovereignty, Justice, and Transcultural Politics* (New York: Columbia University Press, 2016).

Chen, Qin, Li, Gang and Qi, Peifang, *Zhongguo Xiandaihua Shigang* (A Brief History of Modernisation in China) (2 vols, Nanning: Guangxi Renmin Chubanshe, 1998).

Chen, Song-Chuan, *Merchants of War and Peace: British Knowledge of China in the Making of the Opium War* (Hong Kong: Hong Kong University Press, 2017).

Ching, Julia and Oxtoby, Willard G. (eds), *Discovering China: European Interpretations in the Enlightenment* (Rochester, NY: University of Rochester Press, 1992).

Cohen, Paul A., *Discovering History in China: American Historical Writing on the Recent Chinese Past* (New York: Columbia University Press, 1984).

Collis, Maurice, *Foreign Mud: Being an Account of the Opium Imbroglio at Canton in the 1830s and the Anglo-Chinese War that Followed* (London: Faber, 1964).

BIBLIOGRAPHY

Conner, Patrick, *The China Trade, 1600–1860* (Brighton: Royal Pavilion Art Gallery and Museums, 1986).

Costin, W.C., *Great Britain and China: 1833–1860* (Oxford: Clarendon Press, 1937).

Dawson, Raymond, *The Chinese Chameleon: An Analysis of European Conceptions of Chinese Civilization* (London: Oxford University Press, 1967).

Dawson, Raymond (ed.), *The Legacy of China* (Boston, MA: Cheng & Tsui, 1990).

Derks, Hans, *History of the Opium Problem: The Assault on the East, ca. 1600–1950* (Leiden; Boston: Brill, 2012).

Dikötter, Frank, *The Discourse of Race in Modern China* (London: Hurst, 1992).

Duyvendak, J.J.L., *The Last Dutch Embassy to the Chinese Court, 1794–1795* (Leiden: Brill, 1938).

Eames, James Bromley, *The English in China: Being an Account of the Intercourse and Relations between England and China from the Year 1600 to the Year 1843 and a Summary of Later Developments* (1909; reprinted, London: Curzon, 1974).

Elliott, Mark C., *Emperor Qianlong: Son of Heaven, Man of the World* (New York: Longman, 2009).

Elman, Benjamin A., *On Their Own Terms: Science in China, 1550–1900* (Cambridge, MA: Harvard University Press, 2005).

Evans, Eric J., *The Forging of the Modern State: Early Industrial Britain 1783–1870* (London: Longman, 2001).

Fairbank, John K. (ed.), *The Chinese World Order: Traditional China's Foreign Relations* (Cambridge, MA: Harvard University Press, 1968).

Fairbank, John K., *Trade and Diplomacy on the China Coast: The Opening of the Treaty Ports, 1842–1854* (Stanford, CA: Stanford University Press, 1969).

Fairbank, John K., et al. (eds), *The Cambridge History of China* (15 vols, Cambridge: Cambridge University Press, 1978).

Fan, Fa-ti, *British Naturalists in Qing China: Science, Empire, and Cultural Encounter* (Cambridge, MA: Harvard University Press, 2004).

Fay, Peter Ward, *The Opium War 1840–1842* (New York; London: Norton, 1975).

Forman, Ross G., *China and the Victorian Imagination: Empires Entwined* (Cambridge: Cambridge University Press, 2013).

Frank, Caroline, *Objectifying China, Imagining America: Chinese Commodities in Early America* (Chicago; London: The University of Chicago Press, 2011).

Franke, Wolfgang, *China and the West* (Oxford: Blackwell, 1967).

Fu, Lo-shu, *A Documentary Chronicle of Sino-Western Relations 1644–1820* (Tucson, AZ: University of Arizona Press, 1966).

Gelber, Harry G., *Opium, Soldiers and Evangelicals: Britain's 1840–42 War with China, and its Aftermath* (New York: Palgrave Macmillan, 2004).

Gelber, Harry G., *The Dragon and the Foreign Devils: China and the World, 1100 BC to the Present* (London: Bloomsbury, 2007).

Graham, Gerald S., *The China Station: War and Diplomacy 1830–1860* (Oxford: Clarendon Press, 1978).

Grantham, A.E., *A Manchu Monarch: An Interpretation of Chia Ching* (Arlington, VA: University Publications of America, 1976).

BIBLIOGRAPHY

Greenberg, Michael, *British Trade and the Opening of China 1800–42* (Cambridge: Cambridge University Press, 1951).

Gregory, John S., *The West and China since 1500* (Basingstoke: Palgrave Macmillan, 2003).

Hanes III, W. Travis and Sanello, Frank, *The Opium Wars: The Addiction of One Empire and the Corruption of Another* (Naperville, IL: Sourcebooks, 2002).

Hay, Malcolm, *Failure in the Far East: Why and How the Breach between the Western World and China First Began* (London: Neville Spearman, 1956).

Hertel, Ralf and Keevak, Michael (eds), *Early Encounters between East Asia and Europe: Telling Failures* (London; New York: Routledge, 2017).

Hevia, James L., *Cherishing Men from Afar: Qing Guest Ritual and the Macartney Embassy of 1793* (Durham, NC: Duke University Press, 1995).

Hibbert, Christopher, *The Dragon Wakes: China and the West, 1793–1911* (New York: Penguin, 1984).

Hillemann, Ulrike, *Asian Empire and British Knowledge: China and the Networks of British Imperial Expansion* (Basingstoke: Palgrave Macmillan, 2009).

Ho, Ping-ti, *Studies on the Population of China 1368–1953* (Cambridge, MA: Harvard University Press, 1959).

Hodder, Ruppert, *In China's Image: China's Self-Perception in Western Thought* (New York: Palgrave Macmillan, 2000).

Hoe, Susanna and Roebuck, Derek, *The Taking of Hong Kong: Charles and Clara Elliot in China Waters* (Aberdeen; Hong Kong: Hong Kong University Press, 2009).

Holt, Edgar, *The Opium Wars in China* (London: Putnam, 1964).

Howland, R. Douglas, *Borders of Chinese Civilization: Geography and History at Empire's End* (Durham, DC: Duke University Press, 1996).

Hsia, Adrian (ed.), *The Vision of China in the English Literature of the Seventeenth and Eighteenth Centuries* (Hong Kong: The Chinese University Press, 1998).

Hudson, G.F., *Europe and China: A Survey of their Relations from the Earliest Times to 1800* (Boston: Beacon, 1961).

Hummel, A.W. (ed.), *Eminent Chinese of the Ch'ing Period, 1644–1912* (2 vols, Washington, DC: US Government Printing Office, 1943–4).

Inglis, Brian, *The Opium War* (London: Hodder and Stoughton, 1976).

Inoue, Hiromasa, *Qingdai Yapian Zhengceshi Yanjiu* (Studies in the History of Qing Policy towards Opium), trans. Qian Hang (Lhasa: Tibet Renmin Chubanshe, 2011).

Jenkins, Eugenia Zuroski, *A Taste for China: English Subjectivity and the Prehistory of Orientalism* (Oxford: Oxford University Press, 2013).

Jones, David Martin, *The Image of China in Western Social and Political Thought* (New York: Palgrave Macmillan, 2001).

Keevak, Michael, *Becoming Yellow: A Short History of Racial Thinking* (Princeton, NJ: Princeton University Press, 2011).

Keevak, Michael, *Embassies to China: Diplomacy and Cultural Encounters before the Opium Wars* (Singapore: Palgrave Macmillan, 2017).

BIBLIOGRAPHY

Keith, Arthur B., *A Constitutional History of India 1600–1935* (London: Methuen, 1936).

Kerr, Douglas, *Eastern Figures: Orient and Empire in British Writing* (Hong Kong: Hong Kong University Press, 2008).

Kerr, Douglas and Kuehn, Julia (eds), *A Century of Travels in China: Critical Essays on Travel Writing from the 1840s to the 1940s* (Hong Kong: Hong Kong University Press, 2007).

Kiernan, V.G., *The Lords of Human Kind: European Attitudes towards the Outside World in the Imperial Age* (London: Serif, 1995).

Kitson, Peter J., *Forging Romantic China: Sino-British Cultural Exchange 1760–1840* (Cambridge: Cambridge University Press, 2013).

Kitson, Peter J. and Markley, Robert (eds), *Writing China: Essays on the Amherst Embassy (1816) and Sino-British Cultural Relations* (Woodbridge: Boydell & Brewer, 2016).

Kowaleski-Wallace, Beth, *Consuming Subjects: Women, Shopping, and Business in the Eighteenth Century* (New York: Columbia University Press, 1997).

Kuhn, Philip A., *Origins of the Modern Chinese State* (Stanford, CA: Stanford University Press, 2002).

Kuhn, Philip A., *Rebellion and Its Enemies in Late Imperial China: Militarization and Social Structure, 1796–1864* (Cambridge, MA: Harvard University Press, 1970).

Kumagai, Yukihisa, *Breaking into the Monopoly: Provincial Merchants and Manufacturers' Campaigns for Access to the Asian Market, 1790–1833* (Leiden: Brill, 2012).

Kuo, P.C., *A Critical Study of the First Anglo-Chinese War with Documents* (Shanghai: The Commercial Press, 1935; reprinted, Westport, CT: Hyperion, 1973).

Lach, Donald, *Asia in the Making of Europe* (3 vols, Chicago: University of Chicago Press, 1965–93).

Le Pichon, Alain (ed.), *China Trade and Empire: Jardine, Matheson & Co. and the Origins of British Rule in Hong Kong 1827–1843* (Oxford: Oxford University Press, 2006).

Lee, Thomas H.C. (ed.), *China and Europe: Images and Influences in Sixteenth to Eighteenth Centuries* (Hong Kong: The Chinese University Press, 1991).

Li, Chien-nung, *The Political History of China, 1840–1928* (Princeton, NJ: Van Nostrand, 1956).

Lin, Man-houng, *China Upside Down: Currency, Society, and Ideologies, 1808–56* (Cambridge, MA: Harvard University Asia Center, 2006).

Liu, Lydia, *The Clash of Empires: The Invention of China in Modern World Making* (Cambridge, MA; London: Harvard University Press, 2004).

Lovell, Julia, *The Opium War: Drugs, Dreams and the Making of China* (London: Picador, 2011).

Luard, Evan, *Britain and China* (London: Chatto & Windus, 1962).

Lutz, Jessie Gregory, *Opening China: Karl F.A. Gützlaff and Sino-Western Relations, 1827–1852* (Grand Rapids, MI: William B. Eerdmans, 2008).

Mackerras, Colin, *Western Images of China* (Oxford: Oxford University Press, 1989).

BIBLIOGRAPHY

Madancy, Joyce A., *The Troublesome Legacy of Commissioner Lin: The Opium Trade and Opium Suppression in Fujian Province, 1820s to 1920s* (Cambridge, MA: Harvard University Asia Center, 2003).

Mao, Haijian, *The Qing Empire and the Opium War: The Collapse of the Heavenly Dynasty*, trans. Joseph Lawson, Craig Smith and Peter Lavelle (Cambridge: Cambridge University Press, 2016).

Mao, Haijian, *Tianchao de Bengkui: Yapian Zhanzheng Zai Yanjiu* (The Collapse of the Heavenly Dynasty: The Opium War Reconsidered) (Beijing: Sanlian Shudian, 1995).

Markley, Robert, *The Far East and the English Imagination, 1600–1730* (Cambridge: Cambridge University Press, 2009).

Marshall, P. J. and Williams, Glyndwr, *The Great Map of Mankind: Perceptions of New Worlds in the Age of Enlightenment* (Cambridge, MA: Harvard University Press, 1982).

Maverick, Lewis A., *China: A Model for Europe* (San Antonio, TX: Paul Anderson, 1946).

Melancon, Glenn, *Britain's China Policy and the Opium Crisis: Balancing Drugs, Violence and National Honour, 1833–1840* (Aldershot: Ashgate, 2003).

Morse, Hosea Ballou, *The Chronicles of the East India Company Trading to China, 1635–1834* (5 vols, Oxford: Clarendon Press, 1926; reprinted, London: Routledge, 2000).

Morse, Hosea Ballou, *The International Relations of the Chinese Empire* (3 vols, London: Longmans, 1910–18; reprinted, Folkestone: Global Oriental, 2008).

Mosca, Matthew W., *From Frontier Policy to Foreign Policy: The Question of India and the Transformation of Geopolitics in Qing China* (Stanford, CA: Stanford University Press, 2013).

Mullaney, Thomas S., Leibold, James et al. (eds), *Critical Han Studies: The History, Representation, and Identity of China's Majority* (Berkeley, CA: University of California Press, 2012).

Mungello, D.E., *The Great Encounter of China and the West, 1500–1800* (Oxford: Rowman & Littlefield, 2006).

Myers, Henry A. (ed.), *Western Views of China and the Far East* (2 vols, Hong Kong: Asian Research Service, 1982).

Napier, Priscilla Hayter, *Barbarian Eye: Lord Napier in China, 1834, the Prelude to Hong Kong* (Washington, DC: Brassey's, 1995).

Naquin, Susan and Rawski, Evelyn S., *Chinese Society in the Eighteenth Century* (New Haven, CT: Yale University Press, 1987).

Needham, Joseph, et al. (eds), *Science and Civilisation in China* (7 vols, Cambridge: Cambridge University Press, 1954–2008).

Nussbaum, Felicity (ed.), *The Global Eighteenth Century* (Baltimore, MD: Johns Hopkins University Press, 2003).

Owen, David, *British Opium Policy in China and in India* (New Haven, CT: Yale University Press, 1934; reprinted, Archon Books, 1968).

Pelissier, Roger, *The Awakening of China, 1793–1949* (London: Secker & Warburg, 1967).

BIBLIOGRAPHY

Perkins, Dwight H., *Agricultural Development in China, 1368–1968* (Edinburgh: Edinburgh University Press, 1969).

Peyrefitte, Alain, *The Collision of Two Civilisations: The British Expedition to China in 1792–4* (London: Harvill, 1993).

Philips, C.H., *The East India Company 1784–1834* (Manchester: Manchester University Press, 1961).

Platt, Stephen R., *Imperial Twilight: The Opium War and the End of China's Last Golden Age* (New York: Alfred A. Knopf, 2018).

Polachek, James M., *The Inner Opium War* (Cambridge, MA: Harvard University Press, 1992).

Pomeranz, Kenneth, *The Great Divergence: China, Europe, and the Making of the Modern World Economy* (Princeton, NJ: Princeton University Press, 2000).

Porter, David, *Ideographia: The Chinese Cipher in Early Modern Europe* (Stanford, CA: Stanford University Press, 2001).

Porter, David, *The Chinese Taste in Eighteenth-Century England* (Cambridge: Cambridge University Press, 2010).

Pratt, Mary Louise, *Imperial Eyes: Travel Writing and Transculturation* (London: Routledge, 1992).

Pritchard, E.H., *Anglo-Chinese Relations during the Seventeenth and Eighteenth Centuries* (Urbana, IL: University of Illinois Press, 1929; reprinted, New York: Octagon Books, 1970).

Pritchard, E.H., *The Crucial Years of Early Anglo-Chinese Relations, 1750–1800* (Washington, DC: Pullman, 1936; reprinted, New York: Octagon Books, 1970).

Qian, Zhongshu, *A Collection of Qian Zhongshu's English Essays* (Beijing: Foreign Language Teaching and Research Press, 2005).

Rawski, Evelyn S., *The Last Emperors: A Social History of Qing Imperial Institutions* (Berkeley, CA: University of California Press, 2001).

Rawski, Evelyn S. and Rawson, Jessica (eds), *China: The Three Emperors, 1662–1795* (London: Royal Academy of Arts, 2005).

Reichwein, Adolf, *China and Europe: Intellectual and Artistic Contacts in the Eighteenth Century* (London: Routledge, 1968).

Robert, J.A.G., *China through Western Eyes: The Nineteenth Century* (Bath: Alan Sutton, 1991).

Said, Edward W., *Orientalism* (London: Penguin, 1995).

Schrecker, John E., *The Chinese Revolution in Historical Perspective* (London: Praeger, 2004).

Singer, Aubrey, *The Lion and the Dragon: The Story of the First British Embassy to the Court of the Emperor Qianlong in Peking 1792–1794* (London: Barrie and Jenkins, 1992).

Sondhaus, Lawrence, *Naval Warfare, 1815–1914* (London; New York: Routledge, 2001).

Soothill, William Edward, *China and the West: A Short History of Their Contact from Ancient Times to the Fall of the Manchu Dynasty* (Yardley, PA: Westholme, 2009).

Spadafora, David, *The Idea of Progress in Eighteenth-Century Britain* (New Haven, CT: Yale University Press, 1990).

BIBLIOGRAPHY

Spence, Jonathan D., *Chinese Roundabout* (New York; London: Norton, 1992).
Spence, Jonathan D., *The Chan's Great Continent: China in Western Minds* (London: Penguin, 2000).
Spence, Jonathan D., *The Search for Modern China* (New York; London: Norton, 1999).
Struve, Lynn A. (ed.), *The Qing Formation in World-historical Time* (Cambridge, MA: Harvard University Press, 2004).
Tan, Chung, *China and the Brave New World: A Study of the Origins of the Opium War 1840–42* (Durham, NC: Carolina Academic Press, 1978).
Thackeray, David, Thompson, Andrew and Toye, Richard (eds), *Imagining Britain's Economic Future, c. 1800–1975: Trade, Consumerism, and Global Markets* (Cham: Palgrave Macmillan, 2018).
Van de Ven, Hans (ed.), *Warfare in Chinese History* (Leiden; Boston: Brill, 2000).
Van Dyke, Paul A., *The Canton Trade: Life and Enterprise on the China Coast, 1700–1845* (Aberdeen; Hong Kong: Hong Kong University Press, 2005).
Wakeman, Frederic, Jr and Grant, Carolyn (eds), *Conflict and Control in Late Imperial China* (Berkeley, CA: University of California Press, 1975).
Waley, Arthur, *The Opium War through Chinese Eyes* (London: Routledge, 2005).
Waley-Cohen, Joanna, *The Sextants of Beijing: Global Currents in Chinese History* (New York; London: Norton, 1999).
Wang, Wensheng, *White Lotus Rebels and South China Pirates: Crisis and Reform in the Qing Empire* (Cambridge, MA: Harvard University Press, 2014).
Webster, Anthony, *The Twilight of the East India Company: The Evolution of Anglo-Asian Commerce and Politics, 1790–1860* (Woodbridge: Boydell, 2009).
Wells, Byron R. and Steward, Philip (eds), *Interpreting Colonialism* (Oxford: Voltaire Foundation, 2004).
Welsh, Frank, *A History of Hong Kong* (London: Harper Collins, 1997).
Wills, John E., Jr, *Embassies and Illusions: Dutch and Portuguese Envoys to K'ang-his, 1666–1681* (Cambridge, MA: Council of East Asian Studies, Harvard University, 1984; reprinted, Los Angeles: Figueroa, 2009).
Wong, J.Y., *Anglo-Chinese Relations, 1839–1860: A Calendar of Chinese Documents in the British Foreign Office Records* (Oxford: Oxford University Press, 1983).
Wong, J.Y., *Deadly Dreams: Opium, Imperialism and the Arrow War* (Cambridge: Cambridge University Press, 1998).
Yang, Chi-Ming, *Performing China: Virtue, Commerce, and Orientalism in Eighteenth-Century England, 1660–1760* (Baltimore, MD: Johns Hopkins University Press, 2011).
Yang, Tianshi, *Xunqiu Lishi de Midi: Jindai Zhongguo de Zhengzhi yu Renwu* (In Pursuit of Answers to History: Politics and Personages in Modern China) (Beijing: Renmin University of China Press, 2010).
Young, John D., *Confucianism and Christianity: The First Encounter* (Hong Kong: Hong Kong University Press, 1983).
Zhang, Ming, *Kaiguo Zhihuo* (Founding the Nation: A Puzzle) (Chongqing: Chongqing Chubanshe, 2016).
Zhang, Shunhong, *British Views on China at the Dawn of the 19th Century* (Reading: Paths International Ltd, 2013).

Zheng, Yangwen, *The Social Life of Opium in China* (Cambridge: Cambridge University Press, 2005).

Zhu, Yong, *Buyuan Dakai de Zhongguo Damen* (The Chinese Gate Unwilling to Open) (Nanchang: Jiangxi Renmin Chubanshe, 1989).

Chapters in books

Batchelor, Robert, 'Concealing the Bounds: Imagining the British Nation through China', in *The Global Eighteenth Century*, ed. Felicity Nussbaum (Baltimore, MD: Johns Hopkins University Press, 2003), pp. 79–92.

Beevers, David, '"Mand'rin only is the man of taste": 17th and 18th Century Chinoiserie in Britain', in *Chinese Whispers: Chinoiserie in Britain 1650–1930*, ed. David Beevers (Brighton: The Royal Pavilion and Museums, 2008), pp. 13–25.

Blue, Gregory, 'China and Western Social Thought in the Modern Period', in *China and Historical Capitalism: Genealogies of Sinological Knowledge*, ed. Timothy Brook and Gregory Blue (Cambridge: Cambridge University Press, 1999), pp. 57–109.

Dawson, Raymond, 'Western Conceptions of Chinese Civilization', in *The Legacy of China*, ed. Raymond Dawson (Boston, MA: Cheng & Tsui, 1990), pp. 1–27.

Gao, Hao, 'Imagining the Opium Trade: Britain's Justification for the First Anglo-Chinese War', in *Imagining Britain's Economic Future, c. 1800–1975. Trade, Consumerism, and Global Markets*, ed. David Thackeray, Andrew Thompson and Richard Toye (Cham: Palgrave Macmillan, 2018), pp. 21–41.

Jones, Susan M. and Kuhn, Philip A., 'Dynastic Decline and the Roots of Rebellion', in *The Cambridge History of China*, ed. John K. Fairbank, et al. (15 vols, Cambridge: Cambridge University Press, 1978), X, 107–62.

Kitson, Peter J. 'The "Catastrophe of This New Chinese Mission": The Amherst Embassy to China of 1816', in *Early Encounters between East Asia and Europe: Telling Failures*, ed. Ralf Hertel and Michael Keevak (London; New York: Routledge, 2017), pp. 67–83.

Marshall, P.J., 'Britain and China in the Late Eighteenth Century', in *Ritual and Diplomacy: The Macartney Mission to China, 1792–1794*, ed. Robert A. Bickers (London: Wellsweep, 1993), pp. 11–29.

Min, Eun Kyung, 'Narrating the Far East: Commercial Civility and Ceremony in the Amherst Embassy to China (1816–1817)', in *Interpreting Colonialism*, ed. Byron R. Wells and Philip Steward (Oxford: Voltaire Foundation, 2004), pp. 160–80.

Pagani, Catherine, 'Chinese Material Culture and British Perceptions of China in the Mid-Nineteenth Century', in *Colonialism and the Object: Empire, Material Culture and the Museum*, ed. Tim Barringer and Tom Flynn (London; New York: Routledge, 1998), pp. 28–40.

Perdue, Peter C., 'Culture, History, and Imperial Chinese Strategy: Legacies of the Qing Conquest', in *Warfare in Chinese History*, ed. Hans Van de Ven (Leiden; Boston: Brill, 2000), pp. 252–87.

Rawski, Evelyn S., 'The "Prosperous Age": China in the Kangxi, Yongzheng and Qianlong Reigns', in *China: The Three Emperors, 1662–1795*, ed. Evelyn S. Rawski and Jessica Rawson (London: Royal Academy of Arts, 2005), pp. 22–40.
Tuck, Patrick 'Introduction: Sir George Thomas Staunton and the Failure of the Amherst Embassy of 1816', in *Britain and the China Trade 1635–1842*, ed. Patrick Tuck (10 vols, London: Routledge, 2000).
Wong, Lawrence Wang-chi, 'Barbarians or Not Barbarians: Translating Yi in the Context of Sino-British Relations in the Eighteenth and Nineteenth Centuries', in *Towards a History of Translating: In Commemoration of the 40th Anniversary of the Research Centre for Translation, CUHK*, ed. Lawrence Wang-chi Wong (3 vols, Hong Kong: Research Centre for Translation, CUHK, 2013), III, 293–388.
Yang, C. K., 'Some Preliminary Statistical Patterns of Mass Actions in Nineteenth-Century China', in *Conflict and Control in Late Imperial China*, ed. Frederic Wakeman Jr and Carolyn Grant (Berkeley, CA: University of California Press, 1975), pp. 174–210.
Yoon, Chong-kun, 'Sinophilism during the Age of Enlightenment: Jesuits, Philosophes and Physiocrats Discover Confucius', in *Western Views of China and the Far East*, ed. Henry A. Myers (2 vols, Hong Kong: Asian Research Service, 1982), I, 149–82.
Zhang, Shunhong, 'Historical Anachronism: The Qing Court's Perception of and Reaction to the Macartney Embassy', in *Ritual and Diplomacy: The Macartney Mission to China, 1792–1794*, ed. Robert A. Bickers (London: Wellsweep, 1993), pp. 31–42.

Articles in journals

Basu, Dilip K., 'China Xenology and the Opium War: Reflections on Sinocentrism', *The Journal of Asian Studies*, 73:4 (2014), 927–40.
Bayer, Kristin, 'Contagious Consumption: Commodity Debates over the Eighteenth and Nineteenth Century China Trade', *International Journal of Asia Pacific Studies*, 8 (2012), 73–94.
Berg, Maxine, 'Britain, Industry and Perceptions of China: Matthew Boulton, "useful knowledge" and the Macartney Embassy to China, 1792–94', *Journal of Global History*, 1 (2006), 269–88.
Bickers, Robert, 'The Challenger: Hugh Hamilton Lindsay and the Rise of British Asia, 1832–1865', *Transactions of the Royal Historical Society*, Sixth series, 22 (2012), 141–69.
Chang, Michael G., 'Fathoming Qianlong: Imperial Activism, the Southern Tours, and the Politics of Water Control, 1736–1765', *Late Imperial China*, 24 (2003), 51–108.
Chen, Jeng-Guo, 'The British View of Chinese Civilization and Emergence of Class Consciousness', *The Eighteenth Century*, 45 (2004), 193–205.
Chen, Li, 'Law, Empire, and Historiography of Modern Sino-Western Relations: A Case Study of the *Lady Hughes* Controversy in 1784', *Law and History Review*, 1 (2009), 1–53.

BIBLIOGRAPHY

Chen, Song-Chuan, 'An Information War Waged by Merchants and Missionaries at Canton: The Society for the Diffusion of Useful Knowledge in China, 1834–1839', *Modern Asian Studies*, 46 (2012), 1705–35.

Christie, William, 'China in Early Romantic Periodicals', *European Romantic Review*, 1 (2016), 25–38.

Dean, Britten, 'British Informal Empire: The Case of China', *The Journal of Commonwealth & Comparative Politics*, 14 (1976), 64–81.

Eaton, William Joseph, 'The Old Regime and the Middle Kingdom: The French Physiocrats and China as a Model for Reform in the Eighteenth Century, a Cautionary Tale', *Tamkang Journal of International Affairs*, 10 (2006), 55–95.

Esherick, Joseph W., 'Cherishing Sources from Afar', *Modern China*, 24 (1998), 135–61.

Esherick, Joseph W., 'Tradutore, Traditore: A Reply to James Hevia', *Modern China*, 24 (1998), 328–32.

Fairbank, John K. and Teng, Ssu-yu, 'On the Ch'ing Tributary System', *Harvard Journal of Asiatic Studies*, 6 (1939), 135–246.

Fan, T.C., 'Chinese Fables and Anti-Walpole Journalism', *Review of English Studies*, 25 (1949), 141–51.

Fay, P.W., 'The Protestant Mission and the Opium War', *Pacific Historical Review*, 40 (1971), 145–61.

Gao, Hao, 'Going to War against the Middle Kingdom? Continuity and Change in British Attitudes towards Qing China (1793–1840)', *The Journal of Imperial and Commonwealth History*, 2 (2017), 210–31.

Gao, Hao, 'Prelude to the Opium War? British Reactions to the "Napier Fizzle" and Attitudes towards China in the Mid Eighteen-thirties', *Historical Research*, 237 (2014), 491–509.

Gao, Hao, 'The Amherst Embassy and British Discoveries in China', *History*, 337 (2014), 568–87.

Gao, Hao, 'The Inner Kowtow Controversy during the Amherst Embassy to China, 1816–1817', *Diplomacy & Statecraft*, 4 (2016), 595–614.

Gao, Hao, 'Understanding the Chinese: British Merchants on the China Trade in the Early 1830s', *Britain and the World*, 2 (2019), 151–71.

Gerritsen, Anne and McDowall, Stephen, 'Global China: Material Culture and Connections in World History', *Journal of World History*, 1 (2012), 3–8.

Gerritsen, Anne and McDowall, Stephen, 'Material Culture and the Other: European Encounters with Chinese Porcelain, ca. 1650–1800', *Journal of World History*, 1 (2012), 87–113.

Harrison, Henrietta, 'Chinese and British Diplomatic Gifts in the Macartney Embassy of 1793', *English Historical Review*, 560 (2018), 65–97.

Harrison, Henrietta, 'The Qianlong Emperor's Letter to George III and the Early-Twentieth-Century Origins of the Ideas about Traditional China's Foreign Relations', *American Historical Review*, 3 (2017), 680–701.

Hevia, James L., 'Oriental Customs and Ideas: The Planning and Execution of the First British Embassy to China', *Chinese Social Science Review*, 7 (1994), 135–7.

BIBLIOGRAPHY

Hevia, James L., 'Postpolemical History: A Response to Joseph W. Esherick', *Modern China*, 24 (1998), 319–27.

Hevia, James L., '"The Ultimate Gesture of Deference and Debasement": Kowtowing in China', *Past and Present*, 203 (2009), 212–34.

Huang, Yinong, 'Yinxiang yu Zhenxiang: Qingchao Zhongying Liangguo de Guanli Zhizheng (Impressions v. Reality: A Study on the Guest Ritual Controversy between Qing China and Britain)', *Zhongyang Yanjiuyuan Lishi Yuyan Yanjiusuo Jikan* (Bulletin of the Institute of History and Philology Academia Sinica), 78:1 (2007), 35–106.

Kitson, Peter J., '"The Kindness of My Friends in England": Chinese Visitors to Britain in the Late Eighteenth and Early Nineteenth Centuries and Discourses of Friendship and Estrangement', *European Romantic Review*, 1 (2016), 55–70.

Lach, Donald F., 'Leibniz and China', *Journal of the History of Ideas*, 6 (1945), 436–55.

Marshall, P.J., 'Lord Macartney, India and China: The Two Faces of the Enlightenment', *South Asia: Journal of South Asian Studies*, 19 (1996), 121–33.

Melancon, Glenn, 'Honour in Opium? The British Declaration of War on China, 1839–1840', *International History Review*, 21 (1999), 855–74.

Melancon, Glenn, 'Peaceful Intentions: The First British Trade Commission in China, 1833–5', *Historical Research*, 73 (2000), 33–47.

Mungello, D.E., 'The First Great Cultural Encounter between China and Europe (ca. 1582–ca. 1793)', *Review of Culture*, 21 (1994), 111–20.

Peyrefitte, Alain, 'Chinese Protectionism versus Anglo-Saxon Free-Trade', *Chinese Social Science Quarterly*, 7 (1994), 123–34.

Philips, C.H., 'The Secret Committee of the East India Company, II', *Bulletin of the School of Oriental and African Studies*, 10 (1940), 699–716.

Porter, David, 'A Peculiar but Uninteresting Nation: China and the Discourse of Commerce in Eighteenth-Century England', *Eighteenth-Century Studies*, 2 (2000), 181–99.

Qian, Zhongshu, 'China in the English Literature of the Eighteenth Century', *Quarterly Bulletin of Chinese Bibliography*, new series, 2 (1941), 7–48, 113–52.

Qian, Zhongshu, 'China in the English Literature of the Seventeenth Century', *Quarterly Bulletin of Chinese Bibliography*, new series, 1 (1940), 351–84.

Ramsey, Rachel, 'China and the Idea of Order in John Webb's *An Historical Essay*', *Journal of the History of Ideas*, 3 (2001), 483–503.

Rowe, William T., 'Introduction: The Significance of the Qianlong–Jiaqing Transition in Qing History', *Late Imperial China*, 2 (2011), 74–88.

Rubinstein, Murray A., 'The Wars They Wanted: American Missionaries' Use of *The Chinese Repository* Before the Opium War', *American Neptune*, 48 (1988), 271–82.

Rzepka, Charles J., 'The Literature of Power and the Imperial Will: De Quincey's Opium War Essays', *South Central Review*, 8 (1991), 37–45.

Swanson, Robert, 'On the (Paper) Trail of Lord Macartney', *East Asian History*, 40 (2016), 19–25.

Van Kley, Edwin J., 'Europe's "Discovery" of China and the Writing of World History', *American Historical Review*, 76 (1971), 358–85.

Waley-Cohen, Joanna, 'China and Western Technology in the Late Eighteenth Century', *American Historical Review*, 98 (1993), 1525–44.
Wang, Chunlin, 'Shishu Yapian Zhanzheng Qianxi de Xuannan Shishe de Xingzhi (On the Nature of Xuannan Shishe)', *Lishi Jiaoxue* (History Teaching), 12 (1999), 49–51.
Wang, Dong, 'Between Tribute and Unequal Treaties: How China Saw the Sea World in the Early Nineteenth Century', *History*, 355 (2018), 262–85.
Wang, Junyi, 'Guanyu Xuannan Shishe (On Xuannan Shishe)', *Wenwu* (Cultural Relics), 2 (1979), 72–3.
Wong, John D., 'From the Treaty of Nanking to the Joint Declaration: The Struggle for Equality through State Documents', *Law & Literature*, 30:2 (2018), 309–29.
Wood, Frances, 'Closely Observed China: From William Alexander's Sketches to His Published Work', *British Library Journal*, 24 (1998), 98–121.
Wu, Yixiong, 'Yapian Zhanzheng qian Zaihua Xiren yu Duihua Zhanzheng Yulun de Xingcheng (The Formation of a General Sentiment among Westerners in China for Waging War against China before the Opium War)', *Jindai Shi Yanjiu* (Modern Chinese History Studies), 2 (2009), 23–43.
Yang, Guozhen, 'Xuannan Shishe yu Lin Zexu (Xuannan Shishe and Lin Zexu)', *Xiamen Daxue Xuebao* (Journal of Xiamen University), 2 (1964), 107–17.

Unpublished theses

Blue, Gregory, 'China in Western Social Thought: With Special Reference to Contributions from Montesquieu to Max Weber' (University of Cambridge Ph.D. thesis, 1989).
Chen, Song-Chuan, 'The British Maritime Public Sphere in Canton, 1827–1839' (University of Cambridge Ph.D. thesis, 2009).
Collins, Logan P., 'British Periodical Representations of China: 1793–1830' (University of Houston M.A. thesis, 2014).
Eastberg, Jodi, 'West Meets East: British Perceptions of China through the Life and Works of Sir George Thomas Staunton, 1781–1859' (Marquette University Ph.D. thesis, 2009).
Tsao, Ting Man, 'Representing China to the British Public in the Age of Free Trade, c.1833–1844' (State University of New York at Stony Brook Ph.D. thesis, 2000).
Van Dyke, Paul, 'Port Canton and the Pearl River Delta, 1690–1845' (University of Southern California Ph.D. thesis, 2001).
Wood, Herbert John, 'Prologue to War: Anglo-Chinese Conflict 1800–1834' (University of Wisconsin Ph.D. thesis, 1938).
Wu, Xiaojun, 'A'meishide Shijietuan Tanxi: Yi Tianchao Guan zhi Shijian Wei Zhongxin (On the Amherst Mission: with Its Focus on the Practice of the World View of the Celestial Empire)' (National Tsinghua University M.A. thesis, 2008).
Zhang, Shunhong, 'British Views on China during the Time of the Embassies of Lord Macartney and Lord Amherst (1790–1820)' (Birkbeck College, University of London Ph.D. thesis 1990).

BIBLIOGRAPHY

Electronic resources

Oxford Dictionary of National Biography (ODNB) to be found at www.oxforddnb.com.
'The Southern Expedition of Emperors Kangxi and Qianlong', *China Heritage Quarterly*, 9 (Mar. 2007), online at www.chinaheritagequarterly.org/features.php?issue=009.

INDEX

Abel, Clarke 53, 73–4, 76–7, 80, 82
alcohol 156, 159
America/Americans 58, 101–2, 106–7, 113, 142n.24, 150, 174n.4
American Revolution 6, 21
Amherst, William Pitt, 1st Earl Amherst 6–7, 51–62, 65–71, 73–85, 88n.44, 90n.103, 95, 97, 100, 112, 122, 124–5, 168, 181–2
Amiot, Jean Joseph Marie 32, 44
Amoy (Xiamen) 108–9, 180
Anderson, Aeneas 25, 27, 29, 34–5, 40
Anson, George, 1st Baron Anson 13, 37
Anti-Opium Society 156
Asiatic Society 13

barbarians/(semi)barbarians/barbarous 13, 37, 42, 58, 67, 73, 78, 84, 103, 110–12, 126, 131, 140, 182
Barrow, John 25–6, 38, 40, 42–3, 47n.15
Bates, Joshua 107
Beijing 22, 24, 27–9, 32–3, 36, 38, 40–1, 55, 57–9, 64–7, 69–70, 72, 75, 80, 82–4, 88n.53, 95, 125, 130, 132, 135, 137, 139, 160, 183
Bell, Sydney S. 163
Bengal 46n.1, 84, 87n.26, 96
Bogle, George 46n.1
Bremer, (Sir) James John Gordon 175n.29
British-Chinese
  (British) economic interests (in China) 1–2, 7, 61, 107, 120n.54, 158, 166–9, 171–4, 181, 183
  (British) military expedition (to China) 1, 3, 5, 45, 84, 113, 126, 131, 141, 146, 153–5, 167, 169–72, 175n.29, 180, 183
  (British) national honour/dignity/reputation (in China) 1–3, 47n.9, 60, 126, 131, 136, 138, 149–51, 155, 157–8, 162, 164–7, 169, 171–4, 183
  (British) possession of a (Chinese) island/trading post 87n.37, 138, 144n.92, 153, 169
  trade 5, 13–14, 29–30, 32–3, 36, 45–6, 53–4, 95–118, 122, 125, 128, 131, 135, 138, 155, 157, 162, 166–7, 171–2, 180–2
    see also country trade/unauthorised trade; opium trade/smuggling
British government 1, 23, 53–4, 59–61, 65, 84, 96, 106–7, 113–14, 117, 122–4, 126, 129–30, 135, 139, 141n.5, 141n.6, 142n.35, 144n.92, 146–7, 151–4, 156, 165–6, 169, 173, 177n.103, 183
British manufacturers/industrialists 21, 23, 45, 98–100, 106, 114, 141n.6
British merchants 3, 13–14, 21, 66, 76, 87n.37, 95, 98, 100, 105, 113–14, 123, 125, 127, 132, 134, 137, 141n.6, 146–51, 153, 156, 159–60, 162, 165, 177n.103, 182–3
  see also East India Company; free traders/private merchants/country traders; opium traders

[204]

INDEX

British policies in China
  aggressive/firm/uncompromising/
    vigorous 7, 45, 51, 55, 60, 63, 65,
    83–5, 97, 104–5, 108, 112–13,
    123–6, 130–3, 135–9, 141n.6,
    165–6, 169–70, 173, 181–4
  appeasing/conciliatory/peaceful/
    submissive 7, 33, 44–6, 51, 55,
    60, 65, 84–5, 96–8, 104–5,
    112–13, 117, 125, 132, 136–7,
    169, 181–3
  open warfare (war against China)
    6–8, 15n.16, 50n.124, 123–5,
    131, 133–7, 141, 145–56, 161,
    164, 166–74, 174n.9, 175n.28,
    175n.30, 180–1, 183–4
  show of force 113, 117, 122–4,
    128, 130–41, 169, 182–4
British superiority 12, 25, 27, 30, 42,
  78, 84, 131, 140, 171
British views of China
  favourable/positive 4, 11, 14, 23, 27,
    73, 87n.33, 130, 167–8, 173, 181
  unfavourable/negative 5, 12–14,
    23, 25–6, 40–1, 52, 71, 73–8,
    82, 124, 130, 173, 181
  see also Western/European
    images of China
Bullock, T.H. 172

Calcutta 105
Canning, George 66, 88n.51
Canton 21, 24, 31, 36, 40, 53–8, 61, 64,
  67–70, 76, 78–9, 81–3, 87n.26,
  87n.37, 91n.181, 95–100, 104,
  107–8, 110, 116, 118n.6,
  119n.47, 120n.58, 122–30, 134,
  136–40, 142n.35, 146–8, 150–6,
  159–60, 162–5, 168–9, 180, 183
  government 48n.29, 54–5, 57–8,
    63, 83, 97–8, 101, 105, 116,
    123, 125, 137, 139, 142n.35,
    146–8, 150, 160–1, 163, 168
  see also Chinese government;
    Qing court/imperial government
  system (Chinese monopoly) 21,
    98, 100, 102, 106–7, 123, 180

Cathcart, Charles Allan 22
century of humiliation 1
Chambers, (Sir) William 10
Chang, Lin 29, 31, 48n.29
China expert 5, 53, 55, 57, 64, 164
Chinese
  agriculture/husbandry 9, 12, 41
  arrogance/superiority/isolationism
    24, 30, 81–2, 102–3, 109, 138,
    162
  artistic tastes/aesthetic ideas 5,
    10, 41
  backwardness/stagnation/ignorance
    39–42, 52, 71–8, 82, 85, 103,
    111, 123, 135, 138, 181
  civilisation 8–12, 41–2, 53, 73–8,
    81–2, 85, 91n.181, 140, 181–2
  civil service examinations (keju)
    9, 11, 41
  despotism 9–10, 80, 101, 103–4,
    125, 132, 166, 174
  duplicity 34–5, 77, 115, 121n.102,
    168
  emperor/monarch(y) 7, 9–10, 37, 43,
    57, 60–1, 65–9, 75–6, 80–1, 83–4,
    91n.178, 125–6, 132–3, 135–6,
    148, 160, 167–9, 181, 184
  see also Daoguang emperor;
    Jiaqing emperor; Qianlong
    emperor
  environmental changes 52, 71
  forbearance 164, 178n.107
  foreign trade 81, 91n.160, 96, 102,
    109–10, 116–17, 121n.105,
    124, 137–8, 142n.35, 148, 182
  government 7–11, 14, 33, 36, 42–3,
    45, 69, 77–85, 96–8, 100,
    102–4, 109–10, 114, 116,
    131–40, 142n.35, 146–8, 157,
    159, 162–3, 165–6, 169, 172,
    174, 180–3
  see also Qing court/imperial
    government; Canton,
    government
  hospitality/friendliness/civility
    34–5, 41, 67–8, 79, 108–9, 111,
    115, 135, 140, 156, 168, 182

[205]

INDEX

infrastructure 41, 74
language 8, 11, 41, 53, 55, 64, 108, 129
laws 9, 29, 43, 80, 100, 103–4, 111–12, 116–17, 128, 135, 147, 149, 151, 159–60, 164–5, 170, 182
literati 8, 174n.7, 174n.9
merchants 43, 77, 100–1, 107
  see also Hong merchants
military 40, 71, 75, 125, 170–1
officials/mandarins 34–5, 37, 42–3, 67–8, 75, 80, 83, 109, 111–12, 115–16, 121n.102, 134, 159, 171
paternal authority/filial piety/subordination 9, 42, 81, 103, 181
peculiarity/cultural difference 102–5, 108–9, 132, 182
people 13, 32, 34, 36–9, 42–5, 53, 70, 73–81, 83, 85, 91n.181, 98, 103–4, 108–12, 114–17, 121n.105, 124–7, 133, 135, 139–40, 146, 156–62, 167–72, 174, 182
poverty 72–3, 109, 111
punishment 79–80
religion 76–7, 110–11
sovereignty 147, 163–5, 172
stoppage of (foreign) trade 134–5, 137, 146–7, 163
world view 76, 102–3
Chinoiserie 10, 17n.40
Christianity 9, 109, 115, 140, 157–8
clandestine reconnaissance (voyage of 1832) 108–12, 114–16, 120n.54, 120n.58
Confucius/Confucianism 9, 11, 41
contact zone 5, 46, 95, 98
country trade/unauthorised trade 95–8, 106–8, 118n.1, 119n.47
  see also British-Chinese trade; opium trade/smuggling

Crawfurd, John 105–7, 109, 111, 116–17

Dagu 58
Daoguang emperor 125–6, 133, 146–9, 151, 155, 168, 178n.122
  see also Chinese emperor/monarch(y)
Davis, John Francis 53–5, 66, 68, 72, 74–6, 80–3, 91n.178, 122, 182
Defoe, Daniel 4, 12
Dinwiddie, James 25–6, 33–4, 39–40
Du Halde, Jean Baptiste 8

Eades, Henry 26
East India Company 7, 14, 53–7, 60–1, 64–5, 84–5, 87n.26, 88n.51, 95–108, 112–14, 116–18, 118n.1, 118n.3, 118n.6, 120n.54, 122, 129–30, 132, 142n.35, 167, 182
  Court of Directors 54, 97–9, 103–4, 112, 118n.3
  monopoly 54, 95–107, 113–14, 118, 122, 129, 182–3
  Select Committee at Canton 54–6, 87n.26, 97–9, 103, 108, 111, 122
  see also British merchants
economic blockade 137
Eight Trigrams uprising 58
Elliot, (Sir) Charles 3, 6, 145–7, 149–53, 155, 162–6, 170, 173, 175n.29, 177n.103, 180, 184
Elliot, (Sir) George 175n.29
Ellis, Henry 53, 60–4, 66–9, 72, 74–9, 81, 83, 89n.60, 100–3
Elphinstone, John 87n.26
Enlightenment 9

Fisher, Thomas 99, 102, 104, 112
Forbidden City 58
free trade 21–2, 32, 71, 98–9, 102–18, 138, 149, 161, 173, 182–3

[206]

INDEX

free traders/private merchants/ country traders 7, 95–8, 101, 103–18, 119n.47, 120n.54, 182–3
  see also British merchants; opium traders
French Revolution 6
Fry, William Storrs 157
Fu Kang-an 31, 35
Fuzhou 108

George III, King 22, 24
Gladstone, William Ewart 163
Glorious Revolution 12
Goddard, James 129, 138
Gordon, G.J. 126
Gower, (Sir) Erasmus 28
Graham, Alexander 164
Graham, (Sir) James, 2nd Baronet 154, 167, 172
Grand Canal 36, 70–1, 74, 89n.76, 180
Grey, Charles, 2nd Earl Grey 144n.92
Guang (Kwang), Hui 59, 67
Gurkhas 31
Gützlaff, Karl 108–16, 120n.58, 137

Hall, Basil 53, 73, 78–9, 83
Hangzhou 36, 40
Hastings, Warren 46n.1
Hawes, Benjamin 165
Hayne, Henry 53, 67, 83
Heavenly Principle Society (*Tianli jiao*) 58
He, Shen 31, 33, 35
He, Shitai (Duke Ho) 59–60, 65, 68, 88n.47
Hobhouse, John, 1st Baron Broughton 164
Holland/Dutch 39, 61, 88n.53, 107
Holmes, Samuel 25, 34–5, 38, 40
Hong Kong 53, 99, 144n.92, 147, 180
Hong merchants 96–8, 100–2, 107, 122, 163
  see also Chinese merchants
Huang, Juezi 147, 149

humankind/human beings/humanity 21, 42, 73, 110–11, 126, 131, 137, 140, 149, 158, 162, 172
Hume, Joseph 165, 167

India 2, 13, 21, 45, 54, 84, 88n.51, 95–6, 99–102, 106, 113, 116–17, 156, 167, 171–3, 175n.29
Indonesia 52
interpreter/translator 34, 53, 108

Jardine, Matheson & Co. 108, 123, 127, 177n.100
Jardine, William 6, 153, 164
Jehol (Rehe/Chengde) 22, 35
Jesuits 8–14, 17n.37, 23, 41
Jiaqing emperor 22, 51, 55, 57–9, 61, 64–72, 82, 85, 88n.44, 90n.103, 90n.105, 115, 146, 181
  see also Chinese emperor/monarch(y)
Jinzhou 120n.58
Johnson, Samuel 13, 25
Jones, (Sir) William 12

Kangxi emperor 9, 11, 71
Kew Gardens 10
King, Charles W. 113, 150
Kowloon (battle of) 147, 152–4
kowtow/court ritual/diplomatic protocol 22–3, 29, 40, 47n.9, 52, 55, 59–66, 69, 84–5, 86n.5, 88n.46, 88n.53, 91n.178

law of nations/international law 3, 127, 131, 135, 149, 161–3, 165, 172–3
law of nature/natural law/universal laws 127, 131, 160, 182
Le Comte, Louis 8
Leibniz, Gottfried Wilhelm 9
Li, Hongbin 142n.35
Lindsay, Hugh Hamilton 99, 108, 110, 112–16, 118n.6, 126, 138, 159, 171, 176n.55, 178n.122, 183

INDEX

Lintin 159, 164
Lin Weixi incident 145–7, 149, 152–5, 163, 165
Lin, Zexu 145–7, 149–52, 155–6, 161–6, 168, 170, 173, 174n.7, 183–4
local knowledge/experience 6, 55–7, 61–2, 64–5, 85, 102–5, 108, 114, 128–9, 132, 157, 159–61, 169, 182–3
Lu, Kun 122–3, 125, 148
Lushington, Stephen 156, 165, 171

Macao 56, 58–9, 68, 87n.37, 123–4, 128, 146–7, 151
Macartney, George, 1st Earl Macartney 5–8, 14, 21–46, 47n.9, 47n.14, 47n.15, 48n.17, 51, 53–6, 59, 63, 65–7, 69–72, 75, 78, 82, 84, 87n.33, 88n.53, 89n.76, 110, 112, 128, 170, 181–2, 184
Macaulay, Thomas Babington, 1st Baron Macaulay 161, 165
Macleod, John 53, 80–1, 84
Madras (Chennai) 22
Malaya 45
Manning, Thomas 55
Marjoribanks, Charles 111–13
Martin, R. Montgomery 99–102, 104
Matheson, James 127, 130, 132–3, 142n.24, 177n.100
Melbourne, William Lamb, 2nd Viscount 1
Ming dynasty 37, 58
missionaries 2, 5, 8, 11, 13, 17n.37, 32, 53, 57, 108–9, 135, 137, 140, 157
Montagu, Horatio 163, 172
Montesquieu 10
Morrison, Robert 53, 55, 74–5, 77–8
Muke Deng'e (Duke Moo) 59, 88n.47
Murray, John Fisher 172

Nanjing 74, 108, 175n.30, 180
Napier, William John, 9th Lord Napier 6, 122–31, 141, 141n.4, 142n.35, 144n.92, 145, 169, 183
Napoleon/Napoleonic Wars 6, 53, 87n.37
national character/disposition/identity
　British 4, 25, 30, 79, 109, 158, 171
　Chinese 30, 33, 43, 46, 61, 68, 77–80, 82, 104, 108–12, 115–17, 121n.105, 124, 130, 133, 136, 138, 170–2, 182
Nepal 31, 58, 84
Ningbo 91n.160, 108, 180

Olyphant and Co. 113
opium 88n.44, 146–8, 155–61, 164–6, 173, 177n.103, 180
　crisis 6–7, 141n.6, 145–56, 161–9, 172–3, 178n.122, 183–4
　legalisation 146–9
　trade/smuggling 2–3, 52, 88n.44, 96, 108–9, 116, 145–50, 155–66, 168, 173–4, 183
　　see also British-Chinese trade; country trade/unauthorised trade
　traders 127, 146, 148, 150–1, 153, 157–61, 164, 166, 177n.100, 183
　　see also British merchants; free traders/private merchants/country traders
orientalism/orientalist 12, 22, 70, 105–6, 149–50
otherness 7, 84, 162

Palmer, George 145, 173
Palmerston, Henry Temple, 3rd Viscount 1, 6, 125, 138, 152–3, 163
Pearson, Alexander 55
Peel, (Sir) Robert, 2nd Baronet 171, 175n.30

[208]

INDEX

Philippines 45
Philip, Robert 156–7
philosophes 9, 12, 14
pin (petition) 122–3
planetarium 34
Polo, Marco 42
porcelain 5, 10, 26
Pottinger, (Sir) Henry, 1st Baronet 180
presents 33, 52, 67, 80
progress 12, 24, 26, 40–2, 44, 71, 81, 85, 140, 158, 182
public sphere 42

Qianlong emperor 22, 24, 29–31, 33, 35–6, 44, 46, 48n.29, 51, 53, 55, 59, 65–6, 69, 71–2, 87n.33, 90n.105, 181
  see also Chinese emperor/monarch(y)
Qiao, Renjie 38
Qing
  court/imperial government 21–3, 27–30, 32–3, 38–9, 44–6, 54–60, 64, 67–8, 71, 74, 78–9, 82–5, 88n.44, 88n.53, 95–7, 106, 108, 110–17, 122–30, 132–40, 146–51, 157, 159–60, 162–3, 170, 180–3
    see also Canton government; Chinese government
  decline/breakup 14n.1, 15n.16, 44, 57, 71–3, 90n.105, 182
  Manchu-Han difference/relations 30–2, 37–8, 46, 48n.37, 110–12, 124, 182
  suspicion of/policy against foreigners/subjects 38–9, 43–4, 54, 70, 78–82, 102–4, 110, 112, 116, 127, 135, 157, 163
Quanzhou 91n.160
Quesnay, François 9–10, 17n.40
quinine 158

rebellion/insurrection 58, 66, 133
Rites Controversy 11

Robinson, George 122
Russia/Russian 26, 61, 84

Shanghai 108, 180
silk 10, 26, 45, 59
silver/flow of silver 21, 146–8, 165
slave trade/slavery 91n.178, 156–8
Smith, Adam 12, 21
Society for the Diffusion of Useful knowledge in China 3
Songjiang 91n.160
Song, Yun 29, 33, 48n.29
South-east Asia 105–6, 116
southern tours 71
Spring Purification party 148, 174n.7
Stanhope, Philip Henry, 5th Earl Stanhope 170, 172
Staunton, (Sir) George Leonard, 1st Baronet 24–36, 39–40, 42–4, 46, 53, 65, 181
Staunton, (Sir) George Thomas, 2nd Baronet 52–7, 60–6, 71–2, 85, 87n.26, 87n.33, 89n.60, 100–1, 103, 105, 122, 128–30, 138, 164–7
Stewart, D. 158
Su (Soo), Leng'e 59, 67

Taiping Rebellion 14n.1
tea 5, 21, 26, 45, 54, 95–6, 100, 106, 135, 159
Temple, (Sir) William 11–13
Thelwall, A.S. 156–8
Tianjin 59, 66, 74, 120n.58, 135
Tibet 31, 46n.1, 58, 88n.44
Titsingh, Isaac 88n.53
Tongzhou 59, 62, 64–5, 67–8, 74–5, 79, 89n.76
Toone, Francis 55
treaty ports 180

Vattel, Emer de 142n.23
Verbiest, Ferdinand 8
Voltaire 9, 12

[209]

INDEX

Wang, Wenxiong 38
Ward, (Sir) Henry George 159
Warren, Samuel 162, 168–9
Webb, John 4, 11–12
Western/European diplomacy 22, 32
Western/European images of China 8–10, 12, 14
 see also British views of China
Western/European science and technology 8–9, 12, 23, 26, 34, 39, 42, 76, 82, 140
Whampoa 122, 161
William IV, King 122, 132
Wood, William Wightman 142n.24

Xuannan Poetry Club (*Xuannan Shishe*) 174n.7
Xu, Naiji 148–9

Yangtze River 70–1, 180
yes-men 148
yi (barbarian/stranger)/foreign devil 2, 77
Yuan-ming-yuan 65, 67, 79

Zhang (Chang), Wuwei 64
Zhoushan 28, 180

EU authorised representative for GPSR:
Easy Access System Europe, Mustamäe tee 50,
10621 Tallinn, Estonia
gpsr.requests@easproject.com

www.ingramcontent.com/pod-product-compliance
Lightning Source LLC
Chambersburg PA
CBHW071409300426
44114CB00016B/2240